RON PEARSON

Me

Be a Devil – Give It a Go

AN AUTOBIOGRAPHY
1924–2022 AND COUNTING

AUSTIN MACAULEY PUBLISHERS™

LONDON · CAMBRIDGE · NEW YORK · SHARJAH

A CIP catalogue record for this title is available from the British Library.

ISBN 9781035870509 (Paperback)
ISBN 9781035870387 (Hardback)
ISBN 9781398444300 (ePub e-book)

www.austinmacauley.co.uk

First Published 2024
Austin Macauley Publishers Ltd®
1 Canada Square
Canary Wharf
London
E14 5AA

Table of Contents

Introduction

At age 14 Ron wrote his first advertisement. At 19 he co-wrote and appeared in an army revue.

Over six decades he wrote thousands of press and many TV commercials.

On retirement he wrote the award-winning TV script 'Harry's Kingdom' plus the award-winning but never filmed 'Errand Boys'.

A book on his early life, two stage plays and articles in 'Rugby League Review' followed.

Ron is a life member of the Writers Guild.

Ron and Pat were married for 66 years. Now 98, Ron is still living in the bungalow Pat and he designed and had built in their garden.

O.K. let's make a start. Off we go.

Me

I was born on the twelfth of August, 1924, and I'm starting this book on the 12/08/2021. If I don't get to the end of this, you won't be reading it. Think about it? Let's start with the title, more difficult than you think.

'Diary of a nobody' been done.
'Diary of a somebody' not true.
'This is your Ron' Oh no. Please no.
'Diary of a…' Oh come on, it's about me.
So why not call it ME?
So, what do you think so far?
If it's a seven-letter word starting with 'R' and ending with 'H' I'd put it back on the shelf and try not to spoil the covers.

Everybody has friends who aren't really friends and it's those sorts of friends who send people like you books like this. A simple answer, if it's not your kind of book, is to read the first dozen pages, tell the 'un-friend' how much you've enjoyed it and send it on to another sort of friend. A few wise words, making sure the original gifter doesn't know the potential giftee. Or there is always Oxfam.

If this sounds a bit complex, believe me you're not the only one. If you must, read it again and it does make sense. I've read it several times and I think I know what I mean. '*If he doesn't know, what chance do we have?*' Please read on. There are some laugh-out-loud bits and my carer, Ann, has told me and my typist, Kathryn, agrees. Well, they would, wouldn't they?

Nothing to do with this but I've just remembered a sentence regarding actor Edward Woodward.

'Well, Edward Woodward would, wouldn't he?'

It's that kind of book.

Ok, so, let's make a start, only 35,429 days to go. Phew. Alternatively, title 'Gone with the Wind Up'.

So, what is an autobiography? It's memories, isn't it? And if at my age of 98, I get a bit muddled, please forgive me.

Chapter 1:
In the Beginning

So 12 August 1924, I'm told it was a Tuesday at 8.30pm. Some clever devil with a laptop will take a few seconds to tell you it wasn't a Tuesday. I don't do research, bit like Shakespeare and those lads, everything is handwritten.

I'm blessed with a good memory and many are the friends who are surprised that I don't remember 12/08/24. It is of course the Glorious Twelfth. Nothing to do with me, but apparently, it's when the toffs start grouse shooting. So, there's your first bit of useless knowledge. Honestly folks I've got a sackful.

I was a poorly kid, still in my pram, I had convulsions then followed measles (twice) whooping cough, bronchitis, mumps, jaundice and chicken pox. The pox was so rampant, even in my toes, the doctor said to me 'open your mouth' and to my Mother 'if they were in his mouth, it could've been small pox'.

A gypsy lady who came round selling clothes pegs from a big basket said, 'open your mouth love' and to my Mother 'he'll never be right 'til he has had his tonsils out'. A trip to the doctors proved her right and so I was taken to Bradford Royal Infirmary along with Donald the younger brother of my pal Joe Lawrence. I would be seven, Donald, six. We must have been in a men's ward. I don't know whether it was a joke or not but a man in a bed by the window threatened to jump out of it. The procedure started with the dreaded ether mask on your face. I couldn't breathe and struggled until I became unconscious. After two or three days I was back home and that's when I got mumps. My Sister went throughout her early years with only one childhood illness – jaundice.

I was born at home, 23 Westover Road, Bramley, Leeds 13. If you live there now put the book back on the shelf and I'll send you a free copy. I'm not into statistics but, apart from the landed gentry, bank managers and the like, I would think 75% of births in those days were in the family home. Prove me wrong and I'm damned if I'll send you a free copy. The midwife's name was Mrs Tricket or Mrs Trippet and if any of your ancestors was the midwife, you deserve a free copy for their excellent delivery work.

Getting back to the reality of 1924, just six years after World War I, things were pretty tight on the money, so maternity homes and the like were unaffordable to most, so home delivery was not an option it was fact.

So, 'what are my earliest memories?' That's probably the most difficult five words to answer, in this book, or anybody else's book for that matter. People tell you things that they remember when you were but a tot and eventually, they are your memory. Aw, come on we have all done it, if not you must have been a very boring kid.

There's a black and white snap of me in a pram in Bramley Park and apparently, I rocked the pram so hard I fell out in a heap, head first so I'm told. So, there you have it if you'd fallen out of a pram onto your bonce when but a tiny tot maybe this is why I write as I do. Well, that's my story, and I'm sticking with it.

A little bit of family history. Dad left school at 16 and got a job in Royal London Assurance but at 21 he and two others took over a disused chapel and converted into a silent cinema. Silent then 'talkies' in glorious black and white then glorious 'Technicolor' were to be his life.

1914-18 the First World War, bit before my time but worth a mention. My Mum and Dad, not yet married, were on holiday in Bridlington with another couple—strictly no fratting—the girls in one bedroom – the men in another. The ladies travelled by train, the men by motorbike with Dad on pillion. War must have been declared mid-week and the men were keen to enlist. The general consensus of opinion was that it would be over by Christmas. Four years on it still had a few months to go. Sadly, Auntie Edith's husband was killed on November 11th Armistice Day. I've since been told there were still some pockets of fighting for a few weeks after the Armistice.

Dad wanted to join the Leeds Pals or the Leeds Rifles but was unsuccessful. I've forgotten the unit he did join but after a few weeks training in Darley Dale, Derbyshire went abroad mainly in Ypres in Belgium. The next bit is a bit misty. He learnt the Morse code and sent messages but was not in the Signals. I was in the Signals in World War Two and never sent a message: more on that later. He spent most of his time running an entertainments unit with a Welshman with the wonderful name of Lionel De Courcey Gibbons.

Whether the unit was in a building or a tent I know not but it was silent cinema at one end and concert party at the other. There were concert parties in every town in the country usually five men and two ladies singing, dancing but mainly comedy. Mum and Dad had been in a concert party in Leeds, and Dad was the comedian and pianist in Ypres. There were, of course, no girls but two of the men took on these roles and had quite a few admirers!

I think the chairs must have been ones with folding backs a bit like tram seats so that when a film show was over the backs flipped over for the live show. So Dad kept his cinema connections during the war. On demob he took a job as a clerk working for a man who rented out silent films. The only other member of staff was a typist. The first talkie was 'The Jazz Singer' in 1927 mainly silent apart from when, Al Jolson turned to the audience and said, 'Well folks, you ain't heard nothing yet' and then sang the schmaltzy 'Sonny Boy'. The audience gasped and I'm told some of a delicate disposition fainted.

Talkies came in with a murmur rather than a shout and many thought they were a passing fad. Cinema owners were particularly unenthusiastic. This would mean converting to sound which meant throwing out the old and buying expensive new sound equipment. However, talkies came to stay and by 1929 the game was up and so was my Dad's job as his boss closed down his small empire and emerged a little later as a sound film distributor.

After about a year Dad got a job as manager of the Pavilion Cinema in Stanningley. I think the Pavilion had been built as a silent cinema by the Green family who had the Palace in Pudsey as well. The Pavilion was one of the thousands closed with the advent of sound cinema. It was bought and re-opened by the owners of the Tower Cinema in Leeds and re-equipped for sound. They also had the Carlton in Carlton Hill and after the Pavilion added the Capital in Meanwood and Cottage Road in Headingley. At the time of writing, the dear little Cottage Road is still open for business.

Most people thought being a cinema manager was a cushy number. You turned up in the evening, put on a dress suit and welcomed in the audience with a smile. However, with showing Monday and Thursday films in the morning to check for any faults, 'trade shows' on Tuesday and Friday mornings in the big cinemas in Leeds. These were of films available in six months or so time and reports were then written as to their suitability for the various cinemas in the 'Tower' group. Wednesday was pensioners matinee. Saturday morning take out handbills and free passes, Saturday matinee for kids, usually called the 'tuppenny rush' two separate performances Saturday evening with booked seats – my Father's responsibility, day off Sunday. The two matinees were discontinued during and after the war but it was still a heavy schedule for very little pay. That comes to about 60 hours a week. After 4 or 5 years Dad got a night off, from then on he got a night off approx. one a month. OK, it wasn't manual work but the hours were long and the pay was short. The first-year Dad got a week holiday without pay. Year two one week paid one week without pay. Year three Hurray! Two weeks with pay.

The first talkie at the Pavilion was, I think, 'Feet First' a comedy starring Harold Lloyd. He was a bespectacled, straw-hatted comedian who specialised in daring escapades on high buildings. He said he did all his own stunts but to a film studio he was an important property so it was generally thought there must have been some sort of unseen safety device. In one spectacular climb he got onto the clock on a high building, grabbing one of the clock hands to steady himself, the hand bent, the audience gasped, but our hero was unharmed. Amazingly Lloyd had two fingers missing from a hand and always wore a special glove that looked like a hand in his films.

My Sister and I were allowed to stay up and see this very first talking picture at the 'Pav'. For the next ten years or so we rarely missed a film and of course we got in for nowt.

My Sister would leave school at Easter 1937 and got a job at Roneo a duplicating company in Albion Street in Leeds. As a junior she went for typing and shorthand lessons to a lady in Armley, and as always with my Sister, became a very good shorthand typist. A year or so later she moved to R.K.O Radio Pictures or to give it its posh name Radio, Keith, Orpheum. I thought this would have suited her down to the ground as she was now an avid film fan. However, again after a year or so she moved to a cloth importer and exporter where she stayed until her call up to the W.A.A.F. Well, if you need to know the Women's Auxiliary Air Force at the end of 1943.

Here are a few chronological facts. My Father Harold Nelson Pearson the youngest son of John Robert Pearson and Ann Elizabeth Dettmer, here the crystal ball gets a little cloudy. You see Granddad was born in County Durham, in a small place called Shildon. Granny was born in St Pancras which you might have heard of in a place called London. How did they meet? Dad never said. Dad was one of five. Will, Edith, Kitty, Charlie and Dad. I never met Will who lived in Newcastle but Edith had a different accent and was a teacher in London so maybe Granddad had a spell down there. I don't know where Kitty was born but Uncle Charlie always joked he couldn't play for Yorkshire (when only Yorkshire men played cricket for Y.C.C.C.) because he was born in Manchester, another little mystery.

Both my Mum and Dad were born in Burley, Leeds, the reason why my Dad was somewhat reticent about his Dad was that his Dad didn't live at home. Granddad was company secretary for a brewery in Wrexham and lived there with his 'Housekeeper' only coming back to Leeds at Christmas and Easter. Ah well. Granny Pearson is worth a few paragraphs.

A tough old bird who dressed neck to foot in navy, brown or black, she died in our house when I was about five and I do have a distinct memory of this, apparently she was very ill, it was cancer and being a Christian Scientist refused treatment. With Will being in Newcastle and Edith being in London it appeared Charlie and Kitty were going on holiday so poor old Mum was lumbered with this dying lady. Our house was small. There's a section on that still to come, there's no end to the excitement in this book. Upstairs was the main bedroom, a small bedroom and a room known as the 'lumber room' where the holiday suitcases and all sorts of things called 'stuff' were in a jumble.

My parents plus me were in the big bedroom. My Sister moved from the little room to kip down in between my parents and Gran took her room. Stay with it were getting to the memory bit and thanking you for reading so far but it is a real memory

Gran died, the funeral director would come, Mum was cleaning the room with the window fully open.

Ron: 'Is the window open so the angels could come and take granny to heaven?'
Mum: 'Something like that.'

Not exactly a page turner but those are, my friends, the actual words I definitely remember.

To continue with 'the Granny Pearson story' she was born Elizabeth Ann Dettmer of German descent and her ancestors were piano makers, to be more exact pianoforte makers—piano being soft and forte being loud—but you knew that anyway—and if you didn't it's the sort of info you can bore somebody with at a party with a glass in your hand.

Two Dettmer brothers opened a piano shop in the very fashionable Fitzroy Square in London. Going back in history in Germany two older brothers made pianos. One made the woodwork the other brother the clever bits and they specialised in square pianos and I believe oval ones. Now here's the good bit. These two, not the two in London, I get muddled on a regular basis but stay with it, invented the sharp notes (black ones) on pianos. If they'd asked for a Deutschmark on every piano sold worldwide I could have been a million, a billion maybe a trillionaire. There's a Dettmer square piano with sharps and flats in a museum… somewhere in the Netherlands.

I told you I don't do research but the Dettmer story is available on your smart phone or similar contraption.

So what about Mum's family? Granddad Alfred Hillarby was born in North Cave near Bridlington and his wife to be, Annie Pease not too far away in Seaton Carew. How they met and how they ended up in Leeds is another mystery.

Granddad became a Master Bookbinder specialising in bank ledgers which were bound in kid with watered silk inside covers. Granddad was locked in the basement of the bank so he could not reveal the secrets these tomes might hold. He never earned more than £1.50 pence per week during his career and supported a wife and four daughters, Mum, Clarice, Dorothy and Florence on this sum. There was also a boy, Ralph who sadly died in infancy.

Apparently on Saturday evenings Granddad would walk into town, about two miles or so, saving a copper or two on the tram fare. Then he'd go round the various market stalls where they were 'selling off' their produce at 'knockdown' rates. So roast beef and potatoes plus two veg and homemade Yorkshire puddings were on the Sunday menu. He rewarded himself with a tram ride home and probably a tin of his favourite tobacco 'Afrikander'. Not 'Baby's Bottom' but there was, and maybe still is a tobacco with that name. Look it up if you must, another snippet to add to your glass in hand conversation. So where have we got to? Not very far but hopefully I've given you a smile or two and quite a bit of useful (or is it less) info.

A paragraph or three about my Sister Eileen Margaret Pearson and you have the full family. Eileen was born on the 14th of March 1923 being my big Sister. Very quiet, very clever she was always top of her class of 40 or more girls.

In the "Big Boys" my place in class was once no. 2 when I was off with a damaged leg—more later—usually in the top 10 but once in the thirties. Bert Greaves, who had taught at the school seemingly forever, said "Buck up Pearson or I shall need to talk to your Father". That stemmed the flow somewhat.

Eileen always known as Peggy until the day my mother died and from that day on became Eileen. She never told me she hated the name. I was Sonny for the first few years of my life and I knew two more Sonny's in Bramley. I then became Ronnie and on my first date with my future wife she kicked that into touch. And I've been Ron for 70 years.

My sister looked after me, although only a year and a half between us, I was the one who never looked where I was going and she pulled me back onto the pavement. If we went shopping she had the shopping list and the money. I failed the exams to West Leeds High School twice. I don't think she ever sat the exams – I'm fairly certain she would have 'walked them'.

So: Where are we now? If I don't know it's going to be a thin book. OK let's talk about the house on Westover Road. I'm going to pinch quite a few bits from my book 'Bramley as was'. It's now out of print but if you are the proud owner of a copy or read it and chucked it in the bin don't expect a discount on this one.

Westover Road ran off Town Street in what was, known and maybe still is, 'top o' town'. Quite near the park Westover Road was gas lamp lit a, stone cobbled road and stone slab paving. The front of the houses, were also in stone so it looked quite posh. At the back was a dirt street with paving down the first half but none lower down where we were. There were some unusual sort of stones, probably ironstones, in the dirt street and lads who wore boots with steel studs on the heels could get sparks out of these. I begged my Mum for a pair of these boots but to no avail. She thought they were common. We weren't exactly rolling in money but that, as is often said, was that. I think the backs of these houses were brick with a tiny garden, a path, a dustbin and outside lavatory. Many women hung their washing out to dry in the street but not on Tuesday when Mr Knowles the greengrocer came down with his horse and cart. Tattoos were not very popular those days and Mr Knowles was the only man I saw with a tattoo—a small anchor on his wrist—a reminder of his days in the navy during the 14-18 war.

I don't know what 23 Westover Road looks like today but I do know the people who moved in after us made a bathroom, or at least a washroom plus toilet where the small bedroom was.

We had two rooms downstairs and three upstairs. The living kitchen had a stone floor, a cold water tap and a fireside range, I think there would be linoleum On the floor and my Mother made rugs by cutting up old clothes and threading them into a hessian base. Apart from my Mother's sewing machine all the furniture in this room, apart from the dining chairs which were a wedding present, were of poor quality and didn't match.

There's an old saying 'what you don't have you don't miss'. What we and many like us didn't have was;

A hot water tap, electric lights, fitted carpets, central heating, double glazing, electric or gas cooker, a fridge, a freezer, washing machine, tumble dryer, dishwasher (well we did have one – my Mum.) microwave, vacuum cleaner, radio, telephone, electric iron, computers, laptops, etc., etc., etc. and televisions weren't even invented. There was no need for a burglar alarm there was nowt worth pinching, except the piano and you'd have to be Hercules to shift that. We had 2 books in the house, a Bible always placed on top of the piano and at the back of the cupboard "With Roberts to Pretoria", a saga about the Boer war.

One winter we had a big snowfall – a couple of feet in our back garden, Dad dug us out. Westover Road was quite steep and a lad at school – John Birley lived in a little cottage off Bell Lane, which was also very steep just off Town Street. John's Dad had to dig a tunnel to get them out.

'I wish we had a tunnel like John Birley' was my moan
'If that ever happens you'll be doing the digging' was Dad's
response.

Now a paragraph or so about my mother's sewing machine a Singer, good to look at in polished wood. On leaving school my mother served an apprenticeship with a dressmaker and then spent 10 years or so as a dressmaker at Marshall and Snelgrove a top quality shop in Bond Street Leeds. She could make anything and each of her Sisters came with clothes to make.

When Mum died in 1957 my wife became the proud owner of the sewing machine and she too made a lot of clothes for our daughter and herself.

Cut now to March 1973. I was in a production, of 'Fiddler on the Roof' and we needed a sewing machine on stage. How totally chuffed my Mother would have been to see her beloved 'Singer' on stage, for two weeks at the Bradford Alhambra, a beautiful theatre where I appeared half a dozen or so times.

Here's another childhood memory that may raise a smile. The tinny wind-up gramophone was playing a popular tune, Mother was at the sink with her back to me singing along and I was sitting in one of the wedding present chairs beating time on the chair arms. Suddenly the right-hand chair arm came adrift. Now I was particularly partial to a confection called liquorice nougat and took this out of my mouth and put a piece of this into the chair arm without my Mother noticing and continued beating time more heavily. A quarter of a century later my quick repair was still holding fast. Now, as Captain Mainwaring would say in 'Dads Army', 'there's a useful tip'.

13

The other downstairs room, known as the front room and only used on Sunday housed my Father's piano and eventually a three piece suite. Upstairs, apart from a rusting double bed and my cot, eventually made into a bed, I remember little, I don't think there was a wardrobe or a dressing table. Where, our clothes were stored never entered my mind. My Sisters room contained a bed and I think that was it. We've already done the contents of the 'lumber' room in a previous paragraph.

In place of a washing machine, we had a wringer with one of the rollers rotting, a peggy tub and a washboard, the dodgy wringer was still in use ten years or so later. When we moved to Stanningley Road my Dad knew a man who was a vacuum cleaner salesman. Far out of our reach but this salesman being good hearted and knowing we weren't potential customers agreed to leave a machine overnight for us to use. Cut to 4.15pm I'm home from school, panic the cleaner was broken. I think 'jimmied' was the word used. Now my Dad was not a do-it-yourselfer. We had a hammer with a very small shaft, it had been broken and cut down more than once and a screwdriver supplied with the sewing machine. A quick look told me the belt had come loose and releasing one part, putting the belt back on and tightening with the 'Singer' screwdriver, Job done. Mother thought I was a genius and thought high-tech engineering would be my forté. Apart from this my career was never discussed. So, we weren't living on velvet but we were a happy family.

Dad's piano deserves a paragraph or two, a Klingmann bought from Archibald Ramsden the piano people in Leeds for £86, a tremendous sum of money in those days. I've mentioned Dad's day job was as a clerk working for a silent film distributor in one of the Leeds Arcades. At night he played the piano at the Lido cinema in Bramley Town Street until he had amassed this eighty-six quid. It never struck me until writing this that Mr Hobson owned or part owned the Lido and also owned the house. Would this partly explain why the newly-weds moved from Burley to Bramley?

There's an old saying, "If you've a hundred pounds in the bank and a piano in the front room" you weren't doing too badly." Dad never had a bank account or a wallet but there were millions of families worse off than us.

Chapter 2:
Life as a Mixed Infant

Schooldays: both my Sister and I went to Bramley National also known as Bramley St Peters with the church on the opposite side of the road and the vicar's residence alongside the school. My Sister would start school aged 5 and so missed the first class known as baby's class. My pal Joe lived next door but one, was six months younger than me, pestered his Mum to start at 3½ so I would be 4 and started with him, I don't think we had desks. We had rush mats and had to lie down on them quite a lot. I don't remember any girls by name or appearance. There must have been some. It said so above the door in stone. I can only presume they lay on mats at one side of the room and we young gentlemen laid on the other side.

I remember learning nursery rhymes, but not much else. Miss Paul, a very young teacher turned up one day with a fair load of egg sandwiches and the kids formed a queue for these. The next egg sandwich day I joined the queue. Mum was furious 'those are for poor children who don't get breakfast at home'. On more than one occasion, when Dad was out of work, Mum boiled an egg, cut it in two, so my Sister and I could both have egg for breakfast – I believe eggs cost two pence in old money. I know little of my Sister's schooldays except she was very clever but seldom talked about school. It was just something she got on with.

Apart from lying down and nudging each other and the egg sandwich episode all I remember is as a run-up to Christmas a big picture of Father Christmas was hung over the blackboard and we chanted "Santa Claus has come to town in his bright red dressing gown".

Standard two was almost a blank for me starting in September I was hospitalised I'm told in November with a serious lung condition – empyema. There was an egg-shaped lump on my right side. A specialist was needed, Dad was out of work and his Sister Edith gave him the specialist's fee. The specialist came, 'no time for an ambulance' he said I'll drive him down. Mum came with me. I remember it was raining and I'd never been in a car before. It was touch and go. The specialist, the renowned Mr Vining, carried me in. I was, I'm told, unconscious and he didn't gown up before starting the procedure. My life was saved, obviously, but apparently the procedure had to be stopped midway and finished the following morning. For several weeks my right lung had a tube in it draining into a bucket – that's enough of that. I don't know how long I was in LGI but I was eventually moved to Ida hospital, which I think was in Arthington, to recuperate. There we were wheeled out, whatever the weather, except for snow or fog, to benefit from the cold fresh air. My cousin Jack drove me home where I had to learn to walk again and Father Christmas visited 23 Westover Road in early March.

Each autumn a bazaar was held at Moriah and in the afternoon the Sunday School children did a few bits and pieces. I was to be a Crocus in 'Mary, Mary Quite Contrary' who was to come on with an empty watering can and the crocuses were to rise up open their petals and do a little dance. I'd like to say the teacher said "Crocuses rise and reveal your pistils." I'd like to say it's because it's a good line. Exactly the opposite, because of the girls' brown stockings I screamed the place down and didn't appear aged 4 and a bit it looked as though my acting career was over. But no.

The following year I was to be a soldier in the song 'There's something about a soldier'. Mum was against me being a soldier. I think she thought we would be in khaki whereas the uniform turned out to be black shoes and trousers, crepe paper red jackets and black busbies. They look like something you got out of a Christmas cracker. My Mother said she would make my uniform but didn't tell them I would be a sailor, in a white outfit rather than the traditional navy blue.

The afternoon of the show, I was to be in the centre, all started well but half way through I took a wrong turn and hit the kid next to me with my cardboard rifle. The rifle bent and flopped on to my shoulder and the lad I hit broke from the line up went to front of the stage and shouted.

"Mam, that big daft kid in the sailor suit just belted me with his gun". Mums reply, "Then belt him back". The lady producer in the big hat dashed on and peace broke out.

I'd also like to say I sat by the 'phone for a couple of years but suddenly boy croci in girls' brown stockings and soldiers in American sailor suits with cardboard rifles were out, 'cos that's also a good line' but we didn't have a telephone.

Apart from being the head of the dragon up against St George in mixed infants (standard 4) nothing else comes to mind except one lad died – (I remember his name) and we all had to pray. Most girls did but most lads sniggered. Well that's what young lads in Standard four did.

Chapter 3:
I'm in the 'Big Boys'

A bit of a scandal here, Mr Tolson taught Standard Four and lo and behold Standard Five. Apparently a lady teacher and the teacher of Standard Seven and Eight combined 'don't ask' were somewhat sweet on each other resulting in both leaving Bramley Nats and a quick re-shuffle.

Dad always insisted on the first two weeks in September for his summer holidays as it was always fine weather and it seemed to be, consequently I missed the start of term and the first thing I remember is a lad called Arthur Johnson reciting a poem titled 'Vitae Lampardi' the vital spark. 'They've learnt a foreign language in the first two weeks of term' were my first horrifying thoughts.

Probably the most exciting event of my young life occurred in 1933. We moved house. Dad often said he would like a house nearer the cinema but never seemed to do anything about it. One Sunday, I must've looked a real twit in my Sunday best, my Sister and I found ourselves on Stanningley Road, a different part of the world to us, on the far side of Bramley. The Fairfield Estate had been part built and the houses that were on Stanningley Road were a bit different to the rest with fake Tudor beams on the front, very posh. Lo and behold 286a was empty. I'm not sure how we knew it was empty for, being corporation owned property there would be a no 'for sale' sign. Often people leaving put up newspapers on the windows. Do people still do this? Anyhow we peeped through a window, probably the corner and saw the house was empty.

We raced back home with the news. Apparently, my Father's brother 'Uncle Charlie' was in charge of housing stock and having no telephone at home, Dad rang him Monday morning from the cinema and got hold of the keys.

We moved in, imagine – electric light, a bathroom with hot water and inside toilet, a kitchen, a pantry, garden front and back and so many other things to bore you with. Don't go looking for 286a because it's not there. It became 418 shortly after we moved in. It was a new world. I made a friend the first night – looking in a sweetshop window – and for the first time ever I had my own bedroom. I don't know how many houses there were on the Fairfield Estate it doubled in size shortly after we moved but there were only four shops, Mr Rogers, baker and confectioner, Mr Drake's Post

Office, sweets, newsagent etc. Miss Beevers, I don't know quite what she sold, wool, needles, thread I suppose it was haberdashery, and Ramsden's (no relation to Harry) fish and chip shop.

Not exactly front page news but in addition to three unrelated Ramsden Chip Shops in Bramley there was of course the famous Harry Ramsdens in Guiseley Leeds. This is now known as Wetherby Whaler. Both Guiseley and Wetherby are fifty or sixty miles from the coast and I have yet to eat 'Whale, chips and mushy peas'. There are quite a few Whalers including one at Pudsey.

Apart from the nationally known Pudsey Bear the township is also known as the place where the crows fly backwards to keep the muck out of their eyes and the difficult to find treacle mines, plus this rhyme:

> Owd Sammy Knapton.
> Ad a grey mare.
> Took it up to't Pudsey Fair.
> Bumped it's 'ead agane a tree.
> E by gum it's barn to dee.
> Get some traykle in a spoin.
> E by gum that's got it going.
> Reet into 't' barbers shop.
> Where 'es shaved its whiskers slap bang off.

I believe there is a somewhat ruder version.

Back to School, and poverty. Many lads came to school with torn and dirty clothes, many smelt, the lad in the desk in front of me in Standard Four had seeping boils on his neck, a roughly made, torn and mended jacket and no shirt, in its place was a piece of white material with tapes tied round his neck. Another lad was brought to the front of the class and asked to explain why he came to school on odd days. The lad started to cry then he explained he and his Sister only had one pair of shoes between them. On his unwashed bare feet he was wearing girl's shoes. Whether the teacher, the school or the Education Authority paid for shoes and socks. I know not, but next week he wore them. Many lads smelt and had wee stains on their unwashed, short trousered legs. Many lads had a torn piece of rag pinned to their jersey's – a snot rag. It gives an idea of what poverty was really like. Thank goodness those days are far in the past and you very seldom, if ever, see a poorly dressed kid.

1933ish... My Dad only ever hit me once. He had a habit of standing on the fender to get his face close to the mirror above the fireplace. Then he would inspect his face closely step down and say 'I don't look too bad when all's said and done.' On this occasion he looked in my ears and said. 'By crikey you could grow spuds in your lugholes they're full of muck'. Now I have to admit personal hygiene as a lad of 11 wasn't my strong point. After all until I was 8 the only warm water we had was what my Mum boiled in a pan morning and night and a bathtub in front of the fire Friday nights. I relied on my Mum to give me a good clean out when she thought about it. Back to Dad's remark about my ears I said this, I shouldn't have. 'Well at least I don't have a mucky head like you'. Dad hit me hard on both cheeks and shouted 'Don't you ever say anything like that again' he was white with anger. Mum dashed in from the kitchen to see what was wrong. I said "Me Dad says I've got mucky ears and I said he's got a mucky head". Even as a small boy I'd noticed this large dark brown patch at the back of his head. Mum had a look. 'Oh Harold it's awful'. She'd never noticed? I can only presume he stopped washing his hair to make himself look less bald. Mum took him to the kitchen and dealt with it. 'It's black scum', was her verdict. Surely his barber would have noticed it, or his boss or my Mum? It was always spotless from then on and the incident was never mentioned again. As I remember at Westover, we had one small mirror at my Dad's height for him to shave in. I didn't even know what I looked like. When we moved aged 8, I got my first toothbrush.

We were on holiday in Blackpool when war broke out. Returning home Dad was doing his facial inspection by the mirror. 'Well I don't think I look too bad all things considered. If they sent for me I'd go'. 'Go where?', from me. 'Back in the army. We got the last little lot sorted out, now well get this little lot sorted out'.

'How old are you Dad'. "Just 50" was the reply. I didn't sleep much that night. Dad wanted to leave his wife and two teenage children to go back in the army. What would we live on? My starting Army pay was twenty one shillings a week of which I sent seven bob home. He may have got a little bit more being married. I gave my Mum five bob a week my Sister maybe 10 so Mum would be managing on about 30 shillings a week. I'm sure he never bothered to work that out. If he did that makes it even worse. Dad was seldom in the house, except for Sundays. Then he slept on till lunch-time, read the paper in the afternoon and played the piano and cards in the evening. But oh, the freedom of not having a wife and children to bother with, a very odd man indeed my Dad. Well you know what they say? It takes all sorts to make a world.

School hygiene, particularly for boys, was almost non-existent. In the back playground there were half a dozen lavatories and a urinal for around 200 lads. No hand washing facilities and the less said about this smelly and dirty place the better. In the cloakroom there were half a dozen cold water wash basins and a couple of wringing wet, usually dirty roller towels.

The main playground for lads was mud and stones. On a regular basis we lined up at one end, picked up stones, lads in jerseys held the jersey with one hand and picked up and loaded stones onto the jersey. I think I used my blazer pockets.

The sensible thing was to have a dustbin at the other end, but no. We dropped them at the far end for them to be dispersed again.

One afternoon at 3pm the bell was rung. Running to line up to go inside

I fell and my knee it a stone. I saw a piece of triangular flesh hanging by one side and a fair bit of blood. I spat on the wound, popped the flesh back, pulled up my sock and lined up.

Back home at tea-time, I got a warning about being daft. I already knew that – as Mum bathed off the sock, cleaned the wound and applied the ever reliable 'Zambuk'. I still have a grey triangular bit of dead flesh on my knee.

The mixed infants and girls had tarmac playgrounds. The school was around fifty years old and we were playing in the mud and stone age.

Nothing much to report about Standard Four and Five, a lad called Alderson let a stink bomb off in the choir stalls and got the seldom used cane. Alan Alderson had several strings to his bow or notes for his fingers. Mr Tolson played us in to school on piano but Alderson also did. At a school concert he played the xylophone. His Dad ran a plumbing business in Bramley and after leaving school Alan joined the family business. "*What's he on about?* Hang on I'm getting to it." In addition, Alan played trumpet at the Leeds Empire a number one touring date for variety artists. The Empire was a twice nightly-or twice brightly. At the 15-minute interval up to 1.500 people had to be ushered out and another 1,500 ushered in and the band played on. When the Empire closed in the early 60's—television killed it—Alan transferred to the Grand Theatre. Whilst the Empire was 'bright and breezy' the Grand Theatre was high standard with opera, ballet, Gilbert and Sullivan plus musicals and a long run pantomime. Plays were also presented so there was the odd week off.

Standard six: Mr Greaves didn't like me. Thought I was a sissy and he could've been right. You see after having part of a lung removed and knocking on deaths door waiting for me harp, my Mother cosseted me. In cold weather instead of wearing a scarf at the front it was pinned round the back for, as she said the lungs are at the back as well as the front. More importantly the class had started going to the swimming baths. In the beginning it was holding on to the side rails, larking about but eventually I started to swim. One morning I sank to the bottom and the swimming instructor in tee shirt and slacks had to dive in and rescue me, so the baths were out for me. Another lad Eric Lye was also a non-swimmer, I never knew why and we stayed in class playing simple pencil and paper games to be sent home about 11.30am.

On holiday the first two weeks in September, I thought I'd try to swim in the sea, thinking the waves would help me. Once gain I sank. Dad, sitting in a deck chair fully clothed, came in and rescued me. On both occasions I'd no shortage of breath. I just went down feeling a bit tired.

I then had two years with Mr Carr in standard 7 and 8 in the same room. I'm still unsure how this worked? There were some Standard Eight students who, because of birthdays, had to stay on until Christmas and a few more left at Easter. It was very crowded. When I moved to standard 8 three or four tables were set up in what was Standard 4 where a dozen or more of us worked unsupervised until Christmas. What happened to standard 4 didn't bother me at the time but I have wondered about it ever since.

Mr Carr was a very good teacher, not a tall man but with fairish hair that he never combed, it stood straight up giving him and extra inch or so in height. Deep of voice, strict but absolutely fair, no boy put one over on E.T.C.

On Fridays we did woodwork at Broad Lane School about ten minutes away. I've mentioned the lack of tools at home plus my Dad's lack of D.I.Y. skills. On Friday a.m. I'd made a complete hash of something and the woodwork teacher shouted at me, 'Get out of my sight idiot boy, get back to your own school' and opened the door for me. I should've gone home and kept quiet but I went back to school where Mr Carr was writing up the afternoon lesson.

> 'Now then lad what are you doing here?'
> 'Mr Mac says I'm an idiot at woodwork and won't have me in his class'.
> 'Does he now?'

I was in tears and Mr Carr put his arm round me and said, 'Leave this with me and off you go home'.

I wasn't looking forward to the following Friday but Mr Mac changed his tune. He got me some new wood, showed me where I went wrong and how to put it right. I made a tea tray, a Seagrass woven-topped stool, a towel roller and teapot stand with Mr Mac helping me on the tricky bits. The wood was stored on an extra deck with a Jacobs Ladder for access and I became the wood getter, I absolutely loved Fridays am. Mum showing me how to do the weaving of the Seagrass. Mr Mac said how good it was. It also covered a few errors on the top pieces of wood and it was used for many years.

I would be about 10 when Mum took Sister a self to the 'Leeds Empire' the variety theatre in Briggate, Leeds. The Victoria Quarter is now on this site but if you look carefully there is still a sign for the stage door.

I was absolutely bowled over. An Orchestra, a big stage, lots of twinkly lights and Stalls, Circle, Upper Circle and Gallery. The theatre held up to 1,500 – twice nightly.

The show we saw was a Pantomime… 'Cinderella' starring northern comedian Tom Moss. As we were in a 'Moss Empire' I asked Mum if Mr. Moss owned the theatre. The answer was no but Moss Empires had a theatre in most big towns in the U.K. One of the exceptions being the Bradford Alhambra built and owned by local Impresario, Francis Laidler.

On reflection the Panto was not all that good but I was hooked. After a little while I was allowed to go to Leeds on my own, by tram, meet my Sister from work and go to the first house.

If Variety mean nothing to you, from 1920 to 1955 it was the most popular form of live entertainment in the country.

People have always wanted to be entertained from street singers (Buskers) to pub singers and Court Jesters. Before the First World War, Music Hall was what it said on the label. Basically, singers plus jugglers, acrobats etc. Technically Music Halls were licensed for music and singing and theatres for speech, but the Licencing Authority turned a blind eye on comedians who introduced a bit of 'Patter' in their acts and of course the 'Legitimate' theatres also put on musicals, Gilbert and Sullivan and Pantomime.

Variety was based on American 'Vaudeville' which faded earlier than variety which meant more Americans, often of necessity, came over. Laurel and Hardy, Chico Marx, Harpo Marx, singer Alan Jones and his actress wife, Irene Hervey, all toured Britain.

Towards the end of one school year I was crossing the road to catch a tram to go to the 'Pavilion' when a cyclist knocked me down. The chain came off his bike and the cog wheel, ripped through my right leg. It was more or less outside the house and big Sister ran back to get Mum. The cyclist said 'Sorry pal your fault' and ran off with the bike. I looked and there was a deep gash about 9 inches long with a lot of bleeding. My Mum was a very emotional person but on this occasion was surprisingly calm. I think she brought a makeshift bandage with her, probably a tea towel and I hopped along to the chemist. It was a Friday and the chemist stayed open later that day. He cleaned the wound and used some oiled silk in the dressing which impressed me no end. He then said I must get into bed and wait for the doctor whom he would contact. Around 8pm Dr Ogilvie arrived with an anaesthetist, I was put to sleep and the wound was cleaned and sewn before I woke an hour or so later. Apparently, a good part of muscle was gone and I still have the scar to prove it.

Dr Ogilvie was a kind, serious but humorous man who came three times a week, then two, then one until the wound was healed. He usually told me a riddle or conundrum and I had to work it out before his next visit. I never failed. Big 'ead.

Read this:

PARIS
IN THE
THE SPRING

Then read it very carefully word by word. Clever that.

The good news is I missed the exams and my years' work was assessed by

Headmaster Sweetman and I came second, yikes wow and hurrah for that. I'd like to add the kid who came first became Brain of Britain but he didn't.

At the start of the second term in Standard Eight when some lads left and we 'outsiders' were moved into the main room. I was given two desks one at the front and one at the back of the class. It never struck me as odd but each morning I was given four or five national newspapers, a large 'Boots' diary, a pot of paste (Gloy) and a pair of scissors. I then had to read and cut out various news items and paste them into the book. With the Kings Abdication and war in the offing I got to know more than most 12/13 year olds what was going on.

At the back desk I did the odd lesson, particularly 'Composition' which was writing stories. Whilst some lads struggled with this I could manage 20 odd pages an hour. I read a lot of school stories. They were about public schools which of course weren't public at all, they were private fee paying schools. One such was 'Fifth form at St Dominic's' a book my Dad also read when a lad.

On one occasion Mr Carr called me to his desk and said, 'Why have you crossed this out; it's quite funny?'

'I didn't think it was right for that lad to say that,' was my reply. I also became the school messenger taking notes Mr Carr and the Headmaster, Bruce Sweetman, to other classrooms and other schools. Broad Lane, the Council School, Good Shepherd and Sandford were all regular calls. I also had to take the school registers to a man known as the 'board man' who would check for absentees plus a regular letter to a man who was probably a school Governor. He had a big house with a full sized billiards table in the room where I had to wait to see him, very posh.

One day I was on my way there when I stopped to look at a colour poster which was at my height. 'What are you doing there lad?' It was Mr Stones who now taught Standard four. 'These colours are made up of different coloured dots', red, blue, yellow and black and when they overlap they produce greens and purples and that. "So they do" was Mr Stones reply.

This was a process I became very familiar with when I started work. Another bit of useless info, blue was always referred as cyan in the printing trade. Is Cyanide blue?

In Standard 7/8 there was a bench running across the back of the room. I was given postcard portraits of the Kings and Queens of England and told to paint larger portraits to be framed and displayed around the room, I did the portraits-Mr Carr helped me with the faces but I never went back to see if they were displayed and then I think the school burnt down one night. There are now houses there and it surprised me how small that area was.

Friday afternoons 3pm till 4pm Mr Carr read to us, 'Three men in a boat'. He read slowly and had a deep voice. It was absolutely wonderful. Jeremy Paxman, who admits he's a miserable old sod, once said on the telly it was the most over-rated, unfunny book he'd ever read. He should've heard Eric Thomas Carr. At four o'clock he closed the book. Tough, mucky kids who had started smoking and swearing shouted, "Oh no sir, go-on" and he read for another few minutes.

Mr Carr asked the school leavers about their job prospects. Jackie Marsh who sat next to me said 'Inwimidad' this meant 'I'm going to work with my Father' now the Marshes had two shops, a butchers and a fishing tackle shop. I'm not sure which shop he meant.

> My Turn: "Civil Service, Sir"
> Mr Carr: "That's interesting Pearson. What part?"
> Me: "I'm not sure but you get a good pension."
> Mr Carr: "That's forward planning for you. Looking forward fifty one years on before you've started."

For some reason I thought Civil Service meant wearing a black uniform with silver bits on it but I've never told anybody that before. When I found Cousin Eric was a very junior civil servant in a coal mining area of South Yorkshire my interest dimmed a little.

Each year end in July there would be some sort of entertainment. On one occasion a sound system was rigged up, all the teachers were in stand-ard 7/8 and the screens were removed between the classes and all the boys were in this space. The teachers read a comic play, often using silly voices and we had to guess which teacher was which voice. Then the door would open and the owner of the voice revealed amid much laughter. Another Year it was the minstrel show. I have mentioned Alan Alderson earlier. He was the comedian and played the xylophone. He must have had one at home. It didn't matter whether a lad had dark brown, light brown, blonde or ginger hair they all had black faces and big white lips. Very amateurish but very enjoyable. Then scenes from 'Midsummer Night's Dream' were performed on the vicarage lawn. All I remember is one of the Bairstow twins playing one of the lovers got to wear an orange velvet curtain, as a cape on his back, I was envious. Who played the girls? Think about it. Each time anything like this cropped up lads who wanted to be in it had to put up their hands. My heart beat twenty to the dozen but I never dare put up my hand.

We'd had a day trip to the Lake District and on the way home I'd sung a silly song and told a few jokes. Back to School entertainment time. Mr Carr had written a short play based on Robin Hood, in it was a village idiot called Michael. He wasn't in the Errol Flynn version I saw at the Pavilion but there you go. When this part came up Mr Carr pointed at me and said 'Pearson, you're playing Michael'. My heartbeat 29 or more times to the dozen. I think larking on the way home from the Lake District got me the part. I can only remember my opening line in this farrago "It be hot and I be tired". From this I can only presume Robin and his Merry Men had been on a day trip from Nottingham to the West Country. Robin Hood, played by Harry Marsden a really tough kid more suited to Humphrey Bogart that Erroll Flynn, had to hypnotise me. Don't ask. I spent ages in our back garden leaning backwards and forwards without falling. Then I tried it crossing my eyes but fell over but like all hams I kept it in. Add a scene with a pork pie and I was ready for Hollywood.

On Thursday at 4,30pm we gave our first performance. Mums and Dads invited. There was no scenery but we did have costumes and bright orange makeup. Sitting by the tree (desk) with Mr Hood I had a pork pie (always mimed in rehearsal). I broke it in two with the big half nearest Robin. I crossed hands giving him the small piece and got a big laugh and a smattering of applause, I felt absolutely wonderful. After the show Mr Carr said, "You're cut out for this Pearson, make sure Marsden gets the small piece of pie tomorrow."

Come Friday morning quite untypical of Robin Hood he punched me in the kidneys and said "If I don't get the biggest piece of pie you're a dead man". Now this needed some thought and I evolved a cunning plan. Waiting in line for the orange make up I decided to stand in front of Robin A.K.A Harry Marsden. When it was my turn I said, "What did you say to me yesterday, Mr Carr, about the pork pie?"

"Oh, Pearson, make sure Marsden gets the smaller piece. Did you hear that Marsden?" Marsden: a muffled "Yes sir" and another kidney punch. Once again I got a big laugh and some applause. The show was over I'd left school. Several lads came up to me and said, "Was it a real pie, did it taste nice?" etc, etc, etc, a sign of the times in the thrifty thirties.

Hang on I haven't finished. I didn't think Marsden would actually kill me but just to be on the safe side I started to run home. Marsden lived in the opposite part of Bramley but I wasn't taking any risks. It was a boiling hot day, I was sweating through the orange gunge and a touch of lippy and stopped for a breather by a lamp post. A woman came to her door and said; "Eeh, luv, you look badly I think you've caught summat – come in and sit down. I'll get somebody." Me: "No, it's alright. I've been in summat at school and I've just left." What she made of this I know not. I was an actor getting on for fifty years and I put it all down to a twopenny pork pie. Goodbye schooldays, hello Hollywood…. Well not quite.

My Sister was an avid autograph collector and I had a few. Although she was very shy she had no problem asking for signatures. I was the opposite, heart beating etc, so she took my book with her to the stage door of the Leeds Empire.

So, I'd left school and during the second week on holiday. 'Hutch' was top of the bill at the second week in Bridlington. Leslie Hutchinson a West Indian singer and pianist, a big favourite of both of us and the only big name on the bill. There were a couple of acts who were pleasantly enter-taining but it was otherwise a third rate bill. We saw 'Hutch' going into the stage door and Sister got both books signed.

Here's a nice little story about Hutch. A friend of mine, Richard Wilson (not he of *One Foot in the Grave*) but a small 14-year-old apprentice elec-trician at the Bradford Alhambra was 'hanging about' as Hutch, white tie and tails, very handsome, six foot something West Indian took this final, rapturous bow.

> Hutch: "Boy, get me fish and chips."
> Richard: "I do have a name Mr Hutchinson."
> Hutch: "I'm sorry, what is it?"
> Richard: "Richard Wilson."
> Hutch: "Well, Richard, would you please get me some fish and chips with salt and vinegar and get some for yourself (handing over a two-shilling piece)."

> Richard crossed the road to Charlie Brooks then knocked on Hutch's dressing room door and handed over the wonderful Sea Brook fish and chips.

> Hutch: "Thank you very much Richard. Oh, keep the change."
> Richard: "Thank you Mr Hutchinson."

Now I reckon fish and chips plus free fish and finerks six nights a week for Richard would cost about a shilling in those far-off days so young Richard would be six bob better off at the end of the week as this was the standing order every night. It's a bit incongruous to think of the very handsome, Hutch immaculately dressed in white tie and tails opening the newspaper and paper wrapping and tucking into Yorkshire's best with his fingers.

It's often said that fish and chips were eaten 'up north' in newspaper only. This wasn't so.

Continuing the Hutch story, he lived in a flat in a posh area of London and it was an open fact that he and Lady Mountbatten were more than friendly.

Time moves on. Variety theatres and long seasons in seaside shows were no more. Tastes were changing also. Pop groups were 'in', their records sold in millions. His contract was cancelled. He got a summer engagement in an 'end of the pier show'. The venue might hold 300 compared to the 1500 variety theatres. The shows were usually run by a comedian and would comprise of the comedian, a couple of singers, half a dozen dancers and a speciality, in this case Hutch. Business wasn't good, neither was the pay and Leslie A Hutchinson couldn't understand why he wasn't a drawing card anymore. The posh flat had to go, and it was rumoured, Lord Louis Mountbatten paid for his funeral. There's a play there for somebody to write or as the song goes, "Somebody else, not me". If you've never heard it, now's your chance to read the second verse, sung by Phil Harris.

> Two ivory bones with ebony dots.
> Can oft times lead to cemetery lots.
> A game I played the other night ended up in pistol shots.

I was the furthest from the door.
The others… man they got there long before.
And thru' the transom somebody said.
Who's goin' to tell the officer gennleman when he arrive.
This dead brothers … ain't alive?
It's a wonderful opportunity, I agrees with you there.
And opportunities like this are very rare.
There he is, y'know he's dead, so I'm sure that you don't need me.
It's a wonderful opportunity for somebody else.
Yes, somebody else, not me.

Well I think it's wonderful and have done for sixty years or more. It is my book so I'll write what I please. More recently, a mere 54 years ago as my pen touches paper, Mr Harris's dulcet tones were heard in The Jungle Book where he voiced Baloo and sang "Bare Necessities". A unique voice.

It's a bit of a ramble and if you've never heard of Hutch and Phil Harris, it's your loss.

I saw Phil Harris at the Palladium. Top of the bill Jack Benny with Eddie (Rochester) Anderson and Marilyn Maxwell. Wonderful.

Another backstage story about the Alhambra concerns top of the bill act Revnell and West 'The long and short of it'. Ethel Revnell was tall and skinny with a megaphone type of deep voice. Gracie West was small and meek. They often appeared as schoolgirls with Revnell getting most of the laughs.

Band call 11am Monday. Revnell has lost her voice. A doctor is called. Bed. Tonsilitis. A few desperate phone calls to agents. No luck. One of the stagehands mentioned there was a very good comedian in Pudsey. Oh yes. The manager kept ringing around. Still no luck. In desperation the manager asked the stagehand about the man from Pudsey. Use him for a couple of nights then surely they would find somebody. Cliff Rhodes was the Pudsey funny man, the comedian with the *Novelties* concert party. Many people didn't go to see the *Novelties,* they went to see Cliff Rhodes, a very funny man indeed. I saw them several times as a boy and the other members of the cast were also above average as was the general presentation. Cliff Rhodes appeared several times and then had his own spot just before the finale.

He came, he saw, he conquered and played to full houses all week. An agent from Manchester came over on the Wednesday, saw the act and offered Cliff professional terms. Rhodes decline and stayed with The Novelties until they and he packed in.

One day, when I was still at school we had a week holiday away then my Dad had an extra week at home. On a walk on the Friday he said 'Got any money chum?' I said 'A bit'. Can you lend me sixpence for 10 cigarettes?' I did. Returning home we couldn't have tea because there wasn't a scrap of food in the house. We had to wait until my Sister came home from work with her wages when I had to dash to the 'bakers and confectioners' for food. Everyone, including me, laughed, but I vowed to never be broke, and have always had an eye on the money side of things. Oh, Dad gave me my tanner back.

School days over, I enrolled in a book-keeping course at evening school. The tutor was Eric 'Copperwire' Carr, so named because of his unusual hair style. It was at Bramley Broad Lane school. I'd always envied that school as it had an upstairs. Now I was in an upstairs room. Not much different really.

Here's one further episode in my acting career. My pal John Birley joined the Scouts so I joined the Scouts as well. Originally based at St Thomas's in Stanningley, a local mill owner, Mr Huggan gave the scouts a stone outbuilding a few hundred yards from where I lived. It was decided to have a celebratory supper with one or two bits and pieces. 'Albert and the Lion' was a well-known humorous monologue made famous by an actor called Stanley Holloway. It was decided to do an acted version of this. I appeared mid-way through as the judge. Now our house had a front garden plus a wide section of tarmac, and an unkempt piece of grassland plus the original pavement. Being a regular at the cinema and now an actor, I decided to rehearse my part on the tarmac.

The Barrymore family (nothing to do with Michael) were famous actors in America. Lionel, the eldest played a crotchety old doctor in the Doctor Kildare films so I decided I would sit on the wall and 'take off' the senior Barrymore which I did endlessly. Passers-by gave me funny looks but at last I got through a show without an accident and a life-threatening remark from, a fellow thespian. And there were other strings to my bow... Erik Rhodes was a Character actor at R.K.O. I think it was in 'Top Hat' that he said:

> For the woman zee kiss.
> For the man zee sword.

I liked this and added it to my repertoire and that's not all.

'The March of Time' was an American News programme which started with a very deep voice saying "The March of Time" and ending "Time Marches on". On one programme the narrator said.

> "In America today there are 10,000 alcoholic delinquents, victims
> of the cruel depression...."

I'd no idea what an alcoholic delinquent was but I liked the words and repeated this endlessly. No wonder I got funny looks and people avoided me.

Forty years or so later they ran a clip from 'The March of Time' on a British T.V. programme. Imagine Pat's amazement when I read out the exact phrase.

So, crusty Lionel Barrymore, foreign Erik Rhodes and strong American accent for "March of Time" man all done in a pre-pubic falsetto voice, surely Hollywood wouldn't be beckoning, nay, they would be begging for my services.

Dream on.

Chapter 4:
This Sporting Life

I've been a cricket fan from a young age. I would be about six when my Mum, hearing a noise, rushed upstairs to hear me shouting' L.O.B. Fleetwood Smith' over and over. She woke me and I explained Fleetwood Smith was an Australian slow bowler. Years later I found out his full name was the wonderful Leslie O'Brien Fleetwood-Smith. So I must have been reading cricket scores in the 'Leeds Mercury' at an early age.

When I was 7 Dad took my Sister and I to see Yorkshire V Kent at Headingley, Yorkshire were of course the team to beat and very proud to have only Yorkshire men playing for them. Yorkshire ran up a big score on the Saturday and when we were there on the Monday bowled Kent out twice for low scores. Dad said we couldn't stay till the end because of his cinema job but the end was in good time for that. Dad and I were regular visitors to both Headingley and Bradford Park Avenue.

In 1938 I saw my first Test Match England V Australia I went with my pal Alan Green and England were beaten by 5 wickets. Mind you Yorkshires Len Hutton, Maurice Leyland and Arthur Wood were missing from this side. Forward to the fifth test. Len Hutton 364, Maurice Leyland 183, Arthur Wood 53 and the hapless L.O.B. Fleetwood-Smith took 1-298, Figures courtesy Yorkshire C.C.C. 1938 Handbook. It was a world record score for Hutton and I think a world record total. Les Ames (Kent) was the first choice wicketkeeper and a top order batman. Second choice was Price of Middlesex at the eleventh hour neither were available Arthur Wood was taxied down to the Oval in Surrey. Ever the Humorist the Commissionaire at the gate said, 'Oi you can't come in here' Wood replied, 'If I can't come in England will be playing a man short with nobody behind the stumps. Arthur scored 53 runs out.'

When Wood returned to the Pavilion England were 876 for 7. Wood quipped 'just like me to get out in a crisis'. Lancashire and Middlesex were Yorkshire's main rivals their contributions to this match were Edrich (Middlesex) 12, Paynter (Lancashire) 0, Compton (Middlesex) 1.

A lot of my 'stuff' well almost all came from my cousin Eric including cricket bat, two sets of wickets and bails. I got quite a few games in both Bramley and Stanningley Parks 'cos I had the gear. I wasn't very good with bat and ball. However, I was a good fielder. Each day, rain permitting, I practised catching with my Dad, on the tarmac in front of the house, first with a tennis ball, then with a hard sponge ball and finally a sixpenny 'corky'.

Batting: I put my lack of prowess down to being left-handed and my Dad teaching me right handed.

Bowling: I bowled left-handed a bit wild but I was usually put on when the low order lads were in and got the odd wicket or two.

Fielding: I could field anywhere from second slip to outfield and seldom missed a catch.

I was just 14 and left school and a cricketer called Francis Jackson was to give some lessons one evening at Moriah. I fielded for about an hour and did quite well. In the gloom Mr Jackson showed me how to hold the bat properly and the rain started.

> As we were packing up a committee man shouted, 'Oi you,
> you're in the second team Saturday here at 2.30pm'.
> Heart thumping, I said, "I thought you had to be 16."
> Committee man: "How old are you?"
> Me: "Fourteen"
> Committee man: "Aye, well you look older and keep quiet about it."

It was the last week in August and half the players were away on holiday, hence my debut. At home Mum fished out Dad's old flannels and Dad found his cricket boots and cleaned them up a bit, I had a white shirt. Come Saturday we batted first. I was number 10 and a lad from school, Arthur Carrick, a much better cricketer than me was number 11. I tried to get the batting order changed to no avail. The wickets kept falling, my heartbeat faster, I was at the wicket. Missed the first three balls then ran a couple of leg byes. Arthur unlike me hit the ball and we ran two and then he was out.

After tea we fielded, a pal of my Dad's was keeping wicket. I was at mid-off and in about the fourth over the batsman played a defensive shot which rolled gently to me. I fielded and lobbed it back.

Mr Stead, "Lad, the reason I'm wearing these gloves and a box (tapping his groin) is to take it hard."

"But he wasn't going to run Mr Stead" was my reply. "Doesn't matter, lad, throw it hard from now on." A few overs later a fast ball came to my left, Mr Stead shouted to me. I was falling and threw it with all my might. Mr Stead was clapping his gloves waiting for the ball which hit him in the solar plexus. Panic, he was on the grass. One of the tea ladies came on the pitch with a mug of hot sweet tea and someone lit him a cigarette, a cure-all for the sort of situations. Mr Stead was replaced by Mr Burton and I took over at second slip where I took two catches. One was off my boot and bounced into my hand. They had to get the rule book out for that one.

Going to the cinema second house Saturday Dad said, "How did you go on?" My reply, "Nought, not out. I took two catches and laid out George

31

Stead with a throw. Can I have a choc ice please?" Come the following Saturday, holidays over, my cricket career seemed to be over as well.

Jumping forward Cricket Army Style.

In Huddersfield Signals I met a keen cricketer from Essex who told me he'd "be opening for the county if I get through this lot".

Sometime later this lad decided to have a limited overs match. He would captain one side and open the innings and if, and when, he scored 50 would do the gentlemanly thing and retire.

Two sides were picked I was in the fielding side and the Essex potential opened the opposition side. First over was I think a maiden. To non-cricket lovers this meant no score. Second over I think a run scored, and so it went on for a few overs. Now Ron H. of Slough a six foot plus chap captained my side. He got a bit tired of the Essex man talking about Essex County Cricket Club and decided to put himself on bowl. Very fast, very erratic, fourth or fifth ball a stump was uprooted and our hero had no need to retire on reaching fifty. He was out in single figure. I can't remember the result. I took a catch on the boundary, didn't bat or bowl and there was no return fixture.

On Demob I looked at the scores every day and saw Essex at Harrogate and Bradford but my army colleague was, as they say, conspicuous by his absence. Close of play.

This bit is all about Cricket and Rugby League. It's possible half of my readers have never heard of Rugby League but the other 3 will. In short Rugby Union was a game for toffs. Rugby League was a working man's sport. For umpteen years RU didn't have leagues. All fixtures were decided upon by the club secretary who tried to improve the fixture list each season. RU players didn't get paid. Oh yes. Ignoring 'Boot' money was a common practice with bigger clubs.

Rugby League originally Northern Union was a breakaway movement by clubs wanting to openly pay players for win, draw or lose pay. There was a League, Lancashire Cup, Yorkshire Cup and League Cup with a final at Wembley.

I supported Bramley through thin and thinner, mostly thin but they were the 'Villagers' playing at the Barley Mow, a ground behind the pub on Town Street. It was a Bramley player who played a major part in the breakaway. I think his name was Harry Bradshaw Picked to represent England v Ireland meant Friday travelling by rail and boat, playing Saturday. Everything closed on Sunday. Travelling back Monday so missing two and a half days pay. He asked for expenses. No go.

Twenty or so clubs in Yorkshire and Lancashire plus Barrow formed the Northern Union, which then became Rugby League. Over the years the League tried with little success to spread the game further afield.

In my younger days Wigan Highfield became London Highfield. Streatham and Mitcham and Acton and Willsden had a season or two competing among a load of soccer supporters. I'm told soccer is no longer used but it was always used in my younger days. It was of course slang for Association Football. Newcastle had a team in the single league and met the same fate as the others, Cardiff, Bridgend in rugby union heartland also failed. Fulham became London Bronchos. A team was planned for Glasgow in competition with Celtic and Rangers. It never got off the ground, Toulouse, and would you believe it, Toronto and a few like Mansfield, Scarborough, Chorley, it can be seen that Rugby League tried very hard to move out of its Northern heartland.

Liverpool Stanley/Liverpool City/Huyton/Highfield and another name or two I've forgotten is another example of a Rugby League Club trying its luck against Everton and Liverpool.

So let's talk a bit about Bram.

With Leeds to the north and Hunslet to the south and Leeds United also in the south Bramley were always going to find it difficult to be a big club with good gates. However they were our club in our village. You were there, met your friends and the banter was good. Leeds would have gates of 20,000 plus, Hunslet 10,000 plus and Leeds United similar to Leeds. Bramley's top crowd was over 8,000 but in general 3,000-4,000 was a good gate. In the bad days before World War II Bramley were lucky to get 1,000 and played in what was known as 'mucky white' shirts washed and sewn together after many years' service. When Leeds changed their design to blue with a broad yellow band with narrow yellow bands, bottom and top, imagine the excitement when Bramley ran out of the Barley Mow pub in a similar amber and black rig. They looked like a real club and started to play better as well. In 1939 Bramley were drawn away to Swinton in the first round of the cup. In those days Swinton was a top club and Test Matches were held at their Station Road ground. I read a few years ago they moved to the Bury football club ground with gates under 1,000.

I was setting off home from work by train and the Bramley team was setting off to Manchester on the opposite platform. Benny Pearson, no relation, waved to me. The reason I'm writing this is that lowly Bramley beat Swinton in a low scoring game. It was beyond belief. It couldn't happen but it did happen. Bram were beaten in the second round. The club and the score are long forgotten but to play away to Swinton and win was a real David and Goliath event.

Delving back into history Bramley were involved in a record transfer deal. £100 when Lomas moved to Salford. Don't ask me the year, I've lent the book to a friend but it was a bit back.

How did Bramley survive? Brothers Eddie and Denis Murphy lived near me and gave great service to the club. Eddie played centre and stand-off and Denis loose forward. Denis: "We knew we'd never be in the top four." In the mid-fifties Bramley needed one more win at Christmas to be in the top four. They lost away at Featherstone Rovers and then slid down to mid-table. Back to Denis. 'With good gates against top clubs we survived'. Like all the lower clubs the richer clubs poached the smaller clubs. The money was too good to miss. Just before World War II Frank Lingard was a top class centre for Bramley. He signed for Leeds and played mainly in the second team. Players in the first team were often rested or, given a slight injury and had a match or two off giving the second teamers a chance to strut their stuff. I don't think Lingard played again after the war. Denis too was a mover to Leeds.

One day on the tram I asked him about this and his answer was simple, "I'm mainly in the second team. We haven't lost a game all season. Second team winning pay at Leeds is more than losing pay at Bramley and I do get a few first team games."

Denis did return to Bramley and suffered a serious neck injury at home to Workington Town. He clashed head on with Workington's loose forward Frank McTeague. At first it was thought the opposition man got the worst of it but it was Murphy who was rushed to hospital by ambulance. He was in hospital several weeks and told me recently "Frank McTigue had the return trip bus re-routed to LGI and came to see me whenever Workington played in the Leeds/Bradford area. We still send Christmas cards to each other."

Here's a smile or three that I hope will amuse non-Bramley fans, about 55 million at a guess and the few Bramley people who have paid good money to read this book. Let's set the scene.

The Barley Mow pub was the unofficial headquarters of the club and on a Thursday night the snug opposite the main entrance was the meeting place for the selection committee. One bitter Thursday chairman Tommy Bennett in black Crombie overcoat and blue velour trilby made his way to the snug. "Who's in who's out?" shouted a keen supporter. "Birkin after last Saturday's display." Was the curt reply. Frank Birkin was one of the finest second row forwards ever to don the amber and black jersey. Well over six feet tall, granite features he always reminded me of Hollywood actor Jack Pallance in his younger days but Frank was unreliable. He loved the home crowd, worth three men in defence and unstoppable from 10 yards out. The previous Saturday Bramley had been beaten up in Cumbria. When Frank knew the game was well and truly lost he lost heart. There was also the fact that the long journey home would put a limit on Saturday night's conviviality.

Frank enters the Mow. "Tha's dropped" the keen fan informs him. Frank enters the snug. Tommy Bennett was no lightweight. He had been a forward with the Old Boys RU club and Bramley. Now you have to believe this, I was there. The snug had no door. Frank lifted Tommy several feet in the air saying, "If I'm dropped on Saturday you're dropped tonight." Frank played on Saturday.

As mentioned earlier all the big clubs were on the lookout for top class players and Frank moved to Halifax and then Salford.

Now not really a smile but worth a para or five. Long serving member of the Rugby League Council was Bramley stalwart Walter Popplewell. He was appointed tour manager for the 1946 tour of Australia and New Zealand.

Imagine the astonishment when it was announced little old Bramley had signed a top Australian centre for a record £2,000. It's more than likely it was nearer £1,000 but what's a thousand quid or so to an Aussie reporter? Bob Bartlett was his name. We often chatted to him in the Mow and a thoroughly nice man he was. Bartlett's first game was home to the recently reformed Belle Vue Rangers pre-war name Broughton Rangers. Thanks to Bartlett's clever distribution and side stepping, half time 19-0, full time 29-11.

Once again in a couple of years the scouts were out. This time it was Leeds. Bob moved to the North Leeds Club and centre, Denis Warrior and a forward, I think it was Mel Hulme moved to Bramley.

In an attempt to clear up the mystery of why Bramley captured this top player one has to rely on the ever unreliable Mr Rumour. Word got around that the wily Mr Popplewell had got Bob to sign for 'a Leeds club' and not The Leeds Club. Believe what you will, it's a good story.

So what's happened to the game in general and Bramley in particular? Let's look at some basic stats. When Leeds played Hunslet at Elland Road in the late 1930s championship playoff the crowd was a ground record in excess of 50,000 (the book's out on loan). When Huddersfield played Warrington at Main Road in a similar fixture the gate was in excess of 70,000. When it was Halifax v Warrington in a cup final replay at Odsal in Bradford 1966 the gate was in excess of 100,000. I attended all three fixtures.

Here's another smile. At Maine Road I was standing at the very back of the ground with my pal Arthur Baker. He was 6 ft plus and I was 6 ft minus. Standing next to me at around my height was Bert Cook the 5 ft 6inch Leeds full back. We had a chat and he said, "Good job I brought this with me." He was standing on a beer crate. "I'm never without it." Bert was an Australian or was it New Zealand signing? He had a number of interests in Leeds Market. It was said he went to one of his connections for breakfast, another for lunch and one for tea. Rumours make life more interesting don't they? Fancy a top player having to queue to get in to a match like us mere mortals.

So why are the gates down and all the other problems facing this game? Moving to summer where there is so much else going on, holidays, day trips, motor cars, golf, tennis and of course cricket which has been meddled with and as far as I can see with a similar response from the fans.

A 13 a side going from to 13 plus two subs. Is it now four? Scrummaging is now a joke. Why call a man a hooker who doesn't hook? Changing the scoring points and the three man tackle have all played their part. The only good thing is the six play the ball rule. When there were attendances listed in the press, before Covid, they were very much lower than the winter game. What did you do on a winter Saturday afternoon, rain or shine, clear or misty whatever the weather you went to the match.

So what about Bramley in particular? Let's take Hunslet first. Why? Well it's part of the story so just keep quiet and read on. I know it's not *'Gone with the wind'*. Gone with a whiff would be more accurate.

The only name I can recall from the old Hunslet club is Harry Jepson who I believe was long time secretary at Hunslet RLFC. But people get older, take it easier then retire and a new wave moves in. Three Leeds businessmen moved in. I'm not sure of the exact details but Hunslet played a season or so at the Greyhound Stadium. They might have played a few home games at Bramley. I think they went bankrupt and re-formed as Hunslet Hawks started at a newly built ground off the ring road in south Leeds playing to poor crowds. I can only presume the Parkside ground is now housing. Ok so far? Here we go.

Again somewhat of a presumption but the owners of The Barley Mow pub, Bentleys Yorkshire Breweries must have sold the ground for housing. Two lovely ladies, the McClaren Sisters owned the field alongside the Barley Mow ground and once again a presumption, gave it to the rugby club in perpetuity. "Three Leeds businessmen" moved in. Oh yes. After some seasons at the new ground an open meeting was called. I attended. The meeting was called for 7:30pm. One of the directors was missing. The meeting started at 8pm. One of the three announced there was no written agreement or even a scrap of paper that gave the club the right to continue at McClaren Field but Bramley would be staying in Bramley. Houses were built. Bramley played a season or so at the old Headingley RU club in Kirkstall. Another spell of Bramley Phoenix RU, then Headingly the home of Leeds RL and then packed in. The club then re-formed as Bramley Buffaloes, how ridiculous some of these new names are. I've never heard anybody shout, "Come on Buffaloes."

Their new home being the Stanningley RU ground Arthur Miller Stadium. I'm not sure who Arthur Miller was but I know who he wasn't. Arthur Miller the well-known American playwright, more well known for being the husband of Marilyn Monroe for a while than for his plays. I've appeared in five of them. *Oh no, not another plug for Ron, the Artiste …* no it isn't.

To conclude Bramley are now out of the Arthur Miller ground and played a few matches on a local park and the last I heard were back in Bramley at the Phoenix ground and playing in a minor league. What a saga. On a brighter note Bramley's only tin pot was winning the floodlit trophy against Widnes—wait for it—played in daylight—don't ask.

Here's a quickie involving the Leeds Rugby League Welsh Centre Lewis Jones.

It was oft said in the late 50s or was it early 60s, or both:

Leeds relied on Lewis Jones and
Leeds United relied on Jewish Loans.

One day I was attending a textile exhibition in Harrogate and pausing for a few minutes break and a cuppa and was joined by one of the commission-aires. Let's cut it short and call him 'Com'.

Com: I'd just like to thank you for all the happiness you have given me over the years.
Me: Thank you, my pleasure.
Com: Yes, I never miss. I've got my grandson interested now.

Here I began to suspect something wasn't just as it should be. I thought he was talking about Ron Pearson, Actor. He thought he was taking to Lewis Jones, Rugby player. It was often said I bore striking resemblance to Mr Jones. I excused myself, we shook hands and that was that – or was it?

As I departed, he was the commissionaire on the door. He saluted then asked for my autograph. What would you do? Admit you were a virtually unknown actor and disappoint or sign? I signed. Sorry Lewis.

Two Cricketing memories that stick in my mind.

When I was a lad in the 1930s the Leeds Mercury was the popular morning newspaper. The Yorkshire Post being somewhat dry and concen-trating on business affairs. With newsprint rationing at the outbreak of World War II the Merc stopped publication never to return and the YP became more readable to ordinary folk. *What's all this to do with cricket then?* Don't rush me. We're getting there.

Cricket was the summer game and the 'Merc' usually gave a whole page to county cricket scores and cricketing matters. These days cricket is tucked away somewhere, it just doesn't rate much of a mention anymore. Is this the newspaper's fault. Not a bit of it. The game has been altered and does not attract big crowds anymore. Two divisions or is it more?

A friend of mine a keen follower of Yorkshire CCC tells me county cricket is now a Spring and Autumn game leaving the summer months clear for Test Cricket. This can't be true, can it?

Pre-war and for a long time afterwards if you didn't get to Headingley before lunch on a Saturday you didn't get a seat. The gates were locked and you missed Fred Trueman at his best or as Harold Pinter put it:

I saw Len Hutton in his prime.
Another time… another time….

The same applied to Park Avenue, Bradford and Sheffield and other key venues. You had to get there early.

People went to watch cricket not to dress up in silly costumes, getting drunk and very noisy and trying to join plastic beer glasses together in a long string. Do we really need names and numbers on cricket shirts, bat waving, jumping on each other and other silly gestures. What happened to score cards? The last time I attended a Test Match at Headingley I had to open my bag to be checked for the amount of alcohol I was taking in, a bottle of wine. Get inside and you can drink yourself silly on beer. In the 1930s beer was a poor second to the game. I think there were a couple of wooden beer tents in the main ground plus of course bars in the much smaller member's stands. My friend who recently cancelled his membership said a couple of thousand at Headingley was a reasonable turn out. Ah well, as a lad, meddle with something for the sake of meddling you get a broken toy. What about 'huddles' on the ground when they've just come out of the dressing room?

I loved the cricket coverage in the Mercury and could recite most of the county teams in batting order; Kilner, Croom, Ord, Santall, Dollery, they were the first five for Warwickshire followed by RES Wyatt and P Cranmer. Amateurs had initials in front of their names and were in a separate dressing room from professionals. Amateurs were called Sir and professionals Mr. Thankfully this is one tiny part of the game that has been dropped.

I've always loved names and remember this pre-war wicketkeeper for Leicestershire was called Dawkes. A most appropriate name this being a slang word for hands.

The Kent opening batsmen were Fagg and Ashdown. I believe Arthur Fagg held a World Record: The first man to score a double century in both innings.

The Yorkshire side picked itself, Sutcliffe, Hutton, Mitchell, Barber, Leyland, Turner, AB Sellers 'captain' Smailes Wood Verity Bowes. When test duties called PA Gibb opened and kept wicket. NWD Yardley batsman and future captain, Robinson, slow bowler and big hitter and a few second teamers filled the gaps.

In addition to the big test score mentioned earlier, 'Big Bill Bowes' took 5 for 34 in the first innings and Hedley Verity chipped in the 2 for 15 in the second innings.

Hedley Verity once took 10 for 10 I think it was v Nottinghamshire. During the second world war he achieved the rank of Captain and was killed in action.

'It isn't Cricket' is well known phrase meaning that it isn't very sportsmanlike. Well, this isn't cricket in the true sense of the phrase but worth a few paragraphs. It's 1934 and on a bit of unmown grass with a dirt path running through it, a dozen or so lads are having a game, the dirt path being the batting strip. We had a bat but no wickets (probably a discarded orange box) plus a tennis or 'spongy' ball. So it wasn't the playing fields of Eton for sure.

A car pulls up, three or four men get out. One shows me how to hold the bat correctly, another bowls me half-a-dozen balls. Then one of them starts showing photographs of cricketers. I knew every one of them. I was collecting the cigarette cards, Bradman, Ponsford, Kippax, O'Reilly and my favourite the wonderfully named L.O.B. Fleetwood-Smith. All the Australian Touring side with the exception of one, the Captain Bill Woodfull.

Now the plot thickens, when I pointed out Woodfull was missing the man pointed to himself. But he had a moustache and according to card 50 in the series Woodfull was cleanshaven. To end the episode each lad was given a Mars Bar with the exception of one.

This lad was given twopence because they'd run out. This kid about 7 years old, threw the coins into the long grass and ran home crying. What had his mother told him? 'Never accept money from strangers'. His older brother found the coins and took them home to his brother.

Now then, did the Aussie Captain show me how to hold a bat and did 'Tiger' O'Rielly bowl to me or were they Mars Bar Reps?

If they were Australians why were they one picture, the captain short? And if there were Mars Bar Reps, why hadn't they enough bars in the boot?

My Mother had the answer straight away. They were Australians on their way to Pudsey to see Herbert Sutcliffe. This I accepted for many years until I began to question why the wizards from Oz would visit one of England's greatest batsmen during a Test Match.

Were I a betting man I would think it 60/40 in favour of Mars, but secretly I like to think that it could have been men who wore the green floppy caps.

Am I the only living person in Great Britain who remembers 'Van Bars'? They had the same wrappers as Mars Bars and looked and tasted the same. Were they the precursor of Mars Bars? It's more than likely.

Here's another bit about Test sides.

It's hard to believe but in 1939 the West Indies Cricket Team played in a limited overs evening match on the tiny Bramley Moriah Cricket field. One can only presume it was some sort of charity event. George Headley, known as 'the black Bradman' had a neat trick. Going out to field, he looked as though he was about to throw the ball forwards but it came backwards. I caught it. So there you are. The Moriah ground is now housing so if you live to the right on Bell Lane Bramley your lawn could be where the wonderful Mr Headley, Learie Constantine and the rest once stood.

Chapter 5:
Local Entertainments

Every Church and Chapel had a concert party and it may have been where Mum and Dad met. When Dad had saved enough to buy a piano he formed the 'Merrians' concert party with himself as comedian and helping out on the piano. Mum made all the seven costumes including skull caps and ruffles. They were in black and yellow stripes and not very interesting. They also put on a panto at Christmas and during a night scene in 'Robinson Crusoe', Mum made a rat with orange beads for eyes, made out of one of Dad's old trilbys.

It was a night scene with a torch focusing on the rat's eyes being pulled along with an invisible wire, screams all round and kids kneeling at the front were soon back with Mums and Dads. Should've been an 'X' certificate. I was too young to see this but I seem to think I went to the 'Merrians' and slept in my Mother's arms throughout. The 'Merrians' folded and Dad started a new troupe the 'Tatlers' and this time Mum got her way and the costumes were jade green and black. I don't think the 'Tatlers' really got off the ground for when I was six Dad got his six nights a week job at the cinema.

I would be about 11 when my pal, Dennis Ackroyd, was in a musical at Hough (Huff) End, a tiny Chapel and a schoolroom, holding a 100, at most. However, there was a stage, an orchestra and scenery.

All I can remember is that Dennis, a bonny lad, played a sort of 'Boots' running on and off at breakneck speed every now and then. I thought it was wonderful. The comedian was a local 'character'… Reg Hanson. 'Walls' and 'Snow-cap' ice creams had a man on a tricycle with a large ice box in front. 'Stop me and buy one' was the Walls slogan. Reg had a handcart. Imagine pushing and pulling a handcart full of ice cream, ice, not forgetting the ever popular raspberry vinegar on the rough and ready back streets of Bramley. Cornets a penny or twopence, sandwiches twopence. Reg would have to sell a lot to make a few bob profit.

A diversion: In winter we had the 'Hot Peas' man come round.
Peas, Peas, Peas all hot:
Bring your pot and we'll give you a lot.

I think mint sauce was the optional extra at no extra cost. Quite an adventure that. Holding hands with my big Sister and going down an unlit back street to join the queue on a dark November night then running back home, hand over top of hot, mushy supper in a mug.

Back to showbusiness. These musicals were the work of a local man, Herbert Appleyard. He wrote the show, produced (the word used at this time) it and conducted the sizeable orchestra. Hough End wasn't big enough so they moved to the schoolroom of another Chapel.

Heavens above! What's this? The schoolgirl chorus had bare midriffs in a place of Worship.

Onwards ever onwards next stop Bramley Baths, which was a dance hall and an entertainments venue in the winter.

Probably somewhat corny, but so much work went into local entertainment and gave so much happiness.

The only other name I can bring to mind is Carrie Goldspink. When Carrie walked on the stage you watched, you listened. A rare talent.

I can't leave this section without a totally untrue but very funny quote from Diana Riggs book *No Turn Unstoned*:

> 'The prompter, though seldom seen, soon established herself as a firm favourite with the audience'.

Wonderful. Let's move on.

Chapter 6:
Packing Perfect Parcels at Prices

Back home I started applying for jobs and was rubbish at it. Shops, offices, factories, mills, I never got anything then Dad went with me and I got a job packing stationery parcels at a big clothing factory. It was mid-October.

Day 1 – I was shown how to pack a parcel.

Day 2 – I got my own bench. You were given a list of various branches and the items they needed and went to the shelves where the stock was, took what you wanted and marked the stock list.

Day 3 – On my own, I enjoyed packing parcels for Southampton and Edinburgh and far off places thinking this parcel I've packed is going there. It was mind blowing. At 4.30pm we loaded the van and I was the muggins who loaded them onto the man in the van. The lads played tricks on me, throwing a parcel when I was turning and it hit me in the stomach. I threw a parcel back and hit him in the small of the back. The parcel was shattered, the lad was in pain but I never had any trouble after that with parcels.

By Christmas I'd had enough and told my Dad I wasn't going back. He was furious. I pointed out there were five parcel packers ahead of me plus a foreman and the boss. It cut no ice. Nobody realised we'd be in a war in another year and some of the packers ahead of me would be called up.

I had to go to a school in Armley to collect some plastic money and then went to a school the other side of Leeds with 40 odd lads who were looking for work. I can't remember what we did but we were free in the afternoons. They were a rough lot of lads but one lad seemed a bit better than the rest. One Friday he said: 'We could go somewhere Monday if you like'. For some reason I couldn't. Tuesdays 'Leeds Mercury' ran a headline, on the lines of 'Boy steals car and crashes into greenhouse!' It was him. I never saw him again and the report said he was badly injured.

One Tuesday I was given a card for a job. 'Strong lad wanted for packing department in a soap factory'. I was depressed. I got to City Square and for the first time in my life bought a newspaper. It was the turning point in my career. Mum always told me to look under 'clerks assistants' as 'workpeople' were common. I spotted an ad for a boy in an advertising agency at 5 St Pauls Street. I asked the policeman on traffic duty where St Pauls Street was. He pointed right "It's just on there. It starts on Infirmary Street." Which, by the way was nowhere near the Infirmary.

Helsock's was on the fourth floor and when I got there the small reception area was full of lads from the school. Obviously, being a talented parcel packer I wasn't sent for this job. 'Whatever that lad falls into he'll always come up smelling of roses' was a quote of my Dad's. I was in the corridor. The boss came in from the lift tapped me on the shoulder and said, "In, you come." The interview was short and very, very sweet. The boss by the way had a wonderful name, Walter Murray Jubb Carruthers:

Boss: Have you worked before?
Me: Yes.
Boss: Where?
Me: Prices Tailors.
Boss: Who for?
Me: Mr Braham.
Boss: If you can work for him, you can work for me. Ten shillings a week in production department with Mr Johnson, now!
Me: Can I go home and tell my mother?
Boss: Yes, OK but don't be long.

Chapter 7:
I'm an Ad Man (Lad)

Advertising was to be my career and this is how it started. Pure luck.

I still remember my first day at Heslock Ltd. Jack Johnson was production manager aged 23, old to me. Arthur Johnson in my class throughout my school days was his brother but I don't think I ever spoke to him. With classes over 40 you tended to 'pal on' with three or four and ignore the rest. The first thing Mr Johnson (never Jack) said to me is "you talk about ads and advertis-ments not adverts and ad-ver-tise-ments". Nowadays people on television call them adverts and it riles me-just a little.

In addition to Mr Johnson there was Russell Thompson, rather posh lad from Harrogate. Kenneth Weeks who had started as office boy and moved up a rung and a shorthand typist, Connie Levy.

The next room to production was studio, a big room with seven artists. Mr Johnson took me through and introduced me to the studio manager Mr Dobson and the other four male artists and two ladies nodded in my direction as they were introduced. On the far side of the corridor were reception and four more offices. I would meet the users of these offices in due course. In production was a printers galley for taking proofs from printing blocks. You inked the blocks with a sticky black concoction appropriately named Printers Ink put a piece of paper on the printing block and there was a big heavy roller at the end of the galley which you rolled over the galley. Then you pulled off the proof and used a fish and chip shop salt shaker to dust it with powdered French chalk, job done.

If you think I'm going to go through all the processes think again. This was just my first afternoon in a business I came to love. I had a go, over inked, tried again, bit better, third attempt Mr Johnson approved. Success. The hours were 9am to 6pm but you were expected to get there about 8.50am and not in too big a hurry to leave. My last job was to take printing blocks to the two big newspapers in town. Plus calls to blockmakers, printers etc.

The 'Yorkshire Post' printed in the early hours was then very dry with, I believe, classified ads on the front page. The 'Leeds Mercury' a.m. and the 'Yorkshire Evening Post' which had several editions from noon onwards. The Post buildings were on the corner of Commercial Street and Albion Street the 'Yorkshire Evening News' was printed in Trinity Street plus the

'Sporting Pink'. "Get your Pink all the runners and riders" was the news vendors cry.

In summer of 1939 I bumped into my teacher, Mr Carr, and told him about my job in the advertising agency. He told me he'd got a headmaster-ship in Driffield. Wonderful man. Driffield's gain was definitely Bramley's loss.

Newsprint was rationed at the outbreak of World War II and the 'Leeds Mercury' ceased publication and the 'Yorkshire Post' became more read-able. 'The Evening News', always a poor second to the 'Post' struggled on until the early 60s then folded. As for the 'Pink 'un' I don't know what happened to that it certainly won't be printed in Trinity Street.

So at about 6.30pm I set off to both venues.

You'll smile…. I hope.

On my way to the 'Post' there was an ordinary lady standing in a doorway. One of the studio lads told me she was 'on the game'.

It was dark and one night she said to me. 'Do you always work late?'
'Bit like you love' was my reply.
'Cheeky bugger' was her laughing response,
'would you like a Mint Imperial'?

She was a smoker and apparently kept a bag of mints in her pocket in case she got a customer. After that I was a regular Mint Imperial customer but never succumbed to the other product she had on offer. What on ten bob (50pence a week) I must have spent four-bob tram rides a week. Rumour had it that she gave part of her territory to her daughter on the girls 21st birthday. Another street 'character' was 'Cigarette Liz' or 'Woodbine Lizzie'. She would stand on Boar Lane near to the pork shop usually with a fag in her mouth given to her by regular passers-by. Another rumour had it that she didn't wear knickers. This is borne out by the fact that there was often a stream of liquid across the pavement to a nearby grate. She had a tin mug fastened round her waist with a piece of string and somebody told me Liz and a gentleman friend used to go to a yard in Briggate, behind a pub, squat down and fill their mugs from the slops pipe.

One morning my Dad was in his office at the cinema when there was a tap on the door. It was a regular patron he recognised, 'Oh Mr Pearson can you help me?'

'If I can,' was Dad's reply.

'Cigarette Liz' from Leeds has just turned up at my door and says she's my Mother-in-law.'

'What can I do?' It turned out Cigarette Liz was indeed Elizabeth Porter and this was the younger lady's married name. No need to go into further detail but Dad said, 'Where does your husband work?' It was local. Dad rang the firm and that's as much as I know.

Footnote: My wife's maiden name was Porter but my mother-in-law bore little or no resemblance to 'Woodbine Lizzie'.

The only other 'Street' person I remember was 'Little Billy'. His pitch was also on Boar Lane, on the opposite side of the road to Miss E Porter by Trinity Church. Poor man was a cripple. As far as I could make out his legs bent backwards at the knee but they splayed out at the side somewhat. He moved with two wooden blocks which he gripped by his hands. Flat cap and glasses were ever present. There may have been a tin or something else for passes by to drop loose change into. I was on Boar Lane six days a week and Billy was always there whatever the weather, in rain or snow he wore a cape.

When war broke out in September 1939 Billy sported an R.A.F. badge in his lapel. I was told he had a son in the Royal Air Force.

Back to business at 5 St Pauls Street. The Heslock name came from two men, Harry Heselton and Walter Locket. Mr Locket died before I arrived but Harry Heselton was an unusual man. I never really knew what he did. He would occasionally come into the production room and ask for a printing block, a stereotype, for one particular client. I don't think the block was ever wrapped or posted or I would have done that. He also liked to go into the studio and look over the artists shoulder to see what they were working on. He occupied a smaller office with W.M.J Carruthers in the larger office at the end of the corridor. I can only think H.H was the space buyer on the basis that nobody else did that job. Space buying for advertisements in newspapers and magazines etc.

Mr Heselton was a devout Christian Scientist and spent quite a bit of time in the Christian Science reading room in Albion Place. 'You can grow a new arm if you've enough faith. Oh yes it's been done' was an often used mantra to me. As a 14 year old lad I thought how wonderful that would be. As I got older I began to think it out, first of all you've had your arm amputated and tidied up... the arm is connected to the body by bone and muscle so is the elbow, so is the wrist, four fingers and a thumb. To use an often used phrase by actor Richard Wilson in TV's 'One foot in the grave'. 'I don't believe it'.

If you, dear reader, have grown a new arm, or any other part of your body except hair, finger and toenails I'd be interested to hear from you. In later years Harry Heselton and I attended the Advertising Institute monthly meeting in Manchester. I noticed he wore a hearing aid, glasses and dentures. Not much progress there then.

On a sombre note when I told my mother this episode about arm growth she was silent for a few moments then said 'Your Aunty Kitty' (Dad's Sister) had more than one child, my cousin Eric, and a baby, this child contracted meningitis. Grandma Pearson, who late in life became a Christian Scientist, said she would keep all night vigils and the child would recover. The doctor's visits were stopped, the child died. Even with the doctor's visits it wouldn't have lasted long but Granny's interference didn't help. Now I am not saying Christian Science is a rubbish religion. Many people run to the doctors with petty illnesses when a little homecare, medication and most of all a will to get better will do the trick. So that's out of the way.

So, ten whole shillings, fifty pence in today's money, not exactly high finance but how did it pan out? 120 pence, eight pence a day on tram fares for five days, fourpence on a Saturday. At first, I think I gave my Mum half-a-crown so that left a full 24 pence for high living. If these figures are somewhat of a mystery to you each Friday I went to the chip shop for 'a piece and a penn'orth four times please'. To translate fish and chips for four cost one shilling in old money, that's about, five pence today. A chocolate bar was 2 ounces for 2 pence, 4 ounces for 4 pence. Boiled sweets were 2 ounces a penny. I've often wondered about the profit margins on these. The manufacturer, the wholesaler and the retailer all took a cut. I can only presume the profit was in a bottle full. Yes, they were bottles, served by hand into a paper bag. The word inflation didn't seem to exist between 1919-1939 newspapers were 2p, kids comics 1p lads and lasses magazines 2p. I read the 'Skipper' as a boy. These publications ceased at the outbreak of war but resumed in peacetime. I bought the 'Skipper' for my daughter when she was about ten and an avid reader only to find it was mainly hand drawn illustrations with captions below in other words a strip comic. Took me a good week to read mine, took my daughter half an hour. How sad.

In Leeds there were four or five other agencies of a similar size to Heslock plus two or three minnows, each of the others had an ex-Heslockian in a responsible position. H.H's other mantra was: 'We trained them, taught them all they know, then they went and left us. Ten years later I was to find the answer to this oft repeated phrase, "Low wage and not much prospect." So, for now let's leave "Hezzie" in his office, doing whatever he did and move on.'

So how did I earn my weekly stipend? Newspapers, called 'vouchers', came in every morning, usually in two's. One went to the customer—the client—and I had to file the other one on the big shelves at the back of the studio. I loved this job, it was a bit like packing parcels to send to far off places at the tailoring factory. Here were titles from far away 'Inverness Courier', 'Belfast Telegraph', and my favourite, 'Kidderminster Shuttle' and many more. These titles have stayed with me for eighty years or more, I also loved the banter from the artists. There are a bit rude but it made me laugh:

Deep voice: "Are these waters" (high voice) "shark-infested?"
And...
Sex life of a Monk?... None... or Nun?

Apart from taking proofs from printing blocks on the galley which dear reader, I have covered earlier I was always kept busy. Question? How did W.M.J. Carruthers know the manager of a small packing department manager at Prices Tailors? A possible answer could be that Prices Taylors were Heslock's biggest client, but how and where W.M.J. Carruthers met the be-wigged part time club comic remains unsolved. Prices Tailors traded under the name of 50 shilling tailors. £2.50 a suit! Whether this included the waistcoat I know not. There was also a 30 shilling tailors still trading after the war.

'Fifty bob' had about 300 branches, every Autumn and Spring they advertised each week. R.C.N. in London did the national ads and, if we were lucky, the original printing block arrived about 4pm. Richardson's the Stereotypers in Basinghall Street then had to produce 300 duplicates. My job was to collect them on a pair of wheels and after packing then make several trips to Leeds City Station. Jack Johnson, Russell Thompson and Kenneth Weekes did the packing. I was usually sent home at 9pm, they worked on till 11. My pay, overtime one shilling (5p today) the others got 1/6.

On one occasion the original didn't arrive until late evening. I was told to go home, have my tea and return. We all finished at 4am. The remuneration remained unchanged but I was allowed a taxi home. Believe me for 15 minutes that was living the high life, and I was told I could drift in late at about 9.30am. Life couldn't get better than that. Dad didn't agree. I was a muggins.

On a normal day there would be regular visits to Blockmakers, Printers and Newspapers, I would often finish about 6.30pm, but I was learning and Blockmakers and Printers would let me see how they worked and these tricks of the trade would be invaluable to me in later years.

Richardson's the Electrotypers and Stereotypers was the muckiest set of premises I've ever seen. Once a year, Walter Batty—the boss—would call in his men on a Sunday. Everything including cobwebs would be white-washed, Job done. They were a wonderful set of men and taught me quite a lot and let me do some of the processes.

And, without really knowing it, I was picking up engravers and publishers jargon.

Originals, zinco's, half-tones, duplicates, electro's, stereo's and flong. All gone now I presume but essential lingo in the advertising business, formes and quoins were two more memories of the printing trade.

Ear-pieces – the tiny Ads at each corner of a newspaper's title were much sought after. I was becoming a very young, inexperienced and often very wet Ad man.

'Now then lad, get your coat off and make some "flong" was one instruction. In simple terms to make a duplicate from an original you needed "flong". Take a sheet of tissue paper, lather it with a special sloppy paste, repeat 30 or so times, then after some drying time, put this on the original and belt in with a large flat brush. Then this matrix has to be "cooked: until it is very hard and put into a press and very hot metal poured into the press, and an exact duplicate is made." The duplicate is then mounted on to mahogany and you have a printing block. One evening they let me do the whole process under strict supervision, I felt wonderful. For a couple of hours I was a craftsman and who knows that 'stereo' I made might go to the "Kidderminster Shuttle" or the "Falmouth Packet".'

Stanley Atkinson of Burman Norton, the process engravers said every night I called, "Come in lad. Cut yourself a slice of cake, sit down, be with you in a minute". One night I said, "Where's me cake?" Next night, "Come in lad, cut yourself a slice of cake" as he lifted a cover on a plate to reveal a freshly baked fruit cake baked by Mrs Atkinson, plus a knife. They were that sort of people, sometimes rough, sometimes rude but genuine, helpful human beings. Years later when I was running a business, some of them were still my friends.

Come July and war clouds weren't looming they were a racing certainty. Both Walter Carruthers and Jack Johnson were in the T.A. (Territorial Army) and were called up for special training, never to return until demob time. I think Jack became a Sergeant Major and Carruthers, a Major. Jack spent all his working life at 'Hezzies' but Carruthers returned for a little while, couldn't settle and I am told re-joined the army.

The First two weeks in September 1939 there were two major events. 1 war was declared. 2 the Pearson clan went to Blackpool. I may have got these in the wrong order of priority. Returning to work I found several changes. In production with Jack Johnson gone, Russell moved up a rung – Ken Weekes left awaiting call-up so I too moved up a rung and we had a new 'lad' whose name completely escapes me. With paper rationing, news-papers and magazines were drastically reduced resulting in another half-a-dozen of staff leaving. I think I got a rise of two shillings and sixpence. I was on the road to fame and fortune. Well that's what kept me going anyway. Things slowed down, sometimes almost to a standstill. I suppose we were lucky to be employed and, wait a minute, Harry Heselton moved into the big office! Didn't make the 'fudge box', (known as the 'stop press' to mere mortals) in the Evening Post, but there you go.

Here I must introduce Miss Smithies the bookkeeper. How can I explain this? Living in Bramley there were printing blocks to be delivered to the 'Bramley Advertiser' and the 'Pudsey News' every week, Now, Kenneth the lad before me didn't live in this area, were talking high finance here so you could be forgiven for skipping a paragraph or two.

In order to keep the books looking straight I was the given the full six pence and delivered the block on the way home to the Miss Witt's house. Four pence saved. Hang on we're not finished yet, the lovely ladies gave me sixpence for my trouble. Read on. I took the 'Pudsey News' block home and Mr Burrows collected it, another four pence in the bank. Based on the same routine I had deliveries to Greengates and Bingley both on full fare but by going at teatime and a fair bit of walking the cash in the bank began to mount. I also made a few deliveries at lunchtime, riding there and walking back. Is this how Lord Nuffield, Billy Butlin and Lord Sugar started to stash the cash?

At Hezzies smoking and fish and chips were banned. One Friday Mr H was to be out to lunch so I was sent to Youngman's in New Briggate, the best fish and chips in town. I think it was fish and chips seven times and I got mine for nowt. As I went down Lower Bond Street, mission almost completed, who should be coming towards me but the boss. I managed to put the bulky parcel behind my back, holding it with one hand. This must have looked a bit odd and there must have been a delicious smell.

> Mr H: "Now then where've you been to?"
> Me: "The YEP to deliver blocks for tomorrow's Co-op ad." (the truth)
> I think it was at this stage a stray Alsatian started to lick the parcel. Honestly, 'Hezzy' must have noticed an office lad with one hand behind his back trying to ward off a large dog with the other.

Another incident in almost the same place but with me going up and well-known bandleader Joe Loss coming down.

> Loss: "Can you help me. I need the Post Office. One of my trumpets has been taken ill. I need to telegram to get a replacement."
> Me: "Turn left at the bottom, it's on your right. There's also Cable and Wireless there, pointing, where the blue and red sign is."
> Loss: "Thank you very much. Must dash."

To younger readers, anybody below pensionable age, Joe Loss may not mean much. He'd started out with a small group of musicians playing Palm Court type of genteel background music in hotels etc. Loss played the violin. He saw the way things were going. Big bands were in with four sax, three trumpets, two trombones, piano, bass and drums were the usual format. Some bands added a singer who played the acoustic guitar. You never heard the guitar but it looked good and with most of the band with their mouths full and the rest concentrating what they were doing, a nice smiling guitarist did no harm. Big bands played in some of London's biggest hotels, their records were best sellers and they toured the number one variety houses.

Here's another nice tale about Joe Loss. Douglas Isle of Man, the Loss orchestra was doing a summer season at the Villa Marina. Arthur Baker and I were staying at Mrs Kelly's (who else in the IOM?) and their son was on holiday from university and got to know one of the band. We went for a long walk into the countryside.

> The Loss man said, "Wonderful man Joe Loss."
> Me: "Really?"

Loss Man: "Absolutely, marvellous the way he keeps in time with us is astonishing."

Think about it. It was probably an in-joke but quite funny.

I love good comedy and this opening sequence from 60 or more years ago still makes me smile. Harvey Stone was a very dry American comedian who was also an above average trombone player:

> 'Good evening ladies and gentlemen, Mr Orchestra Leader, the boys in the band look a little melancholy tonight; bodies like melons and faces like collies'.

Back to reality. On 14th March 1942 (easily remembered, my Sister's birthday) I was on fire-watching duty at 5 St Pauls Street. You wore your own clothes plus a 'tin hat' that had been passed from head to head. Our equipment was a bucket of sand, a bucket of water and a long handled scoop. When the sirens went off we were obliged to climb through a skylight on to a flat roof, whilst doing this I put my left hand on to something extremely hot which I assumed was shrapnel. This hand has been slightly bent ever since. Not exactly a war wound but something you don't forget. Something I almost forgot, there were two other money makers. Byron Hellyer Tremaine—get that name—the 'contact' man for a number of clients and Kenneth Monkman a copywriter didn't care for fire-watching so I deputised, half a crown from B.H.T. and two bob from K.M.

Monkman had been the drummer in the Leeds University Jazz group. One day he brought me some drumsticks, some brushes and a pad to practice on and gave me a smattering of basic moves and instructions. He also gave me his Yorkshire County Cricket Club Members card to use when he was on holiday. So many nice, kind and generous people. I became 18 on 12 August 1942. They didn't waste any time. They needed me in Dad's often-used phrase "to clear up this little lot". I had my medical mid-September. The Doctors name was Ogilvie. My doctor's brother. During a thorough examination he asked about the scars by my right lung area and right leg and listed me 'on reserve' and unlikely to be called up. The war must have been pretty bad for on the 21st January 1943 they asked me to help with winning it. Up until then, apart from suffering 'shrapnel shock' as previously recorded nothing much seemed to be happening.

No television and radio bulletins strictly regulated and the newspapers weren't much help. Obviously there were no shots of the Stalag Prison Camps where hundreds of thousands of innocent Jewish people ended their lives in gas chambers or starved to death.

Worse than that Hitler was portrayed as a comical figure. Variety comedians combed their hair in Hitler's ridiculous way and added a tiny moustache. We were told his real name was 'Schicklegruber' and he was a house painter. I believe he was an above average water colourist.

We had air raids and my Mum insisted we all came downstairs and had something to eat and drink. We had an easy chair that opened out into a half-length bed, I brought my bedclothes down and was usually back in the land of nod before the refreshments arrived, and if I wasn't asleep I pretended to be.

Apart from work I went to the cinema a couple of times a week and the 'Leeds Empire' was a regular variety venue and, heaven forbid, there were Sunday charity concerts in several cinemas. Where's the cash coming from for all this jollity? Well Russell got his calling-up papers and at 16 and 3/4s I became production manager.... Wait for it.... £1.10.0 per week, not exactly 'untold riches' but 'just a small step in the life and times of Ronald Stewart Pearson.'

However, before I helped King and Country 'win' the war here are a few more random memories. I was never short of friends at 'Westover' and my closest friend, Joe Lawrence lived next door but one. His Dad Walter and Uncle Sam were rhubarb growers somewhere off Waterloo Lane in Bramley. When they worked late in winter we had to take their evening snack to them. Joe's Mum told him to be on the lookout as it was apparently against the law for lads to be out 'sort of' working at 7pm. Imagine then Joe looking down every street end and alleyway for the boys in blue. My reward was in rhubarb, straight from the shed. Absolutely wonderful. The sheds were long, low and dark, lighted by candles and we stayed with 'the men' whilst they ate and we drank tea. I was 7 or 8 at the time. It made me feel very grown up.

When we moved to Stanningley Road, with Joe in a lower class than me we often chatted but the friendship eventually came to an end. As I said I was never short of friends. Alan Green a very quiet lad who lived nearby, went to a different school but became my closest friend for several years, his Father was a bus driver. Once, getting off a tram after work he was knocked down in almost the identical spot where I had my accident years ago. However, his accident was serious. Whether he was killed on the spot or died later in hospital I don't know. Alan and I hadn't seen each other for a year or so but I thought it only right and proper to visit the house and offer my condolences. Alan was a year or so older than me and became a trainee engineer in nearby Armley. When war broke out, I think he was classed as being in a reserved occupation so wasn't called up and worked night shifts. However after the war he did his National Service and I bumped into him at a rugby match and invited him to the Wednesday whist drive at Bramley Recreation Club. He loved cards, he came once and I ever saw him again.

I was never short of lads to go out with or ask to birthday parties. John Birley, Laurie Birley, Dennis Ackroyd, Alan Alderson, David Mann and a few more I've forgotten plus a couple of lads from the office were my pals. My Sister's birthdays were always family affairs.

Here I must mention 'The Doris Waddington's School of Dance', a long narrow room above shops on Boar Lane in Leeds. I'd been to a couple of dances in Pudsey but never had the nerve to ask a girl to dance with me. I sat on the edges and pretended to be enjoying the somewhat corny dance band. There was another reason, I couldn't dance a step. Doris and a tall slim lad stood the newcomers in a line and showed us the basic steps for the waltz and fox trot. Next week it was the quick step. My first partner was the tall slim lad, I had him on the floor in no time. He wasn't hurt but after a few more stumbles he handed me over to Doris Waddington. I didn't floor her but to put it delicately she suggested I wasn't really cut out for dancing and that, as they say, was the end of that. I think being left handed and left footed may have played part but clumsiness and downright thick-headedness were, I think contributory factors. In later years my wife did teach me to waltz and slow foxtrot, she never fell down and the bruises on her ankles and feet soon healed.

Years later I appeared in several musicals at the Bradford Alhambra, only in one did I have to dance with about thirty others, I was hopeless. I suggested to the director and the choreographer that, as I was playing the thick comical boss of a large company it would be perfectly in character for me to go wrong and bump into people with a happy smile on my face. It was a hit with lots of laughter from the audience, but I was never offered a dancing role after that.

Romance, I didn't pull any of the birds during my very brief stay at 'the Doris Waddington's School of Dance' but I have to admit this was my prime motivation, almost every other film you saw it was 'boy meet girl… boy romances girl…. boy loses the girl…. boy gets girl… a kiss and fade out.' I thought that was how it was. My Dad never told me about the birds and the bees and I heard the usual jokes but I was not quite sure what it was all about. I blame the 'Hays Code'. Will Hays (not the school master comedian Will Hay who made several very good British film comedies) laid down some very odd guidelines which had to be held by all studios. For instance: If our hero was trying his luck on a settee and a kiss ensued he had to have one foot on the floor. If a married couple were in bed they had to be in separate beds, so, no 'Hanky Panky' there. If Oliver Hardy (you must know him) was being pursued by a scheming divorcée the film was given an 'A' certificate i.e. unsuitable for those under 16. Ken Maynard, Hoot Gibson, Tom Mix, Tom Keene and another half a dozen 'B' cowboy movie actors could kill countless Native Indians…. Nothing wrong with that…. They all got 'U' for universal certificates.

Back to reality, Harry Heselton's Secretary Madge was quite nice, spent most of her time helping out in the production department but I never plucked up courage to ask her out. When war broke out she moved to another job and when I saw her, she was always seemed to be running to catch a bus or something. I got the hint.

Hezzy moved to the big office and took on a new secretary, red haired, pretty face, and as the pulp fiction writers had it 'curves in all the right places'. I was 15, she was 19. It wasn't exactly 'love at first sight' or, in her case 'love at first fright' but we did break the 'Hays Code' a time or two. We went to the cinema, the theatre and cricket matches but then she got called up into the 'Wrens' which stands for the Women's Royal Navy Services, but the E is a mystery to me, after a couple of letters 'to and fro' the 'Romance' died, or did it? Skip forward to 1975. I was in a production of 'Guys and Dolls' at Bingley playing the comedy lead Nathan Detriot. The B.B.C were running a weekly programme covering gardening, baking, etc and they came to Bingley to give us seven minutes of rehearsal time and what we did for a living. I was shown driving to my office, sitting behind my desk where I was asked, "Why do you do musical theatre?" I replied, "Because I'm a big head and I like the applause." It got a good laugh from the film crew and I thought that was it. But no, I had a duet and one Sunday morning I received a 'phone call from the director. "This number you have with Elizabeth is a bit wonky can you come in at two thirty and we'll sharpen it up?" I arrived promptly to find the BBC camera crew were there. Apparently they were going to film the handsome hero and the other girl in the foursome in a duet but he wasn't interested. The "Beeb" were so pleased with all these weekly clips they gave us a full half hour including "Sue Me" my number with the very talented Elizabeth Nott. It was really her number with my interjections and, thank the lord, I sang my bit kneeling so dancing was out of the question. Oh I don't know I'll try anything for a laugh and not so far to fall.'

So where's all this rambling and self-praise leading? The 'phone rings' are you the Ron Pearson that worked at Heslocks in 1939? 'I am'. 'I'm Kathleen Cooper, remember me?' We both wanted to see the same film but I was a bit iffy due to something else, I had to attend to. I suggested she got in the queue and I would join her if I could, I didn't make it. 'You're not still waiting in the Odeon queue are you?' There was lots of laughter. 'You don't change' we chatted for a few minutes about 'Guys and Dolls' and our marital details and that once again was that, almost. A few weeks later the director of this programme rang and asked me if I would be interested in fronting a similar magazine programme? 'Yes' was my short answer. The short audition script was promised for Tuesday. It arrived 9 am Friday audition 10.30 am. The script was badly typed and needed correcting. The audition was rubbish. I wasn't asked back. The programme went out lasting just two episodes. Finito. A few weeks later I heard the director had gone back to New Zealand. 'Nuff said'.

Now I must mention my other piece of romance. A Dark Beauty I shall refer to as DB. Girls tended to go out in pairs, one pretty, one plain. It was a similar thing for lads, one had it the other hadn't. In the Park one Sunday afternoon the band was playing and me and my pal Leonard got chatting to two girls and we went out a few times together. Leonard with DB and me with the other one. Leonard was in the ATC 'Air Training Corps' and got called up to the R.A.F. I took a chance and asked the pretty one out on a date. She accepted and I had a girlfriend. It was all very innocent. She invited me for an 8pm dinner with her parents. I knew her Father. He worked in the accounts department at a client's office. I used to pass him to the Ad manager's office and we often had a few words about the weather etc. She came to my house for a meal, everything rosy. I got called up. On my last night I plucked up the courage and kissed her. It was like that in those days.

We'll come back to romance from time to time but don't expect any graphic details. They are all in my head but never on paper.

Chapter 8:
Helping His Majesty
to Win the War

On the 21st of January 1943 I got an invitation from the King to help him win the war. Naturally I didn't want to upset his Majesty, I'd used his money for years and I always stood to attention when his signature tune was played at the end of films and variety shows. It appeared he wanted me to appear at 10.30 am promptly at Beckett Park Barracks Leeds. Dad's phrase about coming up smelling of roses came to mind. Beckett Park was near Heading-ley Cricket Ground and I walked home from there many a time and we'd several relations in the area who would be delighted to see me.

Dad had another oft used phrase re World War 1. 'We did everything wrong except win it'. Get this. It was a cold dampish morning and there were about 50 of us stood outside. We were arranged in alphabetical order and one by one we went in to be weighed and measured. This took a couple of hours. Mugs of warm tea were brought out to us. There was then a longish period of doing nothing. At 4'ish we went inside to be fed with undercooked fish, hard boiled potatoes, hard peas and sago pudding plus mugs of warm tea, outside again. It was drizzling, at about 5.30pm a sergeant came out and said there were no beds for us and we were being bussed out to Bradford. Wet and cold we passed Dad's cinema on the way to Bradford. I was homesick already.

We were stationed at the almost completed new Bradford Boys Grammar School. Back to reality, another long wait and some colourful language we were shown our room for the next six weeks – a basement cellar. Another wait and it was upstairs for hot cheese pie, made with mashed potatoes and at last eatable. The cellar was very big with about a hundred or so bunk beds. Running along the full length was a sort of mezzanine floor full of straw. We were each given a palliasse and a rough pillow case and told to fill them with straw. I think we got four blankets and shown how to make an army bed. At 10pm it was 'lights out' apart from some very dim lights in case of fire. The Sergeant shouted 'well lads you're in the army now. Talk about anything you want. Football, birds or dirty jokes… Anything except religion or politics because that's how all wars start'. I didn't believe him but I do now. Finally 'if you hear a rustling it's the rats' so sleep tight lads you'll be up at 7am prompt. There were a few muffled goodnights. Then silence apart from the rats.

I didn't sleep. I was in a cellar full of coughing men kipping down on straw liberally laced with rat dung. I could smell it or was it the unwashed blankets or both. They weren't expecting visitors on Thursday the 21st of January 1943. I didn't cry but had a hankie in my hand and my eyes were definitely damp. I was a soldier.

I tried to rationalise my thoughts. Braver men than me were being killed or badly wounded because a German maniac was trying to take over as many countries as possible and in doing so exterminate the Jewish race in Europe and here was I unhappy about mucky straw and rat dung.

Was his Majesty aware of this? I didn't sleep very well as you can imagine plus before that I had never slept away from home apart from hospitals and holidays. So what was Bradford like? Pretty much the same as Leeds. Next day we stood outside in the rain for an hour or so, they obviously weren't expecting us, the Sergeant called a name you answered 'Here Sarge' and the Lance-Jack ticked off your name on his list. I'm fairly certain the first name was Barry.

Sarge: Barry.
Silence.
Sarge: Barry.
Silence.
Sarge: For the third and final time Barry.
Silence.
Sarge: List him as a deserter and make sure it goes on company orders.

How could he be a deserter when he hadn't been here in the first place? Bit like accusing a sailor of jumping ship when he's still in the N.A.A.F.I. Bit exciting though having a deserter and it was read out every roll call. The deserter turned up Monday teatime, I felt sorry for him. This is his story. He lived in one of the remotest Western Isles and set off Wednesday. His Father rowed him to the next small island and so on till he got to Shetland which he called The Mainland. Here the weather closed down as did transport. Sunday everything closes so on Monday a.m. he started the final stage of his journey.

This amazed me. Jock Barry was the most wonderful jazz pianist. I was a jazz fan and he was very knowledgeable. In the main hall there was a grand piano on stage for visiting bands. We went there one evening and his rendition of 'Honky Tonk Train Blues' and a few other jazz piano standards was superb. Obviously he must have had a piano on his lonely abode, population 3 and he must have had lessons for this was an exceptional talent.

Jock Barry also introduced me to 'tablet', a very sweet, homemade Scottish confection similar to fudge.

Next morning it was bacon and egg and marmalade, toast, butter. Relax I'm not going to tell you about every meal I had in 4½ years' service. Mid-morning a civilian came in to measure us for our uniforms and by midday Monday we were kitted out and given a piece of brown paper and some string to send our civvies home. Proper soldiers or probably improper is a better word. There were two or three squads in the cellar. One bloke was 6'9" and spent the first two weeks in a bright blue suit and a tin hat. I said earlier the war had had little impact on my life but now I realised how desperate they were for men. The chap in the next bed to me had a very bad speech problem with a cleft palate and couldn't read or write. He was A1. Sergeant Spence had to do his best to putting his letters on paper and reading the replies from the man's Sister. There was a butcher from Todmorden 42 with very bad eyesight. His son was already called up so the business had to close. There were many more in this rag, tag and bobtail squad and Powell from Cumbria who stood next to me when we lined up. "I'm not sticking this", said Powell and on Saturday morning his Dad turned up and they found him a bed next to Powell.

Apparently Mr Powell Senior was the signal box man at a very lonely place in Cumberland as was his Father and his Father way back to when Stephenson started things off. A complication. There were some gates and a crossing and the gates had to be manhandled several times a day and Powell Junior had always done this until Senior retired and he was elevated into the signal box. Powell Senior and Junior left for home after breakfast on Monday.

I had a medical and was A2. Weeks later I was B2 then B6 then C1, C2. A pal told me that at C3 you got your ticket. There were many more similar to me but none I knew descended so far and so quickly. Now to the training, I'll put it simply. I was useless. I was the original 10 stone weakling. Couldn't stand up straight, probably due to my months in hospital at 5 years old.

PT... apart from failing repeatedly on the vaulting horse, I didn't do too badly. You had to run up to the end of the 'horse', use your hands to lift yourself on, propel yourself to the other end and do a clean jump and retain your balance and stay at 'attention' at the end. I was hopeless and after 3 or 4 attempts was told to move on. Afterwards I did very little PT—bit like schooldays—and became the squad messenger.

Now a man called Lenny Clough couldn't do a forward roll, the one thing I excelled in. As kids we called it 'tippy, tacky, tails'.

After half a dozen attempts it got nasty. Lenny used some rather choice language regarding the P.T. Sergeant's parentage etc., etc., etc.

That night we were all confined to barracks and a boxing ring erected in the cellar.

Imagine this: P.T. Sarge immaculate in red and black hooped jersey, black shorts and boxers socks and boots.

Lenny G in sloppy vest, baggy shorts, grey socks and PT shoes.

It was a 5 round contest. P.T. man did some warm-up exercises in his corner, Lenny just stood there. You've guessed the result haven't you?

Round 1 K.O. to Lenny, P.T. man received a hard knock to the solar plexus. He was hospitalised for a few days.

Afterwards Lenny G told us he's been the North Staffordshire Middle-weight Mining Champion 3 years on the trot and had volunteered for the Army.

He was never asked again to do a forward roll.

I didn't take the swimming test or run through a gas filled Nissan hut without a mask. Left footed on parade. One day on weapon drill, a Sergeant piled a dozen or so rifles into my arms and told me in the usual colourful terminology to make my way back to barracks. I was very low and in Manningham Lane I chucked the rifles over a garden wall. I was on my way. A kind old lady passed said, "You shouldn't have done that love. They could shoot you for it." I reconsidered, picked up the rifles one by one, cleaning them as best I could and that was that.

On the rifle range I put the implement on my left shoulder and a rather coarse Sergeant said something like, "You're not a chocolate soldier in a pantomime. You're a proper soldier, right shoulder Sunshine". You had 6 rounds. None of mine made the target. The lad next to me got eight including two of mine. Small arms something similar.

When it came to throwing a hand grenade once again it had to be right-handed. Don't ask. So I had to change hands with another spate of ripe language. It was to go into quarry. My right handed throw went about 10 yards and the vocalising Sergeant kicked it over the quarry and it exploded mid-air. I even failed the salute. Again I did it left handed and the bloke next to me got an elbow on his nose.

"Get swep up" was a regular as clockwork, morning cry from Lance Corporal Novells. The floor was untreated concrete and sweeping caused the dust to rise and settle on the blankets which were changed after the first couple of days but soon became dust-bound. I folded up one blanket and got it into my big pack for Mum to wash. I may have been useless but I wasn't daft.

First Monday we 'blancoed our kit'. This struck me as stupid as packs, belt and various bits and pieces were a very similar colour to start with and the 'blanco' came off on everything.

Second Saturday pm we were allowed into town. I went home, kept quiet about my lack of prowess and Mum packed me up a pack of goodies. I managed to squeeze these treasures into my pack which I used as an extra pillow. Sunday morning the food had gone and there was a big corner of the pack missing. The rats had a midnight feast in the dorm. What japes. I got a new pack and on my next visit put the treats in my metal mess tins. This saved the food but once again the pack was eaten as the rats would smell the food. Another new pack.

If you were very bad you did another six weeks and even another six weeks. I was so bad they had to let me go after 6 weeks.

On the Wednesday before we left Bradford a Padre came to give us a talk about praying and having faith that we would come through it unharmed. Any questions?

I went to a Church School and a Methodist Sunday School where I learnt to swear.

> Me: "Will the Germans and Italians be praying too?"
> Padre: "Well they are the aggressors."
> Me: "Hitler and Mussolini and Goebbels and Goering and Ribbentrop are the aggressors. Surely most of the men we are fighting will be like me. So, who does God save, the best shots, the fastest runners or those that stand behind a tree?"
> Some tried to laugh but mostly silence.
> Padre: "Very interesting. I'd like to come back to you on the points you've made."

Knowing we were being posted the next morning.

I was posted to the Royal Corps of Signals in Huddersfield.

Although Huddersfield was only half an hour away I was given half a dozen sandwiches, cake and a Kit Kat and a full water bottle of hot tea for the journey.

I was met at the station by a Sergeant and, as a platoon of one, marched to our barracks nearby. They were a block of condemned houses. No rats, some mice. Makes a change. There were some beds but I was a late comer and slept on a mattress on the floor. One night I turned on my side and a mouse ran up my shirt and out at the top. You didn't get a medal for things like that but it was an upsetting experience.

There would be about 50 or us new signalmen. We were there a couple of weeks but I can't remember what we did. I went to the Ritz cinema and the Palace Variety Theatre and went home Sunday. The cookhouse cat had kittens and they were about to drown them and I put one in my greatcoat pocket and took it home where it lived a long and happy life. The Red Caps on Leeds Station stopped me. "Anything to declare?"

"Yes, I've got a kitten in my pocket." Nothing out of the ordinary there then. Towards the end of our sojourn at Huddersfield a Captain Barker paid us a visit. We were to be Special Operators.

"Some of you men will be dropped over enemy territory with a compass, a pack of corned beef and beetroot sandwiches, a piece of cake and a map concealed in the barrel of a fountain pen. You're on your own." Well, that's how I remember it.

I spent over four years as a Special Operator and never met anybody who was dropped over enemy territory by parachute with corned beef and beetroot sarnies etc. I longed for, but not even saw, a fountain pen with a secret compartment. Nor did I meet anybody who had.

After two weeks of mindless existence we were posted to a nearby mill in Slaithwaite always pronounced Slowit. It was known as Stalag 5. On several floors you had to walk upstairs but not downstairs. Each floor had a fire escape poles which you slid down. There would be well over 100 men on each floor. At one end were half a dozen toilets without doors and each morning men queued up in lines urging the sitting tenants to get on with it. I leave you, dear reader to add your own words. I wasn't for this. The cookhouse had a few lavatories with doors. Each day I was taken short and asked if I could use them. I think I said earlier I may have been a hopeless soldier, sorry Special Operator but I wasn't a 'thicky'.

I think it was a Wednesday when we were posted abroad… to Douglas in the Isle of Man where our barracks were sea front hotels. Once again my Dad's phrase about "Smelling of roses" came to mind. I was to bunk down on the fourth floor on the top tier of a low bunk with a wash basin in the room. Such hardship. My companion was a very broad speaking Scotsman, Ron Curry. Although he was from Edinburgh he was rather proud of the fact that the other half dozen Edinburghians in the squad couldn't under-stand him. All of them were very good in picking up the Morse Code. For six months that's what we did. I was good. I'd done the Morse code in the Scouts. No problem there then.

I think we had one lesson on map reading and a course on E and M, 'electricity and magnetism' at which I was total rubbish. The night before the exam I went with a pal into the exam room. At each desk the papers were laid out plus two pencils and an eraser. I evolved a cunning plan.

The other bloke knew the answers. Wartime pencils were six-sided unpainted cedar wood so I jotted the tricky formulae on one pencil and when the Sergeant left his desk to walk around to see how we were making out I picked up this pencil and put the plain pencil in its place. I think the pass mark was 65%. I got 78%.

On several occasions the Sergeant in charge asked me how I did it. 'Just sort of clicked with me' was my usual reply. On the day we were posted he collared me at 7am and said, 'Come on lad now you can tell me.' I was taking no chances and as the posters said, 'Be like Dad, keep Mum'.

After a few weeks with the other Ron a front bedroom with a sea view became available at Beresford Hotel and I moved in with a Londoner Joe Brown.

It was Morse, Morse, Morse, no 'remorse'. When we became pretty good, about 16 words 5 syllables a minute we played bingo in the final afternoon session. Sixpence in the kitty so the winner took over a quid, well worth winning.

I think we passed out at 18 words per minute. Halfway through our training three of us were taken out of the squad and interviewed separately and the other two were taken off the course and sent back to England. I never found out why although one of them was a Polish Jew with an anglicised name. I wasn't asked about the Dettmer connection but I've often wondered if that's what it was all about. A new lad from Leeds joined the squad. Bit like Doc Martin, he was, as a civilian being trained as a doctor but couldn't stand the sight of blood. A very clever chap but he was hopeless at learning the Morse code and got posted. The RAMC would to me be an obvious choice. He had a lot of medical knowledge and would have been an excellent medical orderly. I don't know the name of the corps but he went back to England to train as a dispatch rider and like me had never ridden a bicycle, nuff said.

The King's visit:

Now it came to pass, as it says in the good book, that His Majesty King George the Sixth was to visit HMS Valkyrie in the Isle of Man. Now the more astute of you would presume that HMS stood for His Majesty's Ship that HMS Valkyrie was some sort of floating contrivance. But no. HMS Valkyrie was a number of hotels painted battleship grey with lots of ropes and pennants and a Union Jack that was raised at sunrise whether the sun was visible or not and lowered at sundown. Back to the plot. Our Colonel was not best pleased. SOTB was not painted khaki with flags and not on the itinerary. Cogs started to click. Suddenly it was on the itinerary. We were to parade in full action dress at 2:30pm on… whatever date it was. One morning I was spud bashing when the Sergeant Major was on his round. Imagine a tall Mr McKay in Porridge with an Irish accent. 'Remember your all on parade tomorrow for the Royal visit'. A tap on my shoulder with his stick 'and that includes you'. A tap on my other shoulder with his pace stick and he was gone.

On a previous potato peeling expedition the heavy cauldron or whatever they called it was dropped on my right foot. The foot turned a funny colour. It was heavily dressed and I was excused boots.

This takes a bit of getting through but stay with it and it all actually happened.

Now Joe Brown liked to be called 'Arry Boy', don't ask why. 'Arry Boy', 'We could make it bit of money if I ran a book on whether you would go on parade in your best denims and going out shoes. You've got the chitties'.

I think 'Arry Boy's family had a bookie connection. It was true. Every time you were excused anything you got a white chitty to put in your pay book and each one itemised.'

Now the battledresses were coated with something that smelt of cat wee. I was told it was to repel a gas attack but I think it was a water repellent but never mind. It gave me a rash from head to foot so I was excused battledress and everything else.

My chitties;
excused steel helmet – 14 days.
excused best battledress – 14 days.

I summed up the proposition.

We could make a fiver each out of this said 'Arry Boy'.

One fiver. When you're on 21/- a week and send seven bob to your Mum that was big money. I agreed. Cometh the day, cometh the deed.

I was somewhere in the middle of the middle row. The Irish Sergeant Major was with the Royal party. The other Sergeant Major was fifty yards ahead checking pocket flaps etc. He got to me and whispered two words beginning with F, the second one being "faint". "Catch him" was his next command. "Guard room" his third. The two lads dragged me, I was feinting a faint, to the guardroom. 'You are in big trouble Sunny Jim' was the blue capped Sergeants, only comment. The parade was over. I had to remain in this small hut that served as a guardroom until company orders were issued. The blue capped Sergeant had a wind problem but never spoke. Company orders arrived. I was on a Court Martial 10:30am tomorrow. 'Arry Boy' was, unlike him, very quiet. Say something I said. A long pause.

> 'Arry Boy', "We could really clean up if you went on your fizzer in that gear."
> "Don't they shoot you if you're found guilty?" I enquired.
> 'Arry Boy' pondered again.
> "You've got the chitties sunshine. Flash your pay book in front of his nibs and you're in the clear."
> I looked at my pay book.
> "They run out tomorrow."
> "What time?"
> "Twenty two hundred hours."
> "Then you're in the clear Yorkie."
> 'Arry Boy's gentle persuasion was irresistible. Plus a 60/40 split in my favour, I agreed.'

10:30am I was marched in by the C.S.M. who gave me the order to appear on parade. Lucky Ron. There was a Major flanked by two Sub-lieutenants. The charge was read out. Improperly dressed on a Royal parade. 'How do you plead?'

> He didn't appear to notice I was still improperly dressed, this time for a Court Martial.
> 'Not guilty, Sir'
> 'Not guilty. You were a disgrace to the unit. This is a very serious matter Signalman'.
> I put my closed paybook on the table.
> 'What's this?'
> 'My paybook, Sir.'
> 'I know it's your bloody paybook. Why is it on my desk?'

My heart was beating 20 to a dozen and I blurted, "I've got chitties, Sir."

'Chitties.' Major opens paybook, reads, looks at me.

'Why the hell didn't you tell somebody?'

I'd played a few aces but now I played my trump card.

'I was told nobody was excused, including me.'

'Who in God's name issued that order?'

Here the Sergeant Major took one pace forward and became my hero, stood to attention, saluted and said, "I gave the order but I was not aware the said Signalman had all them chitties in his pay book Sir." Salute.

I held back a laugh. The Major looked down at the book. Was there a hint of a smile on his lips or was it a grimace or a look of despair? Silently he moved the book to one of the Lieutenants and the other then handed it to me.

'Get out of my sight now'.

I managed a salute with the right hand and was out.

I've a further story involved this wonderful Irish C.S.M. here goes.

It's only hearsay told to me by Titch Morgan who heard—*come on get on with it*—ok here we go.

We usually scrubbed floors on a Wednesday afternoon. This Special Op known as (Sops) was in a room with Ozzie, Signalman Oswald a rather posh chap but just a wee bit scruffy. Enter C.S.M.

'You've missed a bit in the corner there' he said pointing with his stick.

Ozzie: 'Oh right ho well spotted off we go.'

C.S.M.: 'Sir'.

Ozzie: 'Sorry'.

C.S.M: (tapping the crown on his wrist with his stick). 'When you address me you address me as Sir.'

Ozzie: 'Fair enough Sir and you may address me as Lord.'

C.S.M: 'What!'

Ozzie: 'I've just had fourteen days compassionate leave. My Father died. He was Lord Oswald and I've inherited the title.'

The C.S.M, poor man, was speechless.

Ozzie: 'But I'm quite happy with Ozzie.'

Two days later Ozzie had a meeting with the Colonel and was offered a course on OCTU Officer Cadet Training Unit but said, "No thank you. I'm very happy with the lads."

It's a good story but I've checked *Debrett's Peerage* and I knew there was a Lord St Oswald at Nostell Priory but it doesn't mention the 1939-45 war. If I've got it wrong I hope it raised a smile and caused no harm. One thing I am certain of is Ozzie once gave us a very interesting talk on how to lay out a table for a very posh banquet. He wasn't showing off and he certainly knew his stuff. I was there. Let's move on.

Sergeant Burgess, the one who ran the bingo sessions, noticed I was slow with my potato peeling. I was using a right handed peeler in my left hand. A week or so later a note arrived on company orders. A supply of 'left-handed potato peelers soldiers for the use of, are now available in the quartermaster stores.' I got two. Bingo. Thanks Burgie.

'Titch' Morgan. Here's a bit of useful/less info. Titch originally referred to a very large man. Early in the nineteenth century, a man sailed to England from Australia claiming to be the Titchborne claimant, a large estate down south. It went to court and his claim was thrown out. Penniless he toured the music halls to tell his tale of woe and was billed a "Big Titch the Titch-borne claimant". A very small actor I think his name was Relph decided he would be Little Titch and became very famous in his long boots and that's how it all began.

It took six month's training to become a Special Op with one slight snag, lack of high frequency radio sets in the Isle of Man. I think there were about six. From passing out in September to posting the following June I never saw a set. Finally the IOM was not at war with Germany, no air raids, no black out etc. What hardship.

After six months training getting our Morse speed up to 18 words per minute we got 14 days leave. Boat and train. At our final lecture this was said. 'If a bloke wearing black shoes and socks, navy blue suit, fawn raincoat and brown trilby and smokes a pipe and starts a chat-up about what you do stay schtumm otherwise it's the firing squad'. I don't think it would've come to that. However the aforesaid happened, When a man dressed like that got on our train. "Now then lads, where've you been. Where are you going, What do you lads do?" This is how I remember it. 'Arry Boy' chipped in pointing to his shoulder flash he said, "We're signals see. We send signals from one place to another. Nobody's told the Officers 'the telephone's been invented'." Big laugh and we talked about sex, football, sex, food and sex till he got out at Preston.

On the last night of my leave dark beauty and I walked in the rain for a couple of hours, looking in shop windows and laughing a lot. It was a mile and a bit walk home, still raining. Back home I couldn't talk. Next morning worse. The doctor came. Seven days sick leave. He wrote a note which had to be signed by a JP. Dad knew one. The note went to the MO in Douglas.

Saturday and Sunday were pretty grim. Monday evening Doctor Dawson came and said 'Get yourself out tomorrow. Get some fresh air and some exercise. The foul tasting medicine was replaced by linctus. Four more wonderful nights with DB.'

Back at Douglas I found out I'd been posted from a seafront hotel to the biggest hotel on the island, Douglas Bay Hotel at Onchan Head about half a mile away. It was Saturday 7pm and Corporal Stenchion found me a bed and said 'You're in big trouble mate.'

Nothing much happened on Sunday but I realised many of my pals including 'Arry Boy' had got back off leave on Saturday and posted "Somewhere in England" on Monday. Sergeant Major Jack (Busty) Goldberg was a squat man. I was on the front row on the morning parade.

'You Pearson'. 'Yes Sir'. 'I know all about you and your emphysema. I've got that. Cookhouse now'.

Cookhouse now. The cookhouse was very hot and you scrubbed the floor. I can only presume my sickness note mentioned my empyema and Busty had got mixed up between his smoking illness and mine. Dark Beauty wrote and she knitted me a very unwarm scarf which I thought was wonderful. On September leave we saw each other almost every night. Cinema, theatre, meals out – the local chip shop. She now worked at a bank in Leeds. Then I got the letter from DB:

'It's been lovely going out with you but I'm only 16 and don't really want to get tied up to one person at this age'. Plus a few more paragraphs. I was devastated. Who could I talk to? Joe Brown, Ron Curry and all my other friends were gone. I spent days taking out my wallet, looking at her picture, reading the letter with tears in my eyes then I said a few rude words to myself and tore up both letter and picture and got on with my life. Finito… but not quite.

A few years later I was going to the rugby match and she was with a chap I'd remembered from schooldays. She smiled and gave me a wave. I smiled back and waved but then I'd met Muriel Patricia Porter who soon became Pearson for the next 66 years.

There is somewhat 'iffy' but definitely macabre ending to this story. I'll give you a nudge when we get there.

Jack (Busty) Goldberg ruled the roost. I don't think I saw an officer thank the Lord. I was still dodgy on saluting in the sixth months or so I was there. Neither did I see one of the wireless sets. This sounds jokey but it was also a tragedy. We'd spent six months getting up to speed on Morse plus all the other bits and pieces and now we were in a unit with a few inadequate radios.

Busty didn't like me. For the first few weeks I was on cookhouse floor scrubbing duty and staircases and floors. "Report to Corporal Chipperfield in the Cookhouse" was the command. this was often adapted to "Report to Corporal Cookerfield in the Chiphouse". What japes. So what went on?

After a month or so at DBH in the cookhouse, coal heaving and scrubbing floors, I was posted to nearby Castletown, coal heaving, cookhouse and scrubbing floors. If there was a radio set I never saw one. The only thing I remember, it'll come into the book about 50 years later was that a man with a list of names was shouting out names for a nucleus for Captain Napper. I'll remind you when we get there. After a few weeks I returned to DBH – why? Don't ask.

Harry Pevitt was in charge of Busty's geese, honestly. On what had been a lawn was now mud and a big wooden and wire structure held half a dozen geese. Harry had to feed them, clean the cage, exercise them and so on. A lad called Simmons wrote a newspaper that was pinned on the length of one long wall. Later I was to join him as illustrator and jokesmith, Lance Corporal Fox was a PT instructor but we did no PT. Just up the road there was a closed down amusement set up. Every Wednesday Foxy marched us up there on a route march and we slipped under tarpaulins and played the rolling down penny game.

Every weekday there was a raffle. Tickets were sold on when the incoming boat would cross a certain window pane in Busty's office 3.01 3.02 etc. Driver Fitton helped out in the cookhouse. There were no vehicles for him to drive. Don Witty, a Leeds lad stoked the boilers and so it went on.

At teatime the mail corporal came up on his bicycle to dish out the mail. A name was called, a hand went up, a voice said "Corp" and the letter was skimmed across to him. There were a few laughs. Larry Lamb, not 'im on the telly was 'Baaaah'. The star of the show was Driver Bellchamber whose call was, wait for it, "Dingdongpisspot". Honestly and Driver Bellchamber loved it and there was a chap called Puddephat and he got 'me-ow' and happy with it. However Signalman Longbottom was not best pleased with the post corporal's soubriquet and asked his Mum to stop writing him.

After a few weeks I was paired with a chap called Cyril Dix and we did the wash up. After six months training this was our lot. What the rest of them did I've either forgotten or never knew. There were fire drills, floor scrubbings, window cleaning. Cyril Dix was a remarkable man, exactly the opposite of me. Highly educated, very articulate, training to be a solicitor prior to call up. He had a very different sense of humour to me and as the saying goes we got on like a house on fire. No parades we had our own bedroom. Up at 7am, early breakfast. How many eggs? Sausage, bacon, tomatoes, fried bread. We got the best. They got the rest. Wash up and dry the plates. Clear at nine. Similar routine at lunch and tea.

In October Corporal Grayson put on a variety show. It was alright. That was about it, a choir, a crooner, a pianist, a monologue and one or two other bits and pieces.

Every Saturday morning there was an ABCA meeting Army Bureau of Current Affairs which it wasn't. The church parade list appeared on the notice board on Friday with the religion as follows:

14522368 Pearson R S (Meth)

12345678 Dix C (CoE)

Cyril and I didn't do church parades but one Saturday morning Busty fronted the ABCA meeting. His name appeared at the bottom of every list. "Which of you two comedians has put CoE against my name?" The biggest laugh ever, including Busty. It was Dixie.

Busty: "Now we're having another concert, Corporal Grayson's been posted any volunteers?" Nobody volunteered. "Right Dix and Pearson. You'll do it." A massive cheer went up, part relief and let's face it the wash house had become a fun house. We worked very hard on this. In retrospect it wasn't all that good but it went off like a firecracker. I won't give you the whole show because I don't remember it but here are a few bits and pieces.

And, Busty was beginning to like me. The plate washing room was full of laughter, crude jokes, rude jokes, bits of silly songs, rhymes. Here's a couple from the wonderful American Spike Jones.

> Startle startle little twink.
> Who the hell you are I think.
> Up above the world so low.
> You're a better man than I am.
> Old Black Joe.
> And:
> The polar sleeps in his little bearskin.
> He sleeps very well so I'm told.
> Last night I slept in my little bare skin.
> And I got a helluva cold.

I had the Spike Jones records and had a gramophone sent over with more records and we sang alternate lines. Busty heard the gramophone, asked me if he could borrow and a few records for an evening. He lived in a big house next door to the hotel.

Cut to the show.

We started off with morning parade, one bloke in pyjamas another eating a bacon sandwich etc. Lance Corporal Fox, another Jewish person pinched one of Busty's flat hats, stuffed his battledress with cushions and made his entrance, uproar.

> One of Busty's favourite routines was, when standing behind a man,
> "Am I hurting you?"
> "No Sergeant Major"
> "Well I ought to be, I'm standing on your hair. Get it cut this morning."
> Dix had borrowed a long lady's wig for the chap in this gag, laughter unlimited and so it went on.

Geordie Tommy Hall dressed up as a Cub and played the piano badly a'la Les Dawson and then quite well as himself. We had two men in the unit who were hoping to become classical pianists. The piano was the hotel one above average for a so-called army unit but they played a couple of bright classical pieces and a bit of boogie woogie.

What did Cyril and Self do? We decided to do the wash up on the tiny band stage, a bench, a bowl, some plates etc. My Dad had run a Pierrot Troupe and one of his songs was a comedy number "I think of you dear". We rewrote this as "I think of stew dear". Jack Scougal was a tall dour Corporal in the cookhouse. We got a pair of gent's long underpants and pulled them out of the wash up bowl with tongs. It was a bit like radio's

Workers Playtime. The comedian always mentioned the works foreman to thunderous laughter.

"How did Scougal's underpants get in here?" That stopped the show but the biggest laugh came from a short routine by the two pianists and ourselves.

Officers from the main camp were invited including a captain who had risen from the ranks always known as Captain Tommy Butler. It was also known he was a bad sailor, and smoked roll-ups.

"Now the two Pete's, will play a short piece dedicated to Captain Tommy Butler. We mispronounced the piece as The Baccarole by Rizla." Laughter during this piece. We got the lads to play quietly when this happened.

"Very bad sailor Captain Tommy Butler."
"Not surprising. Do you know the Butler family motto?"
"No."
"Sick transit Fleetwood."

Captain Tommy Butler slipped off his chair onto the floor. It was absolutely wonderful.

Corny jokes
Him: "There's a man outside with a funny face."
Me: "Tell I'm you've got one."
Him: "The heats on, the heats on."
Me: "Who says so?"
Him: "Don Witty in the boiler room."
Him: "I've got blue blood in my veins."
Me: "What do you think I've got dandelion and burdock."

Another joke.

Dixie: "I can't do it. You can't do it. Busty Goldberg can't do it."
Me: "What's that?"
Dixie: "Milk chocolate."
The two Petes will now play "The bite of humble flea at Minsky's corset shop."
That stopped the show.
For the uninitiated "The flight of the bumble bee by Rimsky Korsakov."

If a man toadies up to his superiors, he's called a crawler. Dixie asked me if I'd have a word with a Yorkie called Earnshaw about a certain gag. I was amazed he said yes. Halfway through the 'stew' song a curtain rustled and Earnshaw crawled across the tiny stage onto the mess room floor and out of the door. We stopped singing and watched him incredulously.

Me: "Who the hell was that?"
Him: "Earnshaw"
Me: "Earnshaw?"
Him: "Yes, the biggest crawler in the unit."
Both: "Oi Busty he'll be back."
Absolute uproar.

Bit like driver Bellchamber in the letter skimming business Earnshaw was absolutely chuffed.

Top radio comedian Arthur Askey had a signature tune very similar to the middle stanza of The Barcarolle. Our version:

'Big hearted Dixie they call me.
Big hearted Pearsie that's me.
Clean if we're not very clever.
We sing in the wash up you see.
We tell silly jokes and we try hard to please.
And for an encore Busty'll do a striptease.
Big hearted bounders are we.'

The officers went for drinks in Busty's company office. Cyril was missing. He'd somehow got in with the posh lot and had a couple of whiskies.

Dixie: One of the officers works for the BBC in peacetime and said, "If you too lads stay together come and see me."
Me: "What did you say?"
Dixie: "Not me. I'm going to be a solicitor."
So that put the lid on that.

A few weeks later, for no apparent reason, Dixie and I were posted back to the main unit on the sea front. We didn't exist. Never appeared on company orders. We had a room with two beds, probably a Sergeant's Quarters.

One Friday teatime we were issued with Royal Corps of Signals shoulder flashes and told they would be inspected am Monday parade. At call up we were issued with a housewife always called a Hussiff. In was a fold up pack containing needles, thimble, thread, grey wool for darning socks and other odds and ends. Most lads were gobsmacked. Mum's training came in. I did mine and quite a few others. Now we were proper soldiers. Mid-week the big wigs decided the Royal Corps of Signals would become Royal Signals. On Friday we were issued with... for inspection Monday am. Ah well. No comment.

The more intelligent of you may presume that Derby Castle is a castle in Derby or Derbyshire. Wrong. It isn't a castle and it's not in Derbyshire. Pre-war it was a leisure complex in Douglas IOM. There was a ballroom and this is where the Signals dance orchestra played. They were very good.

A traditional twelve piece, four saxophones, three trumpets, two trombones and piano, bass, drums.

One day the drummer, Scotty Howells collared me and said "Are you clear this afternoon?" I said "yes". He said "2:30 Derby Castle ballroom." Cyril was dischuffed. I had a job.

The job was setting up the band music stands and drums, microphones etc. Scotty had a badly injured hand and could only play for an hour or so. There was a deputy drummer but I never saw him. The band had a break every hour or so. I mentioned to Scotty I'd had some sticks and brushes and a few tips and he said, "Get on then let's see what you can do." I was excited and petrified at the same time. I managed a couple of breaks, badly and he put me right on a few things and encouraged me.

Wednesday afternoons at Derby Castle became a regular event. He showed me how to hold the left hand stick properly, slotted between the two middle fingers to give more play. Military drummers still use this technique but pop drummers just clutch the stick and bash. Scotty said he'd been Henry Hall's drummer pre call up. Henry Hall had been fronting the BBC dance orchestra in the thirties. They were fairly straightforward strict tempo outfit then but brightened up considerably after. Henry Hall's guest night was a regular hour programmed on, I think, Wednesday. It was a mixture of music, comedians, singers etc and was billed as 'Henry Hall Idol of Radio Millions and His Orchestra'. Hall was grey haired, bespectacled with a charming rather shy quirky manner. He always sat down and played something on the piano. His drummer was called Jimmy Jack and often did a solo.

Bit of a puzzle there but even more puzzling when I was stationed in Harrogate and went to Leeds Empire with a pal, bought a programme. Henry Hall 'Idol of Radio Millions' was the headline act. Full personnel, drummer Ted Alexander.

Early in the second half the curtain goes up to the urbane Henry Hall and full broadcasting orchestra. Guess who's on the drums – Scotty Howells. You have to put two and three together here to make one – one person. I'm presuming Jimmy Jack was the wartime drummer and Edward Alexander Howells aka Scotty Howells got his job back on demob. If you find this tedious, hard cheese. I'm enjoying it.

Rumour had it Howells injured his hand at Dunkirk. The army's full of rumours. We had a grey haired Sergeant who was rumoured to be well into his seventies and served in the 1914-18 war. He could have done the latter but working on files in the company office I found he was 57. It was my secret and his.

A pal of mine Vernon Moon was second trumpet in the Signals band and his pal was a brilliant saxophonist who had played with a well-known recording outfit. On his firsts leave Moony told me this man went 'AWOL', dyed his hair, wore glasses and played with a rather sedate orchestra on one of the piers. He wrote to the trumpet player at his home address to avoid censorship and told him he was living on egg, chips and other un-rationed delicacies. The trumpeter was full of info. Apparently drummer Howells got drunk one night and tried to open a Jeep door with a pint pot of ale in his hand. Put your own spin on that.

One sun dappled evening Cyril D and I went for a stroll, not far. Alongside Derby Castle is the start of the railway to Snae Fell. We didn't take the railway or stroll on to the highest peak on the island but a short way up the track was a door, curious that. We crossed the track which was closed for the night, tried the door and it opened. A short jump down and we were on the stage of a variety theatre, left, just as it was on the Saturday was when war broke out in September 1939. There was a post of some sort by the back wall and the acts in that show had signed and dated it. I recognised a few of the names from my nights at Leeds Empire. Dixie drew my attention "Hey look at this." It was a small round white table plus two white painted chairs. "We could use these in our room," he said. I can't believe we did this but we did. I don't remember who took what but one of us took the table, the other the chairs.

We carried them half a mile to the guard room, the Blue Cap on duty nodded, we were in our two beds sit. Next day we went shopping. Dix bought a small checked tablecloth, me a few plastic flowers. We got an army sized big jam jar for the flowers from a mate in the cookhouse and there we were, living in luxury. A bit silly but we stopped eating meals in the mess taking our trays a few doors down and nobody blinked an eye. One day there was a room inspection, an officer and an NCO. The officer gaped "What the hell's this?" was his opening remark. Dixie was the world's best in this sort of situation. "They were cleaning out a place in town and we just asked for them." A tiny bit of a lie but a good one. "Good God lad there's a war going on, you must have heard about it," or something like that. He laughed, the NCO followed suit. "You're the clowns from the show at DBH aren't you?" We said, "Yes." He looked around and said, "Well it's certainly clean and tidy." He was by the door when he touched the light switch and repeated his opening phrase, "What the hell's this?"

My turn. "Well I fastened the string to the switch, stapled it over the door and picture rail and by my bed with a loop on the end..." He cut me short. "Stop. I can't take any more." Big laugh. "You buggers, you absolute buggers. Carry on Sergeant." This is almost eighty years ago. It's not word for word but it points out if you've enough cheek you can get away with almost anything.

Hang on a tick. We were at war. Everyday Dixie and I were prannying around like a couple of third rate variety comedians, innocent men on both sides were being killed or maimed. I can't speak for Dixie, I knew his eyesight was very poor but listen please to my case.

At my first medical I was classed as reserve and unlikely to be called up. At my second medical two months later, I was apparently ok. On my call up I was classed as A2, quickly downgraded to B2 then C1 and finally C2.

This meant I could not be sent abroad. Because of my left-handedness, I could carry but not allowed to fire a riffle. I wasn't even allowed to throw a hand grenade with my left hand. Add no swimming test, no gas test due to a dodgy lung and no marching because of a gammy right leg.

What next? Nothing much until I was posted in June. I can only presume Dix went earlier or later for he wasn't in the posting but what was left of 92 squad were. Our destination was a secret. Late at night we arrived in an old bus at an Old Hall in Hertfordshire. A supper was provided by guess who? Corporal Cookerfield from the Chiphouse. Home from home. Next morning we all read and signed the Official Secrets Act. If you let on to anybody even your Mum and Dad you were in big trouble. If you told anything to the enemy it was the firing squad or so it was said.

In December 1943 my Sister was called up into the WAAF and did her basic training at Blackpool. I came on leave that December, landing in Fleetwood, just a tram ride (and they're still there) to Blackpool. Sister found me a bed for the night, presumably in the men's quarter and we went to see a pantomime, at the Blackpool Palace. It was poor and featured a couple of old comics well past their sell by date. One of them had played for Bradford City and whatever part he played always wore a Bradford City scarf. That was the bright spot in the show but it was nice to spend an evening together.

After basic training, my Sister moved to Cheshire and then to Bedford, doing a similar job to mine, without some of the hurley burley in the freezing cold, putting up fallen masts, etc.

One Saturday lunchtime I was walking into town with Charlie Metcalfe and Titch and my Sister was walking towards me. She was taking a chance I wasn't on duty or having a kip. It was supposed to be 'top secret' so I asked her how she found us. "Just asked one of the locals." was her reply. A few weeks later, in exactly the same situation who should be walking up the drive but Cyril Dix. I asked the same question and got the same reply.

Back to Sister. We went to Luton and saw 'Wilson', a film biopic on Woodrow Wilson president of the United States starring Alexander Knox. He founded the League of Nations (Wilson not Knox) and that was a League of Nations to end all wars, an alliance founded in the 1930s. "Gee Woody, ya didn't quite crunch all the right numbers there did you pal?" The film was too long and not enough happened but once again it was nice doing something together.

Top Secret… Get This:
A couple of years ago the Merc mag ran a piece on unusual signs.
Top this. An arrow and caption "SECRET NUCLEAR DUMP".
You're allowed to laugh out loud.

It was one year and three months since we had entered the world of Special Operations and apart from being warned about the blokes in fawn raincoats on the trains sussing us out this was for real. There were three Pearsons, Tom, John and Me all a bit similar. Tom stayed Tom, John became Johnny and I was RS, the only one with two initials and that was my name until demob.

Everything we did was top secret and after a week hanging about we were allowed in the set room, a room with 30 or more sets, a control section and a special section for the Intelligence Corps. I worked with the 'I' Corps for a while... very interesting.

Although it was top secret so much has been written, filmed and televised about Bletchley Park, I feel I can drop a few secrets. If I'm wrong and they shoot me at least I had a good innings.

At first we did afternoons with another set of lads in another room, the White Room, on the same frequencies. Our pads were checked against theirs and with a few instructions we were ready to start what we were trained to do. The shifts were:

> Midnight till 8am.
> Breakfast and kip.
> 4pm till midnight.
> Curled up dry dinner and kip.
> 8am till 4pm.

Then we were off from 4pm to the midnight shift next day. You soon got used to it.

It was sleep-n-eat routine, eight hours on eight hours off. I was on a particularly busy line and if it got really hectic one of the set room supervisors would cover on my frequency to make sure nothing was lost. Always a joker I had to put my hand up asking for cover. I coined a phrase, "They're running out of sauerkraut again." This became a standard one-liner on our watch.

> I had an old hand sitting next to me, a great help. If we were both quiet we could chat in low voices and he told me a few interesting things.
> "Ever hear of a fellow called Didcott?"
> "Was he a Lance Corporal?"

Lance Corporal Didcott gives orders to Colonel Waldegrave who calls him 'Sir'. Bit of a 'con' here. Let me explain. Freddie Didcott was head writer of Hansard the House of Commons word for word 'Bible'. Waldegrave worked for him. Freddie an ever-cheerful man seemed quite happy as a 'Lance Jack' but Waldegrave rose to Colonel. Our old friend 'rumour' has it that the Colonel ushered Freddie into his office, poured a couple of whiskies and apologised profusely for this see-saw changes of circumstances. It would be interesting to know what happened after each were back in 'civvies'.

Another shift he said, "There was a pre-war non-military Special Operations unit in a little village in Derbyshire. When these lads got called up they did their six weeks square bashing then got posted back to work in the village as soldiers. There were some Nissen huts with beds in but they went back home, changed into civvies until their next shift." which is more or less what they did before call up.

> Me: "Bit pointless their six weeks basic training."
> Him: "That's the army for you." Just about sums it up.
> I told him my bit of gossip.
> Me: "You know that bloke called Cocky. He did. He sleeps with
> an attaché case under his pillow. Time off he takes the attaché case
> down to the village gents, changes into civvies and goes home to
> Clapham Junction. The red caps don't bother him. No problem."

I'll come to my experiences with the military police a bit later on.

Another chap who lived nearby said "Look at the windows." They were beautiful stained glass windows and there was a blast wall at foot or so on the outside. He said "Read the names". There was a name at the top of each one, it was Wittewronge. I couldn't quite see the far one and said so. He said "They had to sell up and the bloke who bought it was a northern mill owner". I can't remember this name but it was very northern. Winterbottom would make the point. This was on a stained glass window.

There was a lad in the unit always quiet and sad known as "Buzz Bomb Willy". Now buzz bombs were silent until they started to drop then they buzzed. Walking up the long drive for the midnight shift he heard the buzz and rugby tackled me into a ditch at the side of the path and he followed. I caught my face on a piece of rough stone. Didn't do my teeth any good. The Lance Corporal on guard duty was a pre-war well trained ambulance man so of course in army terms he was totally unsuitable for the Medical Corps but lucky for me he cleaned me up very professionally and I made the midnight shift. Next morning I was driven to the nearest hospital had some dental work and was back for the 4pm shift. Didn't get a medal for it. However it was a close shave. The blast wall outside the wonderful windows was down. Whilst we were on the shift and in the early hours some brickies arrived and started the rebuild. No damage to the windows.

Next day a bit wobbly I went to see Willy to thank him and he told me he'd lived in a heavily bombed area of London prior to call up. Getting to know him took a bit of time but his nickname was rather cruel for a 15- to 18-year-old lad who had had such harrowing experiences. I've not used his real name for obvious reasons.

The unit was well hidden up this long drive but air raids were frequent. The Nissen huts had netting over them with leaves strewn over the top. I can reveal it was somewhere in England between Luton and Watford.

Luton was targeted because the car factories were, like almost all engineering plants, on war work.

A pal of mine Charlie Metcalfe from Nelson had an Auntie who lived and worked in Watford. He took me there for afternoon tea one Saturday. She didn't tell me but he said the Bank of England had relocated to Watford to avoid the bombs and she worked for the BofE. Obviously, the Germans got wind of this. On one occasion I was walking down a small-town main street and the blast from a bomb that landed out of my sight floored the mate I was walking with and I stumbled quite a way but kept my balance. Neither of us was hurt. Another close shave. We'd had leave in December 1943 and our next one was in October 1944, a 48 hour pass.

The Mansion had a number of unusual features. A rather timid man, not a Special Op was sleeping one night when, he heard a low moan. "Whoa whoa let me in" from a panel by his bed. The poor man screamed. I woke up. The panel opened to reveal a drunk sergeant. There was a part of the grounds 'Out of Bounds' to us but this drunk had obviously found a way in and also found the secret entrance. I thought this a bit farfetched but I was sleeping in the room when it happened. One thing I am certain of when I moved up a floor there was a secret panel by my bed. Not being allowed to use a rifle, I still had to have a rifle wherever I went including home. I thought this would be a good place to store my unwanted gun. One afternoon I heard "Rifle inspection, arms at the ready" and a Sergeant walked in. I managed to get the rifle out of its hiding place without the Sarge noticing but as he looked down the barrel a spider crawled out. He put a very stern face on then burst in laughter said something unprintable for quite a while ending "Oh it's you." My reputation seemed to follow me wherever I went. "Get it cleaned" he said trying to suppress his laughter. A bit more ripe language and he moved on. After the laughter I borrowed a pull through from a proper soldier, cleaned the gun then folded up a piece of newspaper in the front end, to make the weapon spider proof with enough sticking out to be easily pulled should a similar occurrence occur.

In the set room, the main hall, there was a fireplace you could stand in, never lit but the fires leading from this upstairs were. One night shift this Sergeant, somewhat inebriated, stood in the fireplace. Whether it was an accident or planned I know not but a considerable amount of soot descended on him. Laughter unlimited.

On Boxing Day 'Titch' Morgan, a driver, a Sarge and myself plus half a dozen others were bussed down to Ashford in Kent to pull and secure two masts affected by a hundred MPH snowstorm. There were a few hundred able bodied men in this unit. But they weren't Signals and only Signals could do this fairly simple, energetic job. That's the Army for you. On return Titch and self were told "Don't settle in, you're going to somewhere in Northumberland in the morning."

How can I explain this without giving secrets away? Here goes. 'Titch' and I were posted, by train from Hertfordshire to London, Leeds to

Newcastle and then the slow train, stopping at every stop until we were picked up by a Jeep and taken to a billet a few miles from the Scottish border. This camp was a bit unusual. It was an Artillery unit firing range. Obvious place to put two Nissen huts for a dozen or more Special Ops? The firing range was in the bottom of an old quarry. We were at the top. Rifles, cannons the lot day and night.

Our workplaces were a few miles away. Two very small square huts both in the middle of ploughed, frozen fields. Big batteries had to be carried over the fields. I managed one without falling. The driver managed one on each shoulder. "There's a knack to it." he said. "One on each shoulder, better for balance. Mind you before this I was a lemonade delivery man." So, the army got it right for once. Inside the hut a foul-smelling stove supplied the heat. It had to be switched off at regular intervals, the door opened to let out the stink. There was some graph paper on the ceiling of the hut to allow for calibration errors but it was black from the fumes and unreadable.

Our shifts were the same as our other place but if you were occasionally prepared to do a sixteen-hour shift 4pm to 8am on your own in a tiny hut with regular air-raids, the Sergeant gave you a travel warrant for a 48-hour break.

It's January 1945, my parent's Silver Wedding. Eileen and I must have been on leave. As a family we went to see a very poor pantomime at the Leeds Empire followed by fish and chips at home.

Later that year I went back off leave on my 21st Birthday. My parents gave me a card, Auntie Clarice and Uncle Bert sent me a card and a £5 note. These things hurt but I came to accept they just didn't know how to do things and I loved both of them for their kindness in my younger days, without their help you wouldn't be reading this.

Back to business – army style. There was an old metal truck at our back door filled with rusty water. The pipes froze for a couple of days. We got a pan from the cookhouse, filled it with rusty water for washing and shaving. We had tans in the middle of January.

I can't leave this without a paragraph on Tommy Hall, The cub playing piano player at the Douglas show. Tommy travelled up from Gateshead/Newcastle to our secret destination, walked a couple of miles to the camp, walked another couple of miles to the cabin in a frozen field, off the road, out of sight. How the hell did he find me? I could've been on leave or having a kip. I brewed up, shared my corned beef and beetroot sarnies. We had a good old natter. Never saw him again.

The small town was about a mile away. There was a cinema with a sloping floor. Every Wednesday the few hundred seats were taken up for a dance on the sloping floor. I didn't try my luck. I was lucky to stay standing on a flat floor. One pub was a warm and friendly place. The landlord had two or three pretty daughters who helped out in the pub. They had lovely, soft Geordie accents. The youngest, all of 15 said to me "I've to go in the kitchen to make some cinder toffee." I said, "I love cinder toffee."

"Then come in with me and you can have some." I've remembered this incident because it was so natural and the cinder toffee was the best I've ever tasted. The other pub on the square was a 'bit posher' with bedrooms and I used it a couple of times a week. There were no proper washing facilities at the camp so I went to the other pub, had half a pint then went upstairs to the bathroom for a five-minute bath. Another half pint and I went. One night the barmaid shouted, "Did you leave it tidy?"

The Sergeant was a big heavily built man and one night he took a short cut across the bay. They were notorious quick sands. He jumped out of the Jeep and it started to sink. One tide and the Jeep was no more. I've often wondered what the requisition notice looked like.

Requirement – Jeeps one.

Reason – Lost at sea, survivors one.

There was a dance upstairs at the hotel and one night one of the other daughters took me across. Not a big room, probably forty to fifty dancers with an accordion and a banjo. This lass said "They're going to do 'Drops of Brandy'. Come on, it's easy." It might have been easy for her but not for me. Just when I thought it was all over it started again and again and again. Hopping, linking arms, twisting round and I introduced an extra move, bumping into people and smiling. It must have got on for 10 minutes. To me it was an hour or more. Still, it was a very happy evening.

Early March I was told "Pack your kit. You're off to Harrogate." I think this Harrogate camp was in a school. In later years, I explained this to my wife and she thought it would be Queen Ethelburga's. They weren't expecting us. Our midday meal menu was Char and Wads plus, Dead man's leg. To translate tea and sandwiches, jam roly poly. Come teatime the lemonade man gave up and having delivered his cargo went back to somewhere near Scotland.

Cushy posting 15 miles from home but what was I doing here? Mid-morning, I found out.

"Pearson 368" bellowed the Sergeant in the crowded NAAFI.

"Here Sarge" was my response.

"Get your kit. You're moving now. Guard room in 10 minutes. Pacey, pacey Sonny Jim. The driver's waiting for you."

Pacey, pacey. He was hardly likely to go wherever it was without his cargo of one.

"Where am I going?" I asked the driver.

"Can't tell you, top secret. You'll know when you get there."

That was about the extent of our conversation in a five-hour drive. Stopping behind a shrub for a leak was the high spot.

We were in Hertfordshire about 15 miles from my previous posting there and very similar big houses up a drive and Nissen huts. A mile down the road there was a similar set up. They were expecting me but not the driver. There was a very small village a hundred or so houses with four pubs. They got him a bed in one of the pubs and I never saw him again.

Hip hip hooray. They had set rooms with radio sets and an added extra, girls. It wasn't as intense as the previous set room; war was coming to a close and we talked quite a bit when things were quiet. The girl next to me said she was Anne Timbernut. "What an unusual surname", I said. A few girls giggled and one said, "She says that to everybody. She's not Timbernut she's Woodhead." Unbounded laughter.

I've just remembered I went out with a girl in Douglas who told me her name was Halfpint. Nothing to do with her intake of alcohol due to the fact that she was Jill.

Back to dreamy Hertfordshire it was nice and sunny and in the daytime breaks on a regular basis I would take my tea to a grassy bank. A girl would join me and we would share a Penguin. Such style:

Auf Wiederesehen: Adolf.

Peace was declared. I was on watch and round about 4:30am took Hitler's capitulation message before he popped into a gas filled chamber or room with his lady friend. "Kaputt Kaputt Heil Hitler" is all I remember on an endless tape. Hang on… where's me medal or even a Knighthood? I'll let the set room supervisor finish this dream. My hand shot up and the set room supervisor came to me. "Don't get too excited. We've had a few calls from other stations and Whitehall but I kept quiet until it turned up here. Well done."

A few nights later we had a victory dance. Everything was gratis, free and for nothing. I drank three whiskies before I was told it was whisky. My Penguin party came up to me, we danced, not in time to any of the music. We got drunk and left laughing a lot. We kissed and cuddled. Things got a bit throbby. A massive thunderstorm. I can't go on calling her after a chocolate biscuit, she was Betty. There were at least six Bettys on the watch so I'm not being very specific. We were wet through, 'she knew a place'. It never occurred to me how 'she knew a place'. It was a small open fronted shelter with a very narrow seat. She undressed, so did I. The 'place' gave us little protection and soon we were wet, glossily wet. Now I ask you. Have you ever been in this position? Naked as nature intended, trying to have an intimate relationship with another naked person wet through and balanced on a narrow seat with the rain bouncing off us. So, there I was … Just a shimmering bare bottom in the moonlight. *'Gee Ron… set that to music.' You could have a spanking great hit.*

Back to the plot.

It was not a success. I sobered up a bit and started to laugh, rain dripping from my nose. She didn't laugh. We got dressed in silence, apart from the noise of the rain. It was about 3:30am. Well, it was V.E. night/morning.

In my hut were two Presbyterian Scotsmen. I think my squelching shoes awakened them. I was not popular. I undressed, yet again, dried myself and put on clean shirt and underpants and slept like a log. Next morning, I took my still wet battledress to dry in the kitchen. There were half a dozen already drying but I found a place. I wonder if the lady friend for the night also found a place to dry her kit?

I must mention here that all entertainments ended at midnight. All dances, theatres and cinemas played the national anthem and most people stood. This was a strict rule due to the Lord's Day Observance Society. Night clubs and discos didn't exist, apart from London. At 10 o'clock in Leeds and other big cities you would be lucky to get a cup of tea except in the big hotels after 10pm.

A few nights later there was another victory dance in the village. I stayed fairly sober, met a girl called Betty from Scotland. After a few months all the girls got posted. This Betty and her friend Betty, no not the wet Betty, got posted to Leeds. On my leave she came home to meet my parents then she went on leave. You've seen newsreels of soldiers, sailors and airmen saying goodbye to ATS, WRENS and WAAFS? Well, that happened to us. Wonderful. The last kiss as I ran down the platform waving. She got home. I got the Dear John letter. On leave she'd met up with a previous boyfriend and that was it. However, after a little sadness I always remember those few months with affection.

I almost forgot I went out with a girl at my first posting to Hertford-shire. Her name was Penny. A nice girl from Sudbury in Suffolk. I had two Uncle Percys and one of them came from Sudbury so we had a number of talking points, including the chip shop, which her family owned. I got posted North. She got posted South. A few letters and that was it.

Another memory introducing Lag Halliday from Leeds. Penny and I never played ping pong. We played table tennis. There were two table tennis tables in the NAAFI. You put your name down on a list and waited your turn and went on. It was our turn. A big stroppy oik told us to... off. He and his three mates were going on. Being from Leeds I got to know signalman 'Lag Halliday'. In the IOM we were issued sten guns. According to legend Lag got drunk and sold his sten for a fiver in a pub. He said "We're never going to fire them and if there is an inspection I'll borrow (winking) one from a mate." A pleasant stockily built man.

Lag: "Trouble RS?"
Me: "It's our turn but…"
Lag: "Oi come here."

The big bloke came over and swore again. When he got close Lag bent backwards onto the table behind him and kicked this oik under the chin. Lag always wore boots. The bloke was bleeding from the mouth.

Lag: "Your table RS."

A lady from the counter came over to see what the trouble was but the big bloke and his mates had gone.

Lag: "Bit of trouble Luv. Nowt for you to worry about."

I think it was the first time I encountered violence and Lag was so calm about it all. I found him a very likeable man. Why he had 'previous' I never asked and he never told me.

Life in peacetime. We were still at war with Japan but things were very much relaxed. The girls were gone and so were most of the men. I was friendly with a Corporal who had a bedroom with nearby bathroom in the house. There was a spare bed. It became mine. I sent home for my pyjamas. Life in the army is so hard. You know what Dad would say.

I was sitting in a pub one evening nursing a half pint of ale when a middle aged lady walked over to me and said, "You've got go-to-bed eyes" and then walked out. Oddly It reminded me of a story told by my Dad. One day a policeman stopped a lad cycling without lights.

Policeman: (with notebook). "Name."
Lad: "Gotobed."
Policeman: "None of that lad. Name."
Lad: "Me name is Gotobed."
Policeman: (writing) "First name"
Lad: "Willie."
Policeman: (writing) "Willie Gotobed. I've warned you lad."
Willie: "But that's me name, Willie Gotobed."
Reluctantly the policeman accepted this. I think there was a Sister Gertie.

Back to the war. Most of the men who manned the sets had served in the Middle East. Quite a few had been boy soldiers during the Depression. They'd been away from home so long they seemed to have an accent that was hard to place also they used a lot of foreign slang. I didn't feel I'd earned the right to use this but others who had not served abroad did but it always seemed not quite right to me. Almost all of them had nicknames: Banger King, Screwy Waterfield, Spiggly Head and Dinty Moore were four I remember. Screwy was from Middlesbrough and he was ok but many of the others thought I hadn't earned the right to join in with them. Spiggly Head – Al Head was married to a girl in the unit but of course they had to sleep in different huts. I couldn't make out Dinty Moore but met several Dinty Moores. In the Bob Hope, Shirley Ross record of "Thanks for the memory" there is a phrase that sounds like "Hash at Dinty Moores" so I wondered if it was a well-known eatery in USA?

Soon even the Screwys and Dintys were gone. There were about 20 of us, three officers, a CSM, a couple of corporals, a couple of drivers and a dozen special ops and 2 girls. I don't know what the officers did but my jobs over many months were Batman, Waiter, Telephone duty, 24 hours shared with 2 others. Company Office with C.S.M. and girl, then wash up. I never found out what the other girl did and where they both slept but they soon moved on.

On company office duty I found an unused book of travel warrants rubber stamped with the colonel's name. Those came in useful. I don't think I ever saw the colonel but there you go. I used the travel warrants on a regular basis and flogged them to the other lads at two bob a time. A nice little earner. I had to start at Kings Cross. On one occasion the red caps pulled me over. "You were here last week lad." I told them my Mother was ill, showed them the warrant and I was through. I don't know why but the Leeds train always stopped at Finsbury Park just a few miles away so I started my journey at Finsbury Park. Problem solved.

I can't remember her name or what she looked like. All I am sure of she was an ATS girl, not in our unit with a pot on her arm which everybody had signed. We'd been out on a few dates when, one Saturday, I suggested we went to Watford, looked around, went to the cinema, went for a meal then came back. All went well until after the meal she said "You've paid for everything up to now, 'this is my treat'," and couldn't find her wallet. A brief look at where we'd been sitting, we then dashed to the cinema which was closing for the night. They gave us a torch, we looked, no luck. On the late night bus she was almost in tears. We were sitting upstairs at the front and I leaned forward, bent down and said, "Is this what you're looking for?" We were on the same bus, sitting on the same seats and the wallet had been on the floor for a good eight hours. She thought I'd had the wallet all the time and started to hit me with her pot arm. Eventually I convinced her what had happened. What an amazing co-incidence, particularly as it was summer and the wallet would have been in daylight most of that time. We never met again.

More romance: There was a hospital nearby and I got friendly with one of the nurses, Irish, quite pretty, lovely accent and very nice in every way. She invited me to a dance in the hospital and I gave her the money for two tickets. We met in the pub. She was somewhat sad. The tickets said "Officers and NCOs only or something like that." I was on nodding terms with a Sergeant from another regiment a mile or so away. "Any problem?" he enquired. We told him the problem. "No problem" was his response. He emptied his pockets and so did I and we swapped battledress. I was wearing ribbons that were issued when I was at school. The next day I was called to the office. The captain gave me a real rollicking but then it occurred to him he would have to involve the Sergeant from the other regiment and that would be rather complicated. "Get out you idiot" were his instructions. I got out. Another near squeak. I can only presume we swapped jackets the following morning but I have no recollection of this.

The officer was a Leeds man. One day after demob I was standing next to him at Headingley.

"So what are you doing?" he asked.
"I'm production manager at my old advertising agency. How about you?"
"Jammy devil. I'm still looking around. My lot went bust during the war."

Back to romance with the Irish Colleen. Everything going smoothly, long walks, afternoon tea, kisses and cuddles and then I was rushed into hospital in London. I was working in the wash up, my skill at this in IOM had obviously followed me. I got very painful boils on both wrists that didn't respond to treatment.

The military hospital was at Mill Hill in London. Many of the men were there recovering from war wounds but they gave me the sympathy because I had to sit or lie down, day and night, with my hands holding kind of stirrups in mid-air. If I lowered hand for more than a few minutes it was very painful. When the wrists were being dressed, I could see the open bone at my right wrist and my left arm became discoloured and ached. My one consolation – there was a big race on the radio. I bought the last ticket. It won. Lucky Ron.

M&B tablets were the cure-all at that time and in desperation the M.O. crushed them into a powder, filled the wounds and bandaged my wrists. On Friday I was allowed out and walked down the hill, probably Mill Hill and I was in Wood Green. The Empire was on my right and Leeds man Syd Seymour and his Madhatters Band were top of the bill. I'd seen them in both Leeds and Bradford and wanted to see how successful they would be in London. They were just as good. I don't think Syd played an instrument but he led the band, did some intricate bowler hat twirling, sang and lots of amusing gags. A good evening out of a military hospital and the Southerners loved him. Marie came to see me and brought me some grapes and I was then sent on two weeks leave with a letter to take to my doctor.

My own doctor was in the forces and a lady doctor read the letter, looked at the wounds and said "Who the hell did this?" The wounds were cleaned and a bright yellow liquid applied daily, that did the trick and for many years, I had scars to show for it.

On the second week Marie came up to stay. Things were getting serious. First the grapes then 'meet the folks week'. It didn't go down well. I was 21 and she was 18, far too young to get serious said Mum. She may have been right but like the girl at Heslocks, and the dark haired beauty, and Scotch Betty, Mum didn't like any of them. The reason became apparent when she met and didn't like my future wife to be.

Dad was out most days and six nights a week. On winter afternoons he went to play billiards and in the summer, he was on the bowling green and had no interest in the home or its contents. He once told me he would have liked to be a county cricketer in the summer and a touring variety comedian in the winter, in other words never at home.

So Mum was going to hang on to her children at all costs. There was no problem with my Sister. She disliked playing out, never had a school friend or teenage girl friend and never went out with a member of the opposite sex. So Mum was determined to hang on to me at all cost. We were the most important part of her life. This was to reach its climax several years to come.

Marie and I went to the theatre in Bradford, the cinema in Harrogate, a day trip to Blackpool, quick snogs on the Ghost Train and the River Caves, a day shop gazing in Leeds then back to our duties. I was taken off wash up and became a servant to the 3 Officers. Dead cushy that, however now the plot thickens. Marie's mother wrote to me.

The wedding was to be in the far west of Ireland. That was a non-starter—if and when I told my Mum—she'd never been out of Yorkshire or Lancashire apart from an evening trip to Cleethorpes and she was a terrible traveller. The letter said the children would be brought up a Roman Catholics. My suggestion was, that as I'd been brought up as a Protestant my children should be old enough to make their own decisions. In any case getting married and having kids was years away. It all ended suddenly when I got posted north to Harrogate. A very nice girl, but that—as is often said—was the end of that. I did hear from a pal who was still down there that Marie had packed in the nursing and was working in a bar somewhere in London. No chance of finding her and writing to her Mother was a non-no. I was sad. We'd had some very happy times but I'm sure I made the right decision. How many kids? The mind boggles.

Then I moved to Harrogate. The barracks were at Penny Pot Lane, the set room a few miles away at Forest Moor. A much bigger American set up is now known as Menwith Hill. Home was a bus and tram ride away. Lucky Ron. You can imagine what my Dad said. Mum was bright and cheerful. So what could go wrong. I was the set room supervisor on my watch. It was my job to tune in the other 18 sets plus my own and help anybody who lost a signal. We had an Officer on the watch but he hadn't been trained in Special Operations, sounds familiar. The Sergeant, a drunk and a Corporal, a bookie did the desk work which mainly involved the handovers beginning and ends of the watch. The bookie took racing tips then both slept 'crashing their swedes' until the handover.

One Saturday at around 11:30am I was at my station on the morning shift when the captain and corporal came up to me and asked me to hand over my headphones to Corporal Pooley. The officer "I've some serious news. I've received a message from Penny Pot to say your mother's died. I've a driver and Jeep outside waiting to take you down. Your Uncle Jack's down there with his car to run you to Leeds."

I was in shock. On my last visit Mum was not too good but she was often what she termed "off it". The driver knew the situation and was very understanding. At Penny Pot I entered the guardroom there was a stranger there. Cut to the chase. I had an Uncle Jack with a car but this wasn't him. This Jack had turned up at the wrong barracks and one can only presume there was another barracks in Harrogate with another Pearson in it. What a set of incredible coincidences but spare a thought for the Uncle Jack at the right barracks with his tragic news.

I went home, went to the rugby with Dad, kept quiet, very quiet. Dad said, "Are you ok chum?" I said "Yeah" gave the impression I'd been on the midnight till 8am shift. "Bit tired that's all." That night I was indeed on the death watch. On the wagon…

> Titch said: "You're in trouble RS."
> "What do you mean?"
> "Desertion and absent from duty."

Monday's company orders went up on Saturday night. Checking up Sunday am Titch was right. 10:30am Tuesday. The charge was read out. It boiled down to leaving my post and my barracks whilst still on duty. No need to say any more. The charge was dropped for as I explained an Officer got me the transport, another Officer was present at Penny Pot and by that time I was not on duty. Lots of sympathy but I was to make another appearance in the charge room a few weeks on. I began to recognise the wallpaper.

Now one Sunday I was walking from the bus station to the tram stop I heard singing at Trinity Church. It was Whitsun, very hot and a back door at Trinity Church was open. I took my forage cap off and stood in the doorway. It was the final hymn. I walked across to Johnson's Engravers, a firm we often used at work to look into their display window. The dreaded red caps approached and charged me with being improperly dressed. I started to explain, one "Shut up you're on a fizzer mate".

> Tuesday 10:30am the charge is read out.
> "That you were improperly dressed such at such a time on such and such a day in Albion Street, Leeds. How do you plead?"
> My heart thumping I said "Not guilty Sir."
> The officer was incredulous. "I've a written statement from the Military Police." I'll read it again, he did. I pleaded again, "Not guilty Sir". There was silence. It seemed like ten minutes, possibly one minute.
> "I'm here to tell the truth."
> The officer nodded.
> "I was born and bred in Leeds and worked in the centre of Leeds for four years and I know every street in the centre and I was never in Albion Street at that time on Sunday etc., etc."

"You realise these men could be in serious trouble if you stick to your story."

"I can only repeat on oath I was never…"

"Get out". I've heard that before somewhere.

My third visit to the Penny Pot guard room started badly. I was walking down the main thoroughfare when I noticed an Officer some distance away. Now saluting has never been my strong suit but CSM Black saw me and put me on charge. I don't think the Officer knew it had happened. I got 48 hours confined to barracks.

Now CSM Black's sleeping quarters were in that area and my last task was to clean his room. It was a shambles and smelt. I tracked the smell down to two mess tins under his bed, makeshift urinals. So, here's the plot, at 11:55am.

An Officer had to be present at the takeover. I placed the offending objects by the door. My rota Officer was the Officer on duty and was on his way to the guard room. I gently held the stinking tins and walked out gingerly.

"What've you got there then, R.S?"

"I don't know Captain but they don't smell too good."

He sniffed and agreed.

"Leave those to me. I'll sign you out."

Success.

Now "Here's a funny thing" as the comedians often said at the start of a joke but this was no joke. We went on strike. *Come on sunshine. If you go on strike in the army it's called mutiny. They shoot you.*

Right – here's the set-up:

There are two sorts of order – standing and company. Standing orders are 'what it says on the label' orders that have to be observed at all times. Your read 'em once and life goes on. Company orders are thing like guard duties, church parades, spud bashing, coal heaving etc. They help us win the war. They have to be read each day.

Somebody changed the standing orders. I'll cut it short. Now, every day your kit had to be laid out for inspection. This would take approx. 45mins. Two items tell the story: broom handles will be sandpapered after use. Water bottles will be laid out for inspection purposes and polished. Now the army-issue water bottles consist of a metal water bottle covered in khaki fabric—nothing wrong in that—wait for it—and a cork consisting of cork, metal spindle, metal cap, metal nut to hold everything in place and they must be polished and laid out precisely in 'military fashion'.

You're on the 8am shift. You get up at 6:45, wash shave, leave your bed tidy, sweep up, have breakfast, get the 7:40 wagon to go on duty. As full inspection layout would take another 45 minutes so you get up at 6am, not on. I think the broom handles broke the camel's back.

What happened?

Each set had, I believe, four aerials. I had two more. I think they were 40-footers bringing in signals from far-off places including Lima in Peru. Now you can't get much further than that. If you do you're on your way back. If you got a signal on a 40-foot aerial, in most cases, you could transfer it to a shorter aerial.

The first thing was for the engineers to 'diss' (disconnect) my aerials and gradually, over several days, take out most of the rest. Harrogate was the top station in the country, now it wasn't.

So the colonel addressed each watch. He was under a lot of pressure from HQ. "Look lads, whatever's wrong, just tell us and we'll put it right". Silence. The one thing that had to be impressed on the newer operators (I was an old hand, almost 23) was to stay silent and never ever mention aerials or standing orders. The colonel went on for a bit with this message, in different forms. Dismissed.

It lasted about a week or more. Another trip to HQ by the colonel. Why was the top special ops station now the lowest? Another pep talk then standing orders were re-written. Nobody told us but rumour had it—oh that wonderful phrase—rumour had it—that 'somebody' put standing orders on the colonel's desk with the key paragraphs underlined. 'Rumour' also had it that a new second lieutenant who was not a 'special op' had changed the orders to standing military practices. Every second lieutenant was the culprit depending on which shift you were on.

You don't believe me? All you need to do is to gain access to top secret documents at special operations headquarters 'Somewhere in England' for May 1947. Piece of cake that.

After the strike demob was looming.

If you could find a business in your line of work 15 miles from Harrogate you could get a month's 'leave'. Harrogate is 15 miles from Leeds so I applied, I got it. Captain Thomas was the pay officer and he called me in and said "You're a Leeds lad, aren't you?" "Yes." "Whereabouts?" It appeared he lived a bus ride away. "Why don't I bring your money with me every Friday to save you the bother of coming over to Harrogate?" Once again Lady Luck was smiling at me.

So I went back to Heslocks for a month, lived at home, had tea then every Friday caught a bus to his house. He was in civvies, so was I. "Do I salute?"

"Please yourself. I'm not in uniform neither are you". Nice chap Mister Thomas.

For my month's training, Harry Heselton gave me a five pound note; big-hearted Hezzy.

Demob was on a Thursday, same day we joined up and we went by wagon with an open back to York for our demob suits. At the gates CSM

Black approached with a check list to make sure there were no extras on the transport. Then. "There's still time to change your mind". Cheers and jeers. "Sign on for a couple of years…" The rest was lost in more cheers and jeers then "Pearson 368, if you sign up you could be a corporal by the end of the year, a Sergeant in twelve months. Think about it."

Being C2 I'd always missed promotion. When I was down-graded in IOM I was told I couldn't finish the course. I asked for an interview with the Adjutant and got him on my side.

As it was CSM Black saying this I felt like saying "What and eat with you?" I resisted and amid the cheers and jeers he shouted "You're not out yet. I can have this wagon stopped and keep you here". The bar went up, we were on our way.

Two Suits, two shirts, two singlets, two pants, two socks, two ties, two pairs of shoes one raincoat were what we got. I always disliked being in uniform and like most of us, changed into my buckshee clobber.

Dad, apparently, loved his uniform and always wore it throughout his infrequent leaves. He delighted in telling me in the trenches they used a lighted taper to burn out the lice from the folds of the uniform and it made a crackling sound.

In addition to the free clobber I also got £179 gratuity. Again my Dad got nowt, no clothes, no money so once more dear folks I was smelling of roses. After 4½ years I was in Civvy Street. Dad told me he stayed on a bit longer to 'clear things up! He loved the Army. Unlike me, I was in a big hurry to get back to my job.'

I never saw a German, or an Italian or a Japanese but along with fellow Special Ops killed quite a few… Mostly innocent men, like me. That's war for you.

I mentioned in my school days I was a boy genius, according to my Mum, mending a Hoover with the Singer sewing machine's small screw driver. We also owned a shortened hammer, that was it.

I've just heard a good line on TV, I think it was John Bishop, 'All my family were musical. Even the sewing machine was a Singer'.

Back to the plot.

On demob I bought some tools. Dad thought I was off my rocker. "We don't own this property" etc was his constant moan. As a lad I was going to make a wireless but never completed it. However somebody gave me a radio cabinet. I turned it into a toolbox. Here's some of the jobs I did, not always successfully at first but 'if at first etc., etc'.

> The garden gate hung loose. I fixed that.
> Dad: "Now we'll have to open and close every time we go out."
> Dodgy curtain rail.

Dad: "It was alright as it was."

We couldn't have a fire in the front room. I fixed the fire bricks.

> Dad: "You'll be the one who'll take the ashes out."
> The bathroom taps were brass with flaky white paint on them. When this was rubbed off they revealed the Leeds coat of arms. I polished them. They looked good.
> Dad: "Now you'll have to polish them every week."
> I tiled the kitchen window shelf.
> Dad: "It's not our property." Etc.

The coal 'ole was underneath the stairs facing the back door. There was invariably coal dust when you stepped in. Some removable planks were the answer. I don't need to print Dad's answer.

My Sister and I helped Mum strip the wallpaper. Mum did the papering.

Dad could have toured the variety theatres with his distempering the ceiling act. Imagine an old 1920s big flat cap, an old raincoat buttoned to the neck, a pair of mucky, unlaced tennis shoes.

> Dad: "These fellers who do this for a living have a knack y'know."

Dad's knack was to get as much liquid as possible on the brush, rush up the steps and let most of it fall on him. Job done, he was covered.

I suggested a pair of steps with a place for the bucket on top, a non-starter.

> Me: "Then put an old cloth on the table, put the bucket on the table, stand on the table, don't put as much on the brush." To no avail.

Chapter 9:
Back to Hezzies

Heslock's: Tremaine had gone to work for one of Ministries in Leicester in 1942. In my months training he was back and I think Carruthers was back and Jack Johnson and Donald (Joe) Lewis in the studio. Otherwise many of the old hands didn't return – lots of new faces.

When I returned a few weeks later Tremaine had gone again, Joe Lewis had gone and so had Carruthers. Rumour (another one) was that W.M.J.C. missed the army so much he re-enlisted.

Some years later I had to call on Tremaine's old London Agency and I was told he had returned to Cornwall and set up a property renovation business.

Jack Johnson ended up as CSM in the Middle East. He would be demobbed a long time before me and had a little office made in the production department. With Carruthers gone, never to return or spoken of again Heselton, once more shuttled to the big office and Jack moved to his old office and I had an office to myself and virtually nothing to do. I wrote a few orders to newspapers, printers and block makers and that was about it. Jack Johnson apologised about the desk. It was a light wood and he decided to stain in dark, the stain never dried properly and a large blotter covered most of it. I scraped off the dark coating, sanded it down then used linseed oil to bring back the original colour. Nothing to do with advertising.

Then Harry Heselton, came in with about a hundred decrepit hymn books and a big roll of imitation leather. I'd made a glass case for the corridor to exhibit a special model of a bus for Heaps Tours which was displayed there. I'd also helped to make the model with an artist called Wilkie for Wilkinson. I never knew his first name. After a month or so he got a job in South Africa. Nice chap. He lived near me and I decided to make some bookends with a cricket theme, wickets, bails, ball and I made most of this at home then went to his house to finish off.

Back to the plot. Harry Heselton said "You're good with your hands. Can you tidy up these books and put new covers on them?" I got a tin of Cow gum from the studio, foul-smelling stuff that could make you light headed if you used it all day. I did. It did. Cow gum? I think the manufacturer's name was PB Cow. Not as odd as Peter De-Witt Kit-Kat an advertising man in London but a lot better than having *Bastard* as a surname which a cloth manufacturer had.

Headline 'Our name is Bastard and we're proud of it.'

There were a lot of pre-war printing blocks on the shelves in production. Mahogany bases and metal tops. JJ gave me a screwdriver to prise the top from its base. He and I took the wood bases home for firewood and I got a pair of wheels and trundled the lead to a scrap dealer down Meadow Lane in Leeds who gave me £190 in cash. I'd never seen so much money. I got half with an instruction from Jack J. to say nowt.

I had yet to bank my gratuity cheque so fishing out my school bank book, went to the Yorkshire Penny Bank which became Yorkshire Bank now known as Virgin Money, with a loss of local facilities. You can go to this bank but you can't ring them. Back to 1947, I'd left school nine years earlier. One of my jobs at school was to take the bank money in on Mondays. Nothing had changed. It was the same bank clerk at the same desk, apparently in the same suit, the same routine without a smile. He said 'I'll make the book up for you', adding my ill-gained cash and Army gratuity cheque plus nine year's interest. I was all smiles with untold riches but what was my job? I did a few trips out and got the sixpence from the Miss Witt's for delivering their printing blocks and that was about it.

Oh, I nearly forgot. I often worked late, delivering last-minute printing blocks to the newspapers. At the long-gone *Yorkshire Evening News* I delivered to the night watchman's office where in addition to the night watchman there was a tall, fair-haired young man. We often had a few words together. He was a cub reporter on minor stories. "I'm a B.M.D. man." he once told me. "Births, marriages and deaths of well-known people." I was told he himself became rather well-known as Peter O'Toole.

This may bring a smile. Fast forward to 1947, on demob, I delivered the block to Miss Witt's house and a shiny sixpence was mine to pick up from the little table by the door. Back to wartime. Nothing much happened, I fell in love about once a fortnight but every time I had a date I got terrible stomach ache and the 'Black Magic' melted in my raincoat pocket. Leeds was probably the least bombed of all the big cities. London, Birmingham, Manchester, Liverpool, Edinburgh, Swansea and the ports were much more heavily hit.

A lady artist kept bringing me a biscuit to have with my tea. Romance beckons. We went out a few times; one time to a hypnotist, Peter Casson. He asked everybody in the audience to link their fingers over their heads and then to remove them. I could. She couldn't. Those who couldn't, about fifty of them, went up to be released and he kept a dozen back for his experiments. She came back.

One night whilst window shopping, we stopped to look in a window. "I'm not going out with you anymore". Apparently she had two horses in the same race. The other bloke was posher, handsomer and had a good job. She'd often said, "You're wasting your time in this dump." I had to agree. On one occasion I decided to empty and clean out the newspaper shelves. Uncleaned for ten years or more, I got very dirty. "You're a muggins" was her remark. I started to think things out. One day an elderly rep and I were walking through town and he said, "You'll run your own business one day." Nothing was further from my mind.

Goodbye bickies am and pm another romance hit the dust. So 'pretty low' until my Mum bumped into somebody when shopping. 'I bumped into Mrs so-and-so' was a well-known phrase. In this case she bumped into Mr Wray, an old friend from our Westover days and he told her his son was a member of the Bramley Ciné Club and they recently moved from Bramley Town Street which was being re-developed (another word for 'knocked down') to Station Parade which was only a short walk from us. More later.

One lunch time a rep took me to lunch at Charlie Brett's fish and chip restaurant in Headingley. He'd just changed his car, got engaged, put a deposit on a house and was getting married. I thought it out. I was a mug in an agency with no driving force. No way could I afford even part-payment on a car and driving lessons and buying a house? I wasn't earning enough to be considered for a mortgage. Ted Dobson, the art director had become a director. A nice enough chap but both JJ and Ted were no go-getters and although I liked both of them, they, together with the boss, Harry H, I still didn't know exactly what he did, were stumbling blocks. Jack Johnson actually helped me pointing out another agency in Leeds were advertising for a production man. I went for a lunchtime interview, got the job. Another thing about Heslocks is that after demob I started at four pounds per week, ten bob rise after a year, another ten bob a year later. Now I was on £8 a week.

I gave my notice to Harry Heselton.

"What are they giving you?"
"Eight pounds a week."
"We'd have given you that." But you didn't was my thought.

I also remembered his old moan that they trained everybody and then they left for other agencies.

"You're earning more than I am." was Dad's first words. I didn't know what he earned but after eighteen years' service and pushing sixty, I was 24 and earned more and giving more to my Mum.

"They took you in when you couldn't get a job." He'd used the same words when I left the parcel packing job.

From then on Dad had little interest in my career and my life in general. Well, as they say, "You can't win 'em all." I certainly couldn't, as far as my Dad was concerned. We weren't enemies but my career was rarely discussed. Don't get me wrong we still went to Rugby and Cricket together.

A new job plus a new lifestyle. It was all happening.

Finally a bit more about Heslocks. The people I met were very kind, very helpful. I learned a lot and very jokey. But I wasn't getting anywhere.

So I, like many others before me I left Hezzies because I was paid little and doing all sorts of jobs that had nothing to do with my career as an advertising man.

Chapter 10:
Leisure time

It was at the Bramley Ciné Club I met four men who were to become my close companions until I got married in 1951: Arthur, Jack, Donald and Jess.

Arthur Baker was two years older than me, tall, fair and handsome. All the ladies fancied him but he lived his own life. His hobbies were running, pubs and racing. He did marry, after me and I bumped into him a few times. In mid-life he put on a fair bit of weight and lost all the hair on his head and face but just got on with it. He was very bright and finished his education at West Leeds High School. He was called up to the Fleet Air Arm and told me he ended in the drink a couple of times but then got the knack of it.

A keen racing man, we visited all the race courses in Yorkshire and quite a few elsewhere. At Redcar on Whit Monday the tipsters were out on the promenade in the morning chalking the horse's names on the promenade but not giving too much away before selling their tips. Most charged two bob a tip but Ras Prince Monalulu in full colourful robes charged 2/6 'I gotta horse' was his catchphrase. The newsreels at the cinemas always showed him on big race days. Good for business that. I think they based their success on giving two or three names out and then claiming "Who gave you, what's its name? in the 2:30?"

Most tipsters moved about a bit so as not to be preaching to the same people. At Redcar, Arthur's Mum and Dad plus his brother, Joe and wife were there, a really good family atmosphere. *Burnt Brown* was apparently the horse that would walk it and all the Bakers had a bob or two on him. I strolled around, placed my bet and won. When I returned to the Bakers they'd torn up their tickets. *Burnt Brown* was nowhere. In my ignorance I backed the wrong horse, *Brown Sugar* which romped home. Here's a list of the Yorkshire courses – Beverley, Catterick, Doncaster, Pontefract, Redcar, Ripon, Thirsk, Wetherby and York. Is Yorkshire the only county without a course in its big cities, Leeds, Sheffield, Hull and Bradford?

Arthur told a good story about a local tipster called Rushton or Rushworth. He had a small band of lady customers and worked as follows:

First he would recommend a 5 to 1 shot. If it won he would send a telegram to his clientele, "Congratulations on backing *Mr Wotsit*. I'm putting your winnings on *How's your father* at Pontefract. This horse would be at 10-1. The same routine was followed until he was nabbed at Nottingham Post Office sending out his usual grams on a 33 to 1 horse. Cut to a court in Leeds."

> Judge: "You're charged with (long speech). How do you plead?"
> Rushworth: "Not guilty your Honour."
> Judge: "Not guilty." Another long speech by the judge ending "Tell me Mr Rushworth: what is that parcel under your arm?"
> "Soap, towel and razor, your Honour."

On the racecourse Tiny was the ladies favourite tipster. A small, round man, well dressed with a polished oval, brass lapel pin with "Tiny" on it. "Get your tips from Tiny" was his call and he was never short of customers and the elderly ladies loved him.

The Cine Club held a fund-raising whist drive every Wednesday at 7:30 plus supper. I would be most welcome. I think I asked my Sister but she was not interested. Then I bumped into my old pal, Alan Green. He'd just completed his National Service as an electrician in the R.A.F. and was a keen card player. He came with me, enjoyed the cards and supper and I said it was up to him if he wanted to come again. He never did.

Jack Dunn, Donald Sutcliffe and Jess Wilson wee my other pals, all in the Bramley Ciné Club. We had holidays together and I kept asking Wray the Younger, "What does the Ciné Club do and when are they going to do it?" The answer was, "Well, we've only moved in here, it takes time." One day, one of the Club members dropped out and I became treasurer and secretary rolled into one. One evening I walked in and there was a projector with enormous spools, some loudspeakers and a screen. An old black and white American B film was shown. How the projectionist had managed to get eight or so reels onto two spools I know not and why choose an unremarkable film didn't make much sense to me. I think there was a short film made of 20 or 30 members getting out of a very small car – stop/go photography and quite amusing. That was the end of the Ciné Club. I called a meeting and as the Club had now nothing to do with cinema, we voted on changing the name to Bramley Recreation Club. There were no votes against and so we continued with the Wednesday whist drive and table tennis every night.

On Saturdays we five would meet in the Barley Mow for a glass or three then fish and chips as we strolled to the Club then played poker until two or three in the morning. One time a policeman, seeing the lights on, knocked on the lower door. We let him in. He played a few hands with us and became a regular caller.

One of the regular visiting table tennis players at the Recreation Club was Barney Colehan long-time producer of TV's much loved. 'The good old days'. I don't know which team he played for but he was above average table tennis player. In other words better than me. Several decades later we were parked alongside each other at Radio Leeds.

> Barney: "I know you".
> Me: "I certainly know you".

A few minutes conversation, a handshake and good luck wishes from both parties. I must have a very memorable face. Leave it at that.

Chapter 11:
Life at Nevin D's

Nevin D Hirst Advertising Limited were in Mount Preston outside the centre of Leeds. Dick Harvey from Hull started the same Monday. On the Tuesday he said to me, "I don't know about you but I'm not impressed." He spent the rest of his career there.

So what was the set-up at Nevins?

Nevin D Hirst, a charming man, a business getter, a drinker who'd missed wartime duty due to a serious stomach operation, late 30s, a bit of a rogue, a real charmer. Nevin ran a one man and a girl business during the war but with his charm and a staff of around thirty his was the agency to watch. In addition to Leeds there were London and Edinburgh offices.

Deryk Hirst, Nevin's younger brother, another heavy drinker, quite good at what he did but without Nevin's charm, thought the agency should be called Hirst Brothers.

Peter Peel on the letter heading listed as P. Mitchell-Peel. That tells you a lot. He had a bad time in the army being a prisoner of war. Again, a dodgy stomach but a very good creative man.

After I'd been there a few months, another man joined the board, Dennis Birkett.

A seven-strong studio and a high standard of work, I was happy to be involved. Jim Gledhill was the production manager and I never really sussed him out. He'd been an officer in the army, came to work in his army greatcoat, hung it by his desk on a hanger, bought a house in the village of Calverley on the same avenue as Peter Peel. Very sociable, he went around each office, shaking hands and wishing everybody good morning etc., etc., etc.

Instead I worked to the well-known principal 'first thing first – get the job done'.

After a few weeks, one member of the production team was sacked and Dick Harvey set up a one man and a girl print department. I took over the sacked man's production schedule on top of my own and was usually clear by lunch. Late afternoon, panic stations so I would help Jim complete his work for the day. It was all very easy going but Jim hadn't come up the hard way, trudging the streets at 7pm delivering stuff to newspapers, engravers, stereotypers and printers and finding out how things were done.

A side issue: Dick Harvey's secretary, Yvonne also lived in Calverley as did junior artist, Brian Hunt as did, eventually, Ron Pearson and his wife. *What's this then? You found a lady who didn't give you the old heave-ho after a few months?* Yes, I did and for almost sixty six years she put up with me.

"Hey, look at that" were artist's, John Harlow's words, looking out of my room window at the new telephonist receptionist who walked towards the offices of NDH. This very attractive young lady was to be the future Mrs Ron Pearson. Yes folks, I finally conned somebody that I was worth living with.

So, Muriel Patricia Porter, yes, the one with the same surname as Cigarette Liz earlier in this tome, was a bit posh with a lovely voice, very happy personality, perfect as a telephonist receptionist. She worked about ten yards from me and in between two young ladies, voucher clerks, opening newspapers and marking any ads produced by the agency. I kept them entertained, with jokes and acting daft when I'd done my work. A side-line, John Harlow's wife to be, was Pat's best school friend.

One day, dear folks, voucher clerk, Ruth Hey said to me, "Why don't you ask Pat out? She's so nice and…"

> So, walking down from the office I said, "I'm going to see the film *The Third Man* tomorrow. Would you like to come?"
> Pat: "Do you mean it?"
> Me: "I wouldn't be asking you if I didn't mean it."
> Pat: "You are the most…" (started to laugh)
> Me: "Is that a yes or a no?"
> Pat: "Yes." And that was the start of it.

Oh, there was one condition. I was to be Ron and not Ronnie. It was a nice gentle courtship. She lived in posh Roundhay, me in ordinary Bramley. I went to meet her Mum and Dad and she came to mine.

Then one November Monday everything changed. No she didn't give me the old heave ho, read on.

I was called into a director's meeting. *Weaver and Weaver*, the multiple men's outfitters were on my list and were opening a branch in Gateshead this coming Friday. They wanted twenty poster sites, three sandwich board men and another bigger board for outside the shop.

> "Poster sites, any ideas?" said Peel. I'd done some work with
> Sheldon's. "I'll give Basil Sheldon a ring and sort out something."
> Posters? "Wilkinson and Dickinson do the posters for my Dad at the
> cinema. I'll ring them."
> Sandwich boards. "John Warrilow, he's the man for that."

I got the job. Moreover, one of the directors chickened out. It could only be either Birkett or Peel who both play major roles in a further 'Weaver to Wearer' episode, and I was to take all the gear to Gateshead, check the poster sites, go to the labour exchange, set on three sandwich board men and generally keep an eye on things Friday and Saturday.'

The person who should have gone had a car. I didn't. I don't know how I did it.

Three sandwich boards, one much bigger display board and a big roll of posters, I loaded them into the goods wagon Thursday evening, got them to Newcastle and unloaded them. What then? My Sister had found me a small hotel in Newcastle. I wouldn't take them there. I must have left them at the station but I have no memory of this.

Friday 8am inspected and approved twenty poster sites. At 9am I went to the labour exchange. Literally hundreds of men sitting on the ground on waste land outside the building. Mr Milburn, the manager was very helpful and three men were set on. At 10am the shop manager was another very helpful Geordie who plotted the routes for the men. I agreed to pay them 7pm Saturday and off the men went with an hour's break at 1pm. Job done.

Friday 4pm the Mayor was about to cut the tape:

"Me bloody braid's broken"

This from one of the sandwich board men it was repeated plus:

"I can't do me round with bloody broken braid"

I managed to get him out of the way, a few chuckles and the assistant manager made some quick repairs.

Why stay until 7pm Saturday to pay them, a 2-minute task and get home in the early hours. Simple answer, get the helpful shop manager to pay them and keep an eye on things so I came back Saturday morning. rang Pat.

Pat: "Where are you, in Newcastle?"
Me: No, Leeds.

Let's move on. We went out Saturday night to the flicks. I said, "Do you think this is it?". Pat said, "Yes" and that, dear reader, was that. After a few 'sort of' girlfriends I had a proper girlfriend. Pat had had a couple or more boyfriends, one who was a pilot in the R.A.F. and was killed in action, another was a Canadian who went back home. After the pilot was killed, Pat was in shock for a while. During the war she'd worked as a civilian for the Admiralty. Based on the coast? Never. The offices were in the centre of Leeds. She'd then stayed at home helping her Mum who, in addition to running the home, did the book-keeping for her husband's businesses, more of that later. Her Mother made her apply for the job at NDH as she was just hanging about being somewhat miserable.

One day Pat said to me, "All my boyfriends were better looking than you, more polite, well spoken…". I cut in "So why the hell are you going out with me?"

"Because you make me laugh. You're good at your job and you get Jim out of jam after jam. Why don't you let him stew in his own juice?"

"Because that's the way I am. I just do it."

That weekend I bought a 78rpm record of Fats Waller singing and playing "My very good friend the milkman said", "That it would make his burden less", "If we both used the same address", "And he suggests that you should marry me". The same Saturday Pat had bought the same record. That was it. I had it played at her funeral.

Back to reality. I haven't mentioned David Renton Peel. Now here's another funny thing. I was on nodding terms with David in a lift. He worked on the third floor, Hezzies was on the fourth floor. At Douglas IOM I was in 92 squad, he in 93.

When I went to work in London, so did he. We shared a bedsit. When I left London, so did he. More importantly, he lived in Roundhay, so did Pat. So I often stayed with him for the weekend and went out with Pat. Who to choose as my best man? Best friends Arthur, Jack, Donald or Jess? Choose one, upset the others. No contest. David Peel it was.

He married a lovely girl called Anne. He was in the insurance business and moved to the Wirral area on the West Coast and we lost touch. However we did get a card to say Anne had died at an early age. I think there was a son or daughter and many years later he moved to North Yorkshire and re-married. He visited us on his own but the spark between us had gone out and then the Christmas cards stopped coming.

So that's out of the way, what next? Crisis. Weaver to Weaver were big business at NDH and there was a price misprint in one of their ads which cost them money. Who to blame? You're ahead of me aren't you?

Peter Peel and Denis Birkett asked me to meet them upstairs. They didn't sack me but said they were reducing my salary to five pounds a week. That's why I left Heslocks. I gave a week's notice. Nevin came back from Scotland and asked me to stay at my original salary. I refused. I said to him, "Each piece of artwork carries a sticker to be initialled by 1 the client, 2 the account manager, 3 the art director, 4 the production executive. All were initialled including Peel as art director." I remember my words, "Thank you but I'm not prepared to work for men who will treat me like this." I've turned over those words for over seventy years and still don't understand why I said them. I came downstairs. Pat was furious. It got worse. Pat was almost in tears. Let's move on.

I worked my notice and on the final Friday discovered a typing error. That very price. What to do? If I went back to Peel and Birkett the girl would lose her job. I said nothing, not even to Pat. I'm no hero but everybody makes mistakes. I left. Over the weekend Pat tried to get me to change my mind.

One London agency, specialising in mail order, were advertising for staff in Leeds. I went for an interview at the Queen's Hotel and was offered a job on the proviso I pinched as much business I could from my present employers. I turned it down and rang Nevin. He was most grateful and again asked me to stay. Daren't tell Pat but I've always had mule like tendencies, so be it.

Before I move on to this, here's a run-down on NDH. I may not have these in the right order or timescale but Nevin bought a boat to sail the Med. It blew up. Nevin had a lot of work on his damaged face. Arthur Emmerson, long-time pal and now media director at NDH had his legs permanently injured. Nevin left his wife and re-married. His first wife was smoking in bed and died. Brother Deryk bought a high-speed car and was killed in a head-on crash leaving a wife and son.

Always bright and cheerful, I was with Nevin in a pub and he said "My life is over Ron." He was 62. I went to his funeral a few years later. Nevin's son took charge and thought he could stay at home and run the business from a computer. He failed.

Peter Peel came out of retirement to try and rescue the agency. He failed. Here endeth the Nevin D Hirst saga according to Ron.

It was certainly the best agency by far in Leeds, possibly Yorkshire but on reflection I was better out than in.

Next week:

Monday I called on half a dozen Leeds agencies and drew blanks.
Tuesday I called on two Harrogate agencies in the morning, two Bradford agencies in the afternoon.
Wednesday I went to Bob Martins in Southport; no luck.
Thursday I went to Rowntree's Store in Scarborough; no go.
Friday I went to London; success.

I got a job in production at John Mitchell, a well-respected technical agency.

Chapter 12:
London Life

First of all, my Sister found me an address in London, The Chase, Clapham South. Quite a nice area to be joined the next week by best man to be David Peel. He was on a six-month course in his new job.

So now I was living in the big city, the smoke. What was it like?

At my interview I asked if I could start Tuesday as I'd several things to sort out at home including conning somebody to take on the secretary/treasurer job at the Club. They were a bit iffy on this but agreed without knocking anything off my weekly wage.

A chap called Greaves was production manager. I was shown to a small desk and given a simple adapt to do. By 9:30am the job was done. Then a more complicated job, now 10:30am and a biggy to get sorted. Lunchtime. There was a big, unoccupied desk in the back of the room. Apparently the poor chap who worked there often had two cigarettes in his mouth at the same time and then had a nervous breakdown. Greaves moved me onto this desk after lunch and I think that's the last time he spoke to me. He and another man worked by the window with their backs to the room and I was at the back. Tuesday: Newcomer Peter Ling, known as 'Tinger' took the small desk. Thursday: Tom Joyce was added. Friday: Another new lad. This got me thinking. John House was the other occupant and he'd been there a long time, almost six months.

The inevitable 'Larry' Lamb gave out the work schedules and ticked off the jobs completed on his clipboard. An ex-Sergeant Major, I became his favourite because things moved quickly from my desk. So 'Tinger', Joyce and the other fellow were told to start at my desk and work the way I worked, so far so good.

John Mitchell was an ex-ship's engineer, tall, broad and a constant user of colourful ship's language. Probably mid-fifties but always referred to as The Old Man. He and the rest of the office staff were downstairs, studio and production upstairs. They were a good crowd. I took a lot of stick being a Yorkie but it was good natured and after a couple of weeks, I was giving as much as I got.

John Mitchell could be 'Mr Niceguy' but when he exploded, watch out. I'd been there about a month when Larry Lamb handed me a job that wasn't technically viable. "The old man wants it this way."

"Well, tell him I'll do it but it won't work." He did. I was summoned to his office. He was purple in the face and used language far worse than army language. I waited. He said, "Why won't it work?" I explained. He replied a one word answer beginning with "B".

Let's cut it short. I did it his way. Sounds like a song, doesn't it? It didn't work. Downstairs again. "Tell me why it didn't work." I did. "Right do it your bloody way you 'Navy Curse'… Yorkie."

After that he calmed down a bit but often exploded for little or no reason. There's a reddish colour in printing called cerise. I re-christened it 'MCP, Mitchell cheek purple' and it stuck.

The offices were near Green Park tube station and one afternoon he caught me on the platform. Heads turned as he stoked up his fury. "What was I doing on the tube station at 3:15pm?" I pointed out that I was working on some tube posters and noticed the tube station signs could be seen from both the platform and the train. Most nameplates were at the bottom of an ad but if you put them in the middle you got double the exposure. Once more he calmed down, had the poster designs done both ways then took me to the clients to explain this idea.

Despite these successes, I was getting fed up with the outbursts which explained the quick turnover of staff.

At Whitsuntide Pat came down and we got engaged. I suggested she got a job in London and she wasn't against the idea. I was beginning to win a few.

Come July, another raging outburst from The Old Man convinced me that I had to make a move. Mitchell shouted, "Do you want more money you Yorkshire (unrepeatable)?" I replied, "Nobody turns down more money." Mitchell: "When I come back from holiday, we'll sort out something. Get out." He left instruction that if anybody left whilst he was away there would be trouble with a 'capital' TROUBLE.

I wouldn't like the reader to think I was superman. I'd spent years making mistakes and trudging the streets after hours and finding out how things were done at printers, newspapers, blockmakers etc.

I came home for the weekend. I developed stomach problems. There was a letter from an agency in Bradford, one of the two I'd visited in February. They needed someone. It changed my life.

I met Pat Saturday evening. I kept quiet about the letter on the simple principle: if they didn't like me or I didn't like them.

Monday 9:30 I'm at the offices of Charles Walls and Partners at North Parade in Bradford. Charles Walls was tall, dark, slim, bespectacled. I'd kept a file on ads I'd done the production work on in London. He was impressed. He asked me a few questions about printing, newspapers and magazines and told me a few things about his agency. I was impressed; £10 a week, one week's holiday this year, two from then on, hours 9-5:30 and 9 to 12:30 on Saturday. "But I'm not keen on clock watchers" he said. I got the job.

Start Monday next. I felt like running the four and half miles home but decided to take the bus.

Someone must have told me that you can give your notice verbally before 12 noon on Monday providing you followed this up in writing the next day. I rang the company secretary at John Mitchells. I can't remember his name but he was a dead ringer for Humphrey Bogart, Hollywood's toughest star and just as tough. He refused to accept it. I told him what I've just told you. He hung up.

Rang Nevins to speak to the receptionist whose name was Pat. Much happiness. I was back where I should be in God's own county. It always annoys me when people get it wrong to I'll say it again "God's own county" not country, never ever.

How did it go down at home? Mum was overjoyed at first but dark clouds were looming.

To give you some idea of her unrest at me having got engaged and about to be married, here's one of many examples of her unhappiness and somewhat mental instability.

One Saturday afternoon Pat and I went shopping. I needed a new raincoat. We chose one in grey. Returning home Mum hated it and cried all weekend and it had to go back. Meeting Pat Sunday afternoon she said, "If you give in now you'll never hear the end of these outbursts." It wasn't easy. On reflection it would be the only item of clothing Mum hadn't bought for me and she just couldn't accept that. I felt so sorry for her but Pat was right and the grey raincoat stayed on my back for many years. However there was worse to come.

Tuesday 9am. I handed my written notice to Bogey. I almost felt like saying, "Here's lookin' at you kid." or one of Mr Bogart's other sayings that became common language in the 40s and 50s. Bogart died in 1957 but if you've never heard of him you ought to have.

Bill Ansell, the quiet kindly middle-aged bespectacled office manager talked to me and tried his best to talk me round but to no avail. Greaves the production manager just got on with his work with his back to me.

Friday I knew if I took my cases to work with me they would pinch them, or would they? I was taking no chances. I got up at 7am and put my luggage into one of the lock-ups at Kings Cross. Bogart had one last fling. "I'm not paying you until the Old Man is back and he decides what we're paying you." It took me two months to get that money. I'd left smoky London for smoky Bradford but more importantly I was back with Pat, back with my pals and starting with an agency that I hoped would be the right one for me and it was. However there's one last footnote to the John Mitchell story.

It's 1957 and my client Downs Coulter, lining manufacturers, had booked a stand at a big exhibition for the clothing trade at Earls Court. I'd come up with the idea of a traditional draper's shop.

The main contractor in London was the Flush Block Company. What an unusual name. I wonder if they are still trading. They were superb. Downs

Coulter made top quality linings and cream flannel cloth for cricket trousers with an office in Bradford, mills in Thornton, Bradford and Chorley, Lancashire and always one member of the Downs family in Australia overseeing a big organisation there. They were a big company.

My design had a mahogany counter with an inset brass ruler, bolts of cloth on the back shelves plus cloths on the sides of each counter. I also tracked down an old-fashioned cash register and insisted the three men on counter duty wore sober three-piece suits and ties plus sensible haircuts. One bloke even had a short-back-and-side traditional haircut and they were all so enthusiastic.

I thought this was about John Mitchells? It is. I'm just painting a picture before getting to the main event. That doesn't make sense but forget it. Read on:

Downs Coulter won the award for best stand. A photographer is at the stand. It's the John Mitchell photographer, Hopkinson. We had a chat. Hoppy told me "He's a changed man, the Old Man. He had some sort of mental breakdown and joined the Presbyterian Church, hands out the hymn books on Sundays, stopped drinking, stopped swearing, a real pussycat."

Me: "Are you still there?"
Hoppy: "Hell no. I'm freelance now. Got out just after you."

A few more reminiscences, a handshake and we moved on. The typist of this saga, the wonderful Kathryn, often says "You couldn't make it up."

What a blockbuster movie that would make with company secretary the Cockney Bogey in a cameo role.

Chapter 13:
Now I'm in Bradford

Monday morning 9am late July, I climb the four floors to Charles Walls and Partners, always known as Charlies, to be greeted by George Scott, another ex-Heslockian who took me to Mr Wall's office. George had been an artist at Hezzies but here worked in production plus calls to a few clients. Charlie showed me around; production George Scott, artist Jack Meynell, new office boy Peter Wilkinson and me. Then I met the telephonist Pam, shorthand typist Barbara, May Walls, accountant Kenneth Wilkinson (Peter's Uncle) and two freelance artists renting a room at the rear of the premises. Oh, I almost forgot, Charlie Walls. First floor creative director Arthur Barthel and a part-time lady copy writer Barbara Swift.

A little bit of history.

Charles Lewis Walls was born in Carshalton Beeches on 6 May 1906 and the family moved to Brixton when he was at an early age. Like me, he started his advertising career at the age of fourteen. After several moves he joined a well-respected agency, Dorlands. There he met his future wife, May whom he always referred to as The Missus. Tragically their baby son was a forceps delivery and didn't survive.

Here's a pen portrait of CLW, six feet tall, bespectacled with a handshake that cracked your knuckles, a chain smoker, a sixty a day plus man but never inhaled. All smokers tell me there's no point in smoking if you don't inhale. His hobby was joinery which he did in the bathroom. He said, "I don't eat sweets, puddings and the like but when the birthday treats come round the office I always pick the sickliest." A complicated man. Dorlands had a number of clients in the Bradford area and in 1937 he and May travelled north never to return.

He got called up and served in the Pioneer Corpe in Italy. Returning to Bradford in peacetime, Dorlands were not interested in keeping their Bradford connection but agreed to him keeping the pre-war business. I think he tried to set-up with another London agency. That didn't work so Charles Walls and Partners was born. You now know all you need to know at this point about Charlie so what about the partners?

Walter Williamson was an ex-pilot officer complete with the moustache. Very outgoing, I think he must have been the business getter. It wasn't a good partnership. Rows were frequent. Charlie often told me when one row got particularly heated he took off his glasses, certain that Walter was going to hit him.

Walter would last a year and a bit before getting a job as a rep for quality magazine' *House and Garden'*. It was however third best to *Ideal Home* and *Homes and Gardens*. Walter then joined newly set-up Tyne/Tees Television and moved to Newcastle. Exit Walter. I think George Scott must have been his replacement as he had known CLW before the war.

Arthur Barthel, the creative director was partner number 3. He too was in the R.A.F. I think he was a Sergeant route planner. A stocky, quiet, humorous man he was without a doubt a steadying influence on Charlie's somewhat erratic creative output. That's all that needs to be said at the moment.

So, what about working in Bradford compared to London? About 200 miles apart, measured by an unsteady crow, it was a million miles apart. Well, not quite but you know what I mean.

A one-man printing business a couple of minutes away. Another printer Valley in one of the highest points in Bradford run by Jack Haggas whom I knew from NDH.

A process engraver who called on us daily. One morning and one evening newspaper in the same building compared to Fleet Street and although it was the wool capital of the world, somewhat sleepy compared to the big city. It is said, so it possibly almost certainly isn't true, that wool men never shake hands, they feel each other's jacket lapel, assessing the quality of the cloth.

Chapter 14:
Pat's Family History

Her Dad was the pleasantest man I've ever met. I could write a saga about the family, boring you to distraction, about people and places that mean nothing to you but I hope you will not skip the next few paragraphs. I found it amazing.

Pat's father, Douglas Porter was the youngest of two brothers. The other one was William. They were rich. Their Mum and Dad had servants, a cook, a maid and an odd job man. Their living room in Harrogate was large enough to hold the Methodist Church bazaar.

William wanted to be an architect and had either won a scholarship or obtained permission to the Royal College of Architects in London. The 1914-18 was broke out. Someone sent him a white feather, the cowardice symbol. He enrolled, became a captain, got a bullet in his head, too near the brain to operate. On demob his father insisted he join the family business.

Pat's Father, Thomas Douglas wanted to be a serious musician, particularly church organs; not a chance. His Father made him take an apprenticeship at Hunslet Engine Company with a view to joining the family business empire.

Father travelled first class with the likes of Sir Montague Burton, head of Burton clothing empire. Young Douglas travelled third class and was not allowed to recognise is Father on the station platform. At 17 Douglas volunteered and served in the Royal Flying Corps as a maintenance engineer. This could explain a lot of the two brothers' future behaviour.

The Porter empire consisted of a pub, a dance hall, three garages with petrol, repairs, taxis, a posh car showroom, a fleet of coal barges, taxis on Leeds City Station and so on. Pat's Dad liked serving petrol, swilling the forecourt and getting under cars. He was a competent engineer on old cars. In 1951 he was driving a mid-size 1937 Austin. They had the Renault agency.

William did some office work. William's son built a sports car for several years at the back of the premises. One by one the businesses disappeared.

Pat's mother was a qualified bookkeeper and did her best to try and get some action to no avail. In the end, William and Alan ran a two-man taxi business. Dad took the bookings and Alan drove the taxi.

When Pat's Mum and Dad moved from the flat above the garage to Davies Avenue he told me the following:

The house was owned by the head brewer of Tetley's brewery. Each Monday he would open the safe in his house and take out a small bottle. He would go down to the brewery and put a few drops of liquid from the bottle into the vat. The secret recipe for Tetley's beer.

I thought about this for a while then asked "How many vats?"

Pat's Dad's favourite answer to many questions was "Don't know". This he repeated in answer to my next few questions.

"How many gallons do they brew each day?"

Tetley's is available throughout the British Isles, certainly in London, so they probably brew millions of pints a week. If he keeps a small bottle in the safe at home, where is the recipe? Who makes the secret recipe and if he does why keep it in a small bottle? If you put a few drops of arsenic or cyanide into millions of gallons what difference would it make? I could of course be wrong however it didn't add up to me but Pat's Dad, invariably happy, enjoyed this story and he always stressed it was only a very small bottle of this secret ingredient he kept in his safe. He always ended the story by saying "the head brewer was done for the week." Me, "So what happened when he went on holiday or was taken ill?" As ever was the reply "don't know". Believe it if you will. I didn't. Cheers.

Pat's Mum and Dad bought a very nice stone-built, double-fronted end terrace house in Calverley for £1100. It had dry rot that cost them a good few quid to get it sorted and I spent many evening with Pat's Dad adding fitted wardrobes and other bits of joinery. In 1957 Pat's Mum decided they needed an income so put the house on the market for £2200. It was snapped up by Pat and I. We moved in late February. By late June they were still with us with all our worldly goods stacked in one room. Pat's Dad was content, his wife, his daughter, grand-daughter plus me all living happily together.

I pointed out to Pat they were living rent-free and we were paying the mortgage. Eventually moving in July and after living in a caravan for a year they bought the village post office in a delightful village in North Yorkshire. A snag, this property was on a slip road with no passing traffic so the only customers were the very small community in the village. They were losing money. Next venture was a general store in South Yorkshire between a fish and chip shop and a railway line. Pat's Dad was quite content whilst Pat's Mum was worn out running the shop single-handed. One Sunday Pat's Dad, as a treat, took me to the local rubbish tip to search for anything that might come in handy. Eventually in 1964 they retired to a small cottage back in the village of Calverley.

Chapter 15:
Harry Secombe, J. B. Priestley,
Richard Harris, Spike Milligan
and Michael Gambon

How was I settling in? Very nicely, thank you.

I knew the job but didn't know the city. Although we lived about 4½ miles away, I had only been to Bradford a few times and then to particular places, Park Avenue for cricket, Odsal Stadium for Rugby League and once to a pantomime at the Alhambra.

I found a couple of places for an eatable one shilling and sixpenny lunch and began to find my way around. Swan Arcade was a delight and there were many good shops – Brown Muff, Fattorini, Busby's, Christopher Pratt, Taylor and Parsons, sadly all gone including Swan Arcade.

I began to appreciate the Bradford humour, distinctly different from Leeds, droll rather than sharp. Here are two examples to hopefully raise a smile.

Comedian, singer Harry Secombe from Swansea was a middle of the bill turn at the Alhambra. Strolling around the town one bright and sunny morning a man approached him.

> Man: "You're 'im, aren't you, that Secombe fella?"
> Harry: "Yes, that's me."
> Man: "I was in the other night. You'll do alright, you will. You nearly had me laughing once."

Bradford born, J B Priestley heard this one-liner. He had a play running in London that hadn't done too well. When it went on tour and played Bradford, he decided to travel north, go to the theatre, sit by the door on an end seat at the back of the stalls, nip out at the final curtain and listen to the comments as people came through the foyer. One middle-aged couple was enough.

> Man: "Well, you would come, wouldn't you?"

Nothing to do with Bradford but three more showbizzy bits of humour.

Actor Richard Harris spent his last few years of his life in a suite at the Savoy Hotel. Now very gaunt and pale, the ambulance men were wheeling the trolley through the foyer as a crowd of Chinese people were being registered. He propped himself up and said "It's the food." then fell back and didn't move.

Another of his quotes: "On a morning I lie in bed with my eyes closed, put my hands on my chest, press outwards and if my elbows don't touch wood I get up."

Comedian Spike Milligan was passing an undertakers, stopped, lay down in the doorway and shouted, "Shop!"

Here's a nice story from actor Michael Gambon.

He was being interviewed by an overzealous young reporter who asked:

Reporter: "Is there anything else you'd like to say?"
MG: "Yes…. I used to be homosexual."
Reporter: "Used to be?"
MG: "Yes. I gave it up."
Reporter: "Gave it up?"
MG: "Yes. It made my eyes water."

Going off at a tangent. That's a thing I do on a regular basis. Stay with it. Soon be back on track. Hopefully.

So what was Charlie's like? In two words, much quieter. Everybody got on with their job and I felt at home with the work and the humour. One day artist Jack Meynell said to me, "Y'know that Morrison's shop in Rawson Place?" I didn't. "Well it's really different. When you go in you pick up a wire basket, put it on some rails and pick up things as you walk around." Big trees from little acorns grow. Was this the start of the supermarket revolution in the north? I think it must have been.

Things were jogging along nicely but there were a couple or three clouds on the home front. I knew Dad had waterworks problems. On holiday we would have to jog trot along the prom to get to the gents. Once inside there was time to read a slim novel before he'd finished. This got critical. I'll spare you the details but Mum took him, under protest, to the doctor's surgery. He came back trembling and for the first time I remember sat in an easy chair then lit a cigarette as Mum put the kettle on. He always sat on an upright chair with his feet on the cross rail which gave him a gnomish appearance. I'll cut to the chase.

"I never thought Dr Dawson would say that to me."

"Say what?"

"That I needed to go into hospital now." I asked him, "Is there an alternative doctor?"

He said, "You could be dead in a fortnight."

He coughed, spluttered and trembled.

I said, "Let's face it, Dad. If he hadn't said that you wouldn't be going."

He went to St James in Leeds, had the operation. On Sunday Pat and I went to visit him. It was a very foggy day. By the time I got home I couldn't stop coughing and it was very painful. Once more Doctor Dawson enters the scene. He visited and tested me. It was pleurisy. If you've never had pleurisy, don't. You want to cough and it's agony. I was off work three weeks and had a week's holiday in September and only started late July. The firm was very understanding and didn't dock my pay.

Happily Dad recovered. He was 61 and finally pegged out at 82 after seven hours in hospital. He'd had mumps at 21 and apparently that can be a factor in prostate problems. Just think he went through the First World War with this condition as a soldier and World War 2 as a civilian.

John Bell, a wonderful artist, a dour Scotsman, a good joke teller and an awkward so-and-so all rolled into one compact package at 40+ joined us as well as a young man who was a friend of a friend's son. He had a brief spell as I don't know what then Ken Allen joined us as print manager. A lovely, slow-speaking man from Otley. Here is the basis of his first words to me. "Mr Pearson, I am not a print man. When my neighbour got his calling-up papers, he passed me some very basic printing machinery and a lot of carrier bags. He supplied Otley market stall holders and I carried it on." How he came to the agency I've forgotten or never found out. A delightful man we used to go to Charlie Brook's fish restaurant every Friday. Just as good or even better than Harry Ramsden's. If, like me, you are partial to potato crisps and have tried Seabrook, they are indeed Charlie Brook's – C. Brook. Totally useless knowledge but I hope it keeps you reading.

Ken must have been with us a year or so then moved on. Years later he came to see me. He was at Hezzies but wanted to move. I would have liked to have him back but for two things. The business he was handling at the salary he was getting did not show a profit. Secondly, although Heslock was a stumblebum sort of set-up, I didn't poach. Ken left me on the best of terms and I once bumped into him in Otley and we had a happy few minutes together.

The IPA (Institute of Practitioners in Advertising) had strict rules about poaching. Years later a local agency with a lay preacher at its head was deliberately calling on our clients. I put a stop to that and got a letter of apology from the lay preacher cum poacher.

Mentioning Charlie Brook's fish and chip emporium brings me back to Charlie Brett's, that other fish and chip emporium in Headingley. It became a regular Friday visiting place for advertising folk in Leeds and one Friday I met David Walls, Charlie's younger brother. Bright and cheery his main topic of conversation being horse racing, now there's a darker side to this story.

On my first day Mr Walls, I never really got used to calling him Charlie but I'll have to use it in this book, told me "Bradford has the worst postal service in the country." David had left before I arrived but Jack Meynell told me this.

David used the postal money to back horses and when the horses lost he burnt the printing blocks of wood and metal on the production room stove which eventually became bunged up with metal. David went back to London, suddenly the postal system in Bradford improved. There's a tragic end to this story. David died of a brain tumour. Nobody ever told Charlie of his brother's betting and printing block scam.

Most of Charlie's creative output went to Arthur Barthel who did a bit of tidying up but occasionally Charlie would bypass Arthur and the rough idea went direct to John B. or Jack M.

One day he called me in and said, "I want you to take this to the client, Glynn Martin. You'll get on with Frank Morton. He opens the innings for Great Horton in the Bradford League."

Glynn Martin was I think a 3-people set-up, M.D. office manager and typist. There were many companies like this in Bradford. I believe they rented looms to produce their wools.

The ever smiling office manager said "Well, Mr Pearson, it's certainly different. I'll take it in and see what Mr Morton has to say." Mr Morton came out with the ad in his hand and went straight to a calendar on the wall. "Just checking it's not April Fool's Day. If you can't do better than this we'll have to look elsewhere." It's hard for you to visualise but the ad had a some-what rambling headline, 'Glynn Martin Wools are like beautiful flowers they stand watering, watering, watering'. Below each word 'watering' was the word 'washing' in brackets, a weak line drawing of a watering can and some flowers, a slab of copy, nameplate and address. Of course, it wasn't true. Too much rain or water from a can and the flowers droop and fade.

Back at the office Charlie said, "Y'know your problem? You're a lousy salesman." Good bye Glynn Martin. This was my first brush with CLW's somewhat unusual creative talents.

Charlie started sending me out to new prospects and I built up a small but profitable client base. He called me in one day and said "I'm not giving you a rise, I'm putting you on 5% commission." After six months he called me in again and said, "The Missus says you're earning more than me." so I did get a rise after all. I took a fair amount of work home. My Mum thought I was God's gift to the advertising industry. The main reason I did this was I was engaged to be married and the last thing I wanted was to lose my job and it was fairly ordinary routine work.

Burras Peake were a smallish, well respected men's outfitters with quite a few branches in the north. The head office was in Leeds quite close to one of my calls. I knocked on the little window, as you do, and who should open it but Captain Thomas. They weren't really into advertising but he took my card and said he would pass it on to his Managing Director. I heard no more but it was nice to meet Captain (sorry Mr Thomas) on equal terms.

George Scott had been an artist at Hezzies but here worked in production plus calls to a few clients.

He was an unusual sort of chap. Before the war he'd been a woodwork teacher. After the war he became an artist at Hezzies. Now a production man at Charlie's whom he'd known before the war, doing what?

In his late thirties he often said, "Never hurry anywhere at any time," and he stuck to this. Each morning he would say "I'm just popping out for ten minutes." and half an hour later he returned.

Chapter 16:
Wedded Bliss, Almost

23 July 1951, not a public holiday but the day pencilled in for our marriage. Pat's Dad said we could have a posh wedding or £200 deposit on a house. No question to answer. My parents had lived in rented property all their married lives. Not for me. Some years later I was surprised to find out so had Pat's parents until their mid-fifties. When Pat was born they lived over the garage in Roundhay Road with the council school opposite. When Pat was 11 they moved house to a stone-built detached house which I presumed they owned. They rented and in 1955 Pat's Father and his brother sold the remaining business in their crumbling empire.

So back to Spring 1951 I was on the property trail. I must have looked at a dozen or more houses in our price range before I found the one that was to become our home for almost six years. Pat was very good about this. She was living in a largish house at Roundhay within walking distance of the beautiful park. She accepted that if I was to make a career with CWP I would need to be in Bradford. I doubt if she'd ever been to the city. Eventually I saw a semi in Undercliffe which I really liked and it was the Leeds side of Bradford. The sellers, a Mr and Mrs Robinson couldn't have been kinder. Mrs Robinson made a list of the best shops in the area and in Bradford. Mr Robinson had been a ship's carpenter and made quite a few improvements to the house. It's an odd feeling and I don't know if you dear reader have every felt this, it felt like our house. It was a warm and friendly house. I wanted it.

Pat came to visit and although the road and path were unmade, she was happy and felt the same way as I did. The cost, £1,750. The mortgage? Well, after six years we still owed a fair wedge but that's mortgages for you. All sorts of things happened before the big day but just everyday things that were important to us but not real page turners. We were married late morning at Leeds register office with lunch at the Metropole Hotel. There were nine of us; Pat and I, Mr and Mrs Porter, my parents and Sister, best man David Peel and Pat's best friend, Betty Oldham.

After lunch Pat and I had a lovely experience on the station platform. No it wasn't a flash oik telling us we'd won a lot of money but I need to wind the story back a few years to set the scene.

When I re-started at Heslocks, I usually sat on the lunchtime tram with a chap who worked at the Yorkshire Post. He was a process engraver on the evening shift. He said they could probably help me out with rush work. I met his boss, an elderly (to me) rather short tempered at times Scotsman with a very ordinary name, Smith. I got loads of work through them but Mr Smith impressed on me he was doing me a favour and if I told anybody else that would be the end of a beautiful friendship.

So we're on the platform about to board the Kings Cross train and who should be approaching us, going on the late shift was Mr Smith. We weren't dolled up in wedding gear, I think a rose for Pat and a carnation for me (we wore clothes) and Pat's friend Betty trying to throw confetti over us, somewhat gave the game away. Mr Smith with the softest Scottish accent said – the exact words:

> Mr Smith: "May I have the pleasure and privilege to be the first to kiss the lovely bride"? … "With your permission, Ron."

What a wonderful and gracious way to start our marriage.
The plot thickens.

> The scene: The Waverley Hotel, London.
> The cast: Two happy people and a hotel receptionist.
> Receptionist: "I'm sorry Mr Pearson. We've double-booked your room and the other couple got here earlier and we haven't a room for you."
> Now read on. We'd ditched the floral adornments but I think it was fairly obvious this was our wedding night. In later years I would have caused a real rumpus but we just looked gobsmacked. "But it was booked weeks ago by phone."

This could go on quite a long time but eventually they found us a ground-floor suite with its own garden in their poshest hotel. Do you really want to know what happened on our wedding night? We played Canasta – don't you believe it.

It was Festival of Britain year. We spent a day there, full of interest from a man making cricket bats to a wonderful water feature. I'll try to explain, 30 or 40 feet high, a small metal scoop with water dripping into it. Below was a slightly bigger scoop and so on until a really big scoop. When this tipped over into a pond with a mighty crash, wonderful.

Many years later a property developer wanted a feature for a shopping centre. I tracked down the maker of this crowd puller but the client settled for a rather rude sculpture on the lines of Epstein's Adam. It didn't last long.

I'm convinced that kids would have wanted to see the water feature and so taken their parents – who spend the money, but it cut no ice.

We went to two shows: '*Touch and Go*' at the Prince of Wales featured

Desmond Walter-Ellis, a very good comedian somewhat similar to Michael Barrymore. You've never heard of him have you? He tried his luck on TV but never really made it. A Hollywood comedian Red Skelton was our other visit at the Palladium; very good particularly in his party piece Guzzlers Gin.

On Friday we arrived at 27 Killinghall Drive, Undercliffe, Bradford, our home.

Pat's Mum and Dad had been up earlier, set out a wonderful tea and a big bouquet of flowers; absolutely brilliant. We ate slowly. We couldn't stop smiling at each other. We were in 'our house'.

Pat took to Undercliffe and Bradford, enjoying the compact shopping area at the crossroads, getting to know the neighbours. Her only moan was hanging out the washing, if the wind was in the wrong direction the washing became speckled with soot. We were so happy.

Chapter 17:
Dogs 1951-2022

When we got married, I made a joke if I didn't take the dog, I didn't get the girl. Pat's dog was a wire-haired terrier called Tuppence, her Mum being Penny.

Tuppence was a lovely dog but for some reason never had a full coat. Pat made her a waterproof, fluffy lined coat for walks. Somehow, I became the owner of a rather large pullover, which I wore in the evening. Tuppence used to be inside the garment with her head poking out at the top. Another foible, daughter didn't like me wearing gloves. So, there I was in winter pushing my baby daughter in the pram, dog on lead, ice-cold hands, sort of frozen to the pram handles.

From then on Dog after Dog. Our next dog was a red (or ginger) Chow. It had one of its paws stood on when it was a pup. It didn't limp but it was obvious the paw wasn't right. Shan was not very sociable, preferring to sit in a corner and watch the world go by. Shan lasted about 8 years then we got Ming, a black chow. What a dog. When I took her out for "walkies" kids said "Mr is it a bear?" We got her from a top breeder near Halifax. Still reserved, which all Chow's are, but a really wonderful dog. I think she lasted until 14 then it was Sasha our first Golden Retriever. Once you've had a Goldie that's it you're smitten.

Sasha was absent quite a bit when the bungalow was being built. The builders loved her and she loved them, particularly at lunch time. Next came Jem our only male dog. A different personality to Sasha with an odd smile when he wanted something. Finally, Honey. We were told by the breeders she was the quietest of the foursome. I wouldn't like to have met the other three. As a pup she was very strong and lively. One of her specialities was to race around the room half a dozen times using the settee to jump on, run on and onto the floor. Walking around the park, when we got to the bowling green hut which was basically white she pulled like mad. If we passed a metallic noise, a two part steel ladder with the top half being hoisted, this was another big pull on the lead. I've thought about this quite a bit and I don't think it would be noises she heard or saw a colour before we owned her as she would not be leaving the house or garden.

On two occasions she pulled so hard I ended up on the ground, flat on my face. On the second time my face was very bloody and one eye was closed. It was a Sunday and our best bet would be a smaller local hospital in Otley. My nose wasn't broken but when I was cleaned up my left eye was purple and badly swollen. Some help was needed. I took Honey to the village training school. I held her on a special harness. "We don't use these, would you take it off please?" I did. She dragged me forwards and backwards a time or two. Then the trainer said, "Let me show you." Quite a small lady she had to run to keep up with super-dog. "I don't think there's much point in you coming anymore." I replied, "How about the dog?" She failed to see the humour.

Next I rang our vet. Now you may have seen him even if you live in Banff or Lands' End. He was a regular presenter on TV, a Scotsman called John Baxter. One day in Guernsey we were on a bench chatting to two ladies who lived there. When we got around to dogs and vets we mentioned John and they'd heard of him. He was grey haired and if you're reading this John a real lady's man. Back to the plot.

He recommended a lady behaviourist, who I believe often appeared on his programme. After watching Honey do her speciality of racing around the room, she came up with the following advice.

"Honey has to know who's boss". Each morning get up, get dressed and leave her in her room no matter what. Get the breakfast ready then let her out and be eating something. We decided on a couple of Pringles each. After a few days she calmed down. Next, "When you go shopping put her back in her room. Unload the shopping and talk so she hears you then let her out." Again success. However the racing around the room and over the settee continued. John suggested he and the behaviourist come again. "Make sure she's in her room before we enter." We did as we were told.

The sun lounge is an add-on to the main room. John said "We three will be admiring the view from the sun lounge. You Ron will open her door and join us. I'm hoping she will be interested in what we are doing and join us." She did but not after the settee steeplechase. We tried a few times. The same result. To conclude I spent a couple of weeks in the garage every day and with little treats every success taught Honey to stay, come on and settle down. It worked. Oh, we donated the settee to Ilkley Playhouse.

I've often said to Ann, 'This is Missy's house and we just happen to live here. It's so wonderful to have a dog in this house again, it makes the house into a home.' She is like a mobile dustbin. Missy is a German Shepherd cross Collie and for the first seven years of her life lived mainly in a sort of cage in the house until Ann took over. Missy is the most loveable dog, you could stroke her ears forever.

Chapter 18:
Back to Charlies

I'm going to jump a bit now. I was sent on a weekend course to Lyme Hall near Stockport and on my return Charlie asked me to write a report on the weekend which I did. George went on a course to Leicester and asked to write a report which he didn't.

Let's look at George Scott and the ten minutes/half an hour break.

Charlie was convinced that George had never been on the course. I'm convinced the Missus was the major factor in George's dismissal.

May Walls and a friend were in the habit of going to Busby's Department Store for the occasional morning coffee. George Scott was in the habit …

On several occasions at advertising do's he often said "I've no idea why I got the push." I did… the Missus. Goodbye George.

The Missus was to be a deciding factor in more than one dismissal later on in the story.

George got a job at Chapmans, a well-respected agency in Halifax run by the wonderfully-named brothers, Lemuel and Aked of that ilk.

Enter Peter Henry Ralph. He joined the agency after the departure of George Scott. About my age, he had a decided limp. Many thought it was a war wound. "Let them think that." Peter said to me. I think the truth was he'd sat on a cracked toilet seat as a child.

A bit like 'Arry boy' in the Army he liked to be called 'Enry'.

Ralph senior was the head honcho at Whitehall Advertising, an offshoot of Petty's, a big printing concern on Whitehall Road, Leeds. Why Peter didn't go there I never found out. Peter had a car so he did some contact work, handled some printing work, some production work and some media work, eventually ending up as media buyer. We were both made directors in November 1952. I was totally chuffed. My Dad was indifferent "It'll be half a crown to speak to you before we know where we are." was his comment. I don't think my Sister spoke but Mother followed me to the gate and said, "What is it they've done to you at work?" I explained as best I could and I think she was happy for me.

There was a 3-year course to get you through the IPA exam. Always a bighead I decided I could do it in one year. I failed. Years later I took the written exam and passed. I was then invited to London for a verbal exam and passed. One of the examiners was from New Zealand. I had a very bright lad who was emigrating to New Zealand. He gave me his card and told me the young man could contact him for an interview. It was all very friendly and I passed the exam on the spot. The lad and the boss of the New Zealand agency, both wrote to me to say how happy they were with each other.

Early 1953 Pat announced she was pregnant. We were overjoyed. However it was not an easy pregnancy. Aside: I've often thought if men had babies there would never be a population boom. Pat was in hospital for a few days in July, August, September and most of October with blood pressure and related problems. I went to St Luke's every night in October. Now this is one of the worst bits in this book but it has to be said. One Sunday I'd gone down to Mum's for tea and early evening I said, "Well that was lovely, it's time for me to go." or something similar. Mum said "Oh, please stay a bit longer. We'll get the cards out and I'll make a lovely supper like the old days." My reply was simple, "Pat's not too good and I told her I'd be there at opening time and I'm looking forward to seeing her." Mum—out of it completely—"I hope they both die in hospital then you can come back here and we can be happy again like the old days."

I was in shock and replied that "I wouldn't be coming to this house again." But I did of course. I was in tears and my Sister quiet as ever thought it was awful. Dad followed me to the gate and said, "She doesn't mean it chum." I said, "The trouble is, Dad, she does mean it." I managed to sort myself out a bit before I got to St Luke's but Pat knew there was something wrong. I fobbed it off by saying, "The usual rows at home." I never told her the appalling truth.

On Monday my Sister came up, cooked me a good meal and tried to smooth things over. Dad phoned me from the cinema and on Tuesday Mum wrote to me. Sadly none of these things happened. I was alone in a cold house living on corn flakes and fish and chips. All Pat's Aunts and Uncles lived in Harrogate and came over to St Luke's plus Pat's Mum and Dad. There were no visits from the Pearson family. Try to imagine how I felt. I was an outcast. A leper. I'd done the unthinkable, fallen in love, got married and was about to become a father. That's enough of that.

After being in and out of labour part of Friday and all of Saturday, our daughter was born. Throughout the pregnancy she was Nesbert (don't ask why). I've a few loose screws in my head. Well, you know that already, don't you? With the difficulties of birth, Pat had a really rough time. They were in a separate room and I was only allowed ten minutes or so to hold my wonderful daughter and cry myself silly with happiness. Oh dear me, I've jumped the gun now read on.

> On October 31 at 9pm at St Luke's Hospital, Bradford there was a virgin birth.
> "Oh no there wasn't."
> "Oh yes there was."

Let me set the scene. With birth imminent, I was ushered into a side room with another Dad to be. We were on nodding terms. He was Don Alred, the sports and crime reporter on the Bradford T&A. Enter the third member of the cast, a small man in a flat cap, thick glasses and a buttoned up raincoat.

> Small man: "Nay it beats me does this lot. I mean, we love each
> other but we've never done owt like that…" and so on. I kid you not.

Don gave me a wink. Exit small man. Don and I started to laugh and I pinched a line from northern comic Norman Evans: "I never did like that coalman." Talk about laugh. We did but with an undertone of nervousness.

Don was the next to go. His wife had twin girls. The Alreds moved to the village, the twins went to school with our daughter and one became an Olympic gymnast.

On Sunday Pat and baby were still in a single room. She'd had a really rough delivery and lived at home with her parents under doctor's orders and daily treatment for several weeks. On Monday she was in the main ward and at the far end was the gentleman in the flat cap.

> "You see that bloke in the flat cap?"
> "Yes."
> "His wife…", "Don't tell me. The virgin birth?"
> "Yes."
> "Well it's true. Doctors have come from Leeds, Sheffield and
> Manchester etc., etc."

I've recently read of this extremely rare condition. A billion to one chance, a carer informed me. It has a name; I think it begins with a "p". This is quite irreverent but it made me smile. "What did the Bradford doctor say on delivery?"

"Jesus Christ." There endeth the unknown testament according to the prophet Ron.

We did the usual round of visiting all Pat's relatives who had helped us plus Dad's Sisters and Brother, Charlie and all we very happy and kind and later sent things for the baby. Cousin Jack sent a really big tea tray which is still in use. My Mum was very pleased to holding little granddaughter. Dad put out his fag and said, "All kids love to be held by me." and started to cough. Granddaughter cried very loudly but at least we were on visiting and speaking terms again. Both my Mother and Sister were avid knitters but I don't think anything was knitted for Granddaughter. Mother visited us three or four times in almost six years, once to view the premises, two for the Christening and once on Boxing Day is all I can remember. Dad and Sister came fairly regularly with the excuse, "Your Mum's been off it all week." Other than that everything was rosy but there was a very dark cloud on the horizon.

Christmas 1953 I got a surprise. The chap delivering a job from a printers shook my hand, wished me all the best and stuffed some white paper in my top pocket; 50 quid in five pound notes. The one man printer we had used when at North Parade had gone in with the printer so I rang him to thank him and the delivery man for their generosity. "He's not the delivery man, that's Norman Morrell, the gaffer, the chap who runs the wrestling in Bradford, Lime Grove, London and elsewhere." He always wore an open necked shirt when everybody else wore ties. On one occasion he booked a room at the House of Commons to give a lunch to the press and some MPs and was refused entry because he was tieless. They have a selection of ties for such occasions but Norman refused them and got a lot of national press coverage for that.

There was a wrestling ring next to the printers and on one occasion Hassan Ali Bey from Egypt with a northern accent was collecting some cartons for an embrocation he was developing. "Fancy a few rounds next door?" was his opening remark, plus a wink. My reply, "Not with you I don't." Laughter all around. "You won't get hurt." I still refused. Norman Morrell had been an Olympic Lightweight Wrestler just before the war.

Switch backwards to 1949… Chinese food was a new fad. In London with my pals we went to Freddie Mill's place. Freddie was world light heavyweight champion and coming around the table patted me on the shoulder and said, "I bet you could do a few rounds." My reply as I said to the Egyptian wrestler, "Not with you I couldn't." Laughter all around. Mills had a mysterious death. He was found in the back of his own car with a bullet in his head. I seem to remember he had got into debt with some of the London heavies.

> Now it's the cup final replay at Odsal in front of 102000 plus.
> Norman Morrell: "Are you going up there to Odsal tonight?"
> Me: "Not a chance, no ticket."
> Norman: "Now you have."
> A ticket was in my top pocket.

I was sitting 3 or 4 rows down from where the presentation took place, end of a row. Warrington won after a 4-4 draw at Wembley. Their brilliant winger Brian Bevan sat on the edge of my seat as the ribbons were put on the trophy and said, "I'm glad we won but they didn't deserve to lose." That to me was what the old RL was all about.

Brian Bevan was a most remarkable player, turned down by Leeds because of his slight physique. On the field he looked even more fragile, balding, toothless and not very tall. 796 is all you need to know about BB. That's the number of tries he scored for Warrington. Just think about it. Scores were much lower than they are today and 796 is a helluva lot of tries for a spindly legged man who seemed to evade the most determined of tacklers.

123

The agency moved to premises that November. Charlie was none too happy about climbing four floors to get to his office so delegated many of his trips to Arthur, Peter and me. Cyril Williams a small-time Bradford publisher climbed the four floors to Charlie's. Somewhat out of breath he asked, "Is God in?" Our new premises were a bit of a rabbit warren on the first and second floors at 35 Morley Street, alongside the Alhambra Theatre. We did need more space and from that aspect it did prove an improvement. Several more staff were added, some good, some bad, some indifferent.

One visualiser was on trial for three months, did absolutely nothing and when I fired him, threatened to commit suicide. Apparently, his wife ran a small successful retail business and he was frightened to go home and tell her. Charlie hired him, I fired him. This was to be a familiar pattern in the years to come. I gave him another month and then he had to go.

One of the best shorthand typists we had stole the petty cash on Friday and never came back. Kenneth Wilkinson tracked her down and went to the address she gave at the interview and found out she was a lodger there and had flown. There were several more similar occasions. One girl lost her wage packet, another girl cried in sympathy, the police were called. I knew the copper. He lived near me. "We know who it did, we just can't prove it." was his assessment. Fast forward six months or so and a client said to me:

"A girl called... Work for you?"
   "Yes."
   "Did you have some money problems with her, a pinched wage packet?" End of story.

The Missus wasn't keen on Peter Henry Ralph. He went for what reason I know not. He put a large rather rude sign on his office door in order to say "goodbye" in a rather unpleasant manner. Ray Gledhill a good visualise stayed a couple of years then went to Nevins.

Colin Moore stayed a while longer, became my assistant and then joined Nevins. Eventually he formed his own agency Clarendon Advertising. He was a very bright and likeable man whom I met at do's, always on a friendly basis and then there is Tom B.

Quite a clever man, quite a heavy drinker, a bit of a middle-aged lad, Tom got himself a secretary, the barmaid at one of Bradford's bigger hotels. Tom asked for time off to go to some sort of rehabilitation centre down South for ex-servicemen. His secretary was on holiday.

The Yorkshire Post printed a picture of two people with bunches of spring flowers in the Scilly Isles. Guess who? I don't think the Missus could have seen this. However on August Bank Holiday Tom failed to return to work but sent a telegram to the effect of enjoying a few days extra in the Lake District, see you Monday. The Missus opened the telegram; tarrah Tom plus 'secretary'.

It would be Whitsuntide in probably 1954 that Charlie accused me of lying to him about a certain job that had gone wrong. He was very unpleasant. I hadn't lied. I can't even recall the incident however Arthur Barthel had warned me to beware of these outbursts. On one occasion he and Charlie had gone out to dinner for another 'clear the air' get together and Charlie had blown his top about who was right and who was wrong about a certain incident. It got so heated they went back to the offices at ten in the evening for Arthur to be proved right.

I said I hadn't lied but in my case I had no proof. It got really nasty. "If I'm a liar you don't want me on your board of directors and working my socks off for you. I'm giving a month's notice and I'll see Kenneth when we come back about this." I was gone.

Pat, of course, was very worried and said, "This is you. You never climb down, do you?", and of course she was right. We'd a lovely baby daughter and I couldn't afford to be out of work. Friends of both agencies Jack Haggas, John Hall and Fred Dawson had all told me Nevin wanted me back on my terms. Jack Haggas took me out to lunch and said "Name your price and you'll probably get it." OK, it would mean a walk to the bus stop, a longer journey but I would be better off so don't worry. We both did.

Come Wednesday I told Kenneth what had happened and he said, "Leave it a day or two. Let things settle down."

I was always in and out of Charlie's office. This Wednesday I wasn't. At 5:30pm he buzzed me. I went in.

"I haven't slept a wink over the holiday about what you said. This company needs you Ron. Have you seen Kenneth?" My answer was, "Yes." Silence. "I didn't lie. I've many faults but lying is not one of them. You made a mistake and tried to pass it on to me. Hold out your hand and admit your mistake and it's all over."

An hour's silence or so it seemed, apart from my beating heart, Charlie took off his glasses, dabbed his eyes and said, "Don't go." I thought of the Jack Haggas lunch. "That's not what I want. You made a mistake and didn't admit it. We shake hands admit you were wrong and that's good enough for me." This was so difficult for Charlie. He was never wrong. As I was to find out in the next few years he couldn't ever, never be wrong as you will discover.

He stood up, held out his hand. I didn't. He tried another wriggle. It cut no ice then "Yes, I did get it wrong. Can we shake hands?" We did. Both were in tears.

I think I was able to put a reason for this extraordinary 'never wrong' behaviour but that's a fair way off at the moment.

On a lighter note…

Dad was in his office one morning when a salesman called, persuading, almost begging Dad to take a full-size cut-out of Esther Williams, one time swimming star and now a popular film star. Dad was running an Esther Williams film the following week and this poor bloke had to dash around the country getting cinema's to take in this life size cut-out. Dad really hadn't the room for this but it was free, gratis and for nothing. Signing the acceptance form Dad noticed the name 'Du Croix'. 'My lads Colonel was a Du Croix,' said Dad. 'That's me,' said he. 'Your lad put on a revue once, bright lad. What's he doing now?' 'He's a Director of an Advertising Agency.' For once I think my Dad was proud of me.

Here's another odd, not so funny incident.

Dad on the phone: "We've a film on this week you'll really enjoy, *Hobson's Choice* with Charles Laughton. Your Mum and Peggy are coming on Tuesday. We'd like you and Pat to come then I'll stop off for fish and chips to finish off a really good night."

I won't bother you with the rest of the conversation but basically Pat was still breast feeding our daughter etc., etc. Dad suggested I came on my own. I pointed out I hadn't a car. If the film finished at 10:30 plus supper I would have difficulty getting home. This went on for a while. Dad said, "Your Mother's going to be very disappointed." What an unhappy family I'd left behind.

In 1955 Charlie and Arthur had another bust up and Arthur, the remaining partner in the original trio left. He'd rescued Charlie's work for too long. Don't get me wrong, Charlie had some good ideas but his bad ones were real stinkers. He taught me a few things including "When you've written the copy for an ad, re-read it and you can often cross out the first sentence." 'It's just to get you going'. It worked.

Arthur had formed a small company with another man selling mail order floor covering plus a small shop and I invested £200 and was to write the ad. I'd had considerable success in the mail order field. It wasn't doing well and after about six months I was asked for another £200 and dropped out. The Missus found out about this shop and Charlie's solicitor found a loophole in the terms of agreement. Arthur didn't even argue. He set up an art business taking Jack Meynell and new artist Frank Pennett with him. That didn't last long. Jack Meynell told me, "We didn't get paid one week and next week I'd get double money. I've a wife and two lads to support." He moved to the Pickersgill agency in Leeds. Frank Pennett became advertising manager at Hammonds Brewery.

In 1957 Charlie added another 'expert' to the staff... 'the Creep', who had worked for the Halifax Building Society. Charlie and the Missus were going to the Channel Islands. The creep went to the airport to wish them bon voyage but missed them. Pat, our daughter and I went to Filey. 'The creep' drove to Filey in the hope of bumping into us. Happily he failed. There is more about the creep as we go on in the book.

On the Wednesday of our holiday in Filey, Pat and Lo and I were looking in a shop window when someone tapped me on the shoulder. It was Mrs Cammish who ran the guest house where we were staying. "I'm very sorry Ron but your Dad has just phoned to say your mother died in the night." I packed a bag and came to Bramley. Apparently Mum had felt quite good on the Tuesday and had done some work on the sewing machine but then died peacefully in bed. She was being treated for mild diabetes but I don't think that was the cause of death. I never did find out but I think it must have been her heart. Her 68th birthday was on 3rd June. She died mid-June. A happy woman in a sad life. I went back to Calverley on Thursday. Pat and Louise were still in Filey. Pat's Mum and Dad did their best to help me but had only met my Mother three times.

I don't remember much about the actual funeral. It was a burial. Apart from the minister there were no speeches. The bun fight afterwards was quite a pleasant affair. Aunts and Uncles from the Pearson and Hillarby clans happily mixing. Sadly, there were no friends or neighbours.

A bit more about the 'Creep'. I was responsible for producing the Building Society magazine. According to Charlie the Creep was a print expert. Monday, I handed it over to his nibs. A week later he asked me to sort it out for him. Apparently whilst at the Halifax, having a car, he'd taken the material to the printer.

One afternoon the 'Creep' knocked on our front door and handed over to Pat a few seed packets apologising for not being able to bring more because money was tight.

Then at Christmas the 'Creep' Left the Office Christmas Party early to knock on our door to give Pat a Christmas present, once more apologising for its smallness.

'Tuppence' our wire haired Terrier was dying and Pat was waiting for the vet. Pat tried to explain. The 'Creep' wanted to come in. Pat was in tears. She shut the door on him. The vet arrived. Goodbye to a very lovely and funny dog.

Finally after a year, the 'Creep' was supposed to be a business getter. £200 in a year. He had to go. Guess who did it? He sent me a very nasty poison pen letter. I photocopied a page from his diary and sent it to him. Something like this:

> Mon: Raining, said hello to CLW. Pauline's birthday, had a chocolate éclair.
> Tues: Still raining. Popped in to see KW nice chap. RSP always busy.
> Wed: Bit brighter. Toured the offices, good set-up, RSP in London.
> Thur: Read the Yorkshire Post. Humphrey Bogart died.
> Fri: Tony in production gave me a lesson on press advertisements, very interesting. Wage day, not much but bought a few seed packets and delivered them to RSPs wife.

This is not exactly word for word what happened but all of this happened in one week or another.

Cheerio Creep.

RON'S PICTURE GALLERY

(With apologies for 'fuzziness' on the older prints.)

The Pearson Dynasty + Mum

Grandad Pearson – Grandmaster in North Wales

Grannie Pearson with Sonny (Me) and Peggy (Eileen)

Dad in his 20s

Mum at 21

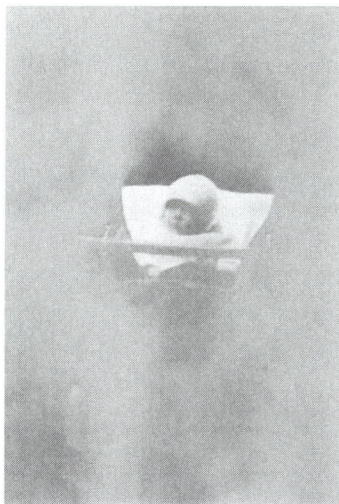

Ron in pram before fall on bootees or bonce

A family portrait

Peggy and Ronnie on holiday

The Hillarby Clan

Grandad Alfred Hillarby – Master Bookbinder

The Hillarby Sisters Florence, Elsie (Mum), Dorothy and Clarice

Grannie and Grandad in holiday attire

Curtain Up

The Summervilles
Mum far left, Dad far right

The Merrians
Dad lower right

There would be 100s if not 1000s of similar concert parties
between the two world wars

Yesteryears

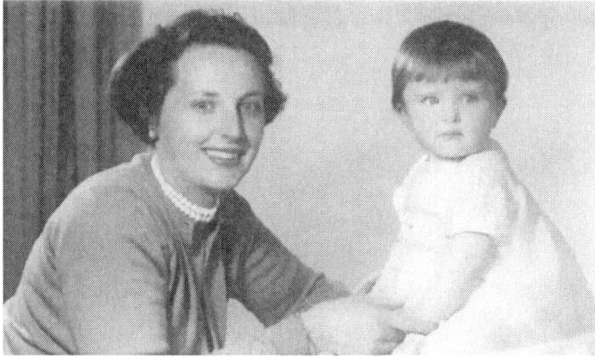

A lovely picture of Pat and Daughter

The Christening – Proud parents with Daughter and various relatives including Dad and Mum, 7th and 9th from the left.

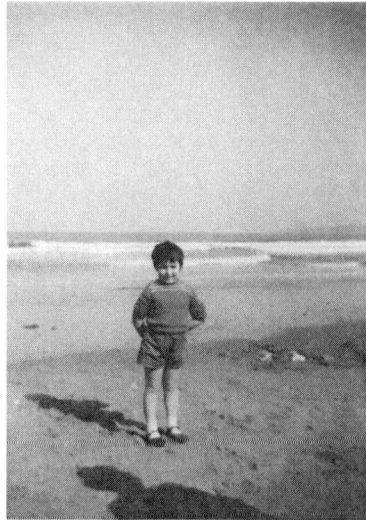

Lo unable to paddle because of plastic Seascale in Cumbria.

Happy Days

My favourite – Daughter and self – Holding hands on top and tunnelling below until hands touching and laughing a lot.

Happy pictures of daughter and sons a few years ago.

Before and After

Me with hair and girlfriend's shoulder

Trying to look business-like

Ron's favourite car with Charles Walls Advertising in the background

With poker players in 'The Odd Couple'.

Give 'em the old razzle dazzle in 'Chicago'.

The Scheming Lawyer – 'Inherit the Wind'.

Here, There & Sainsbury's

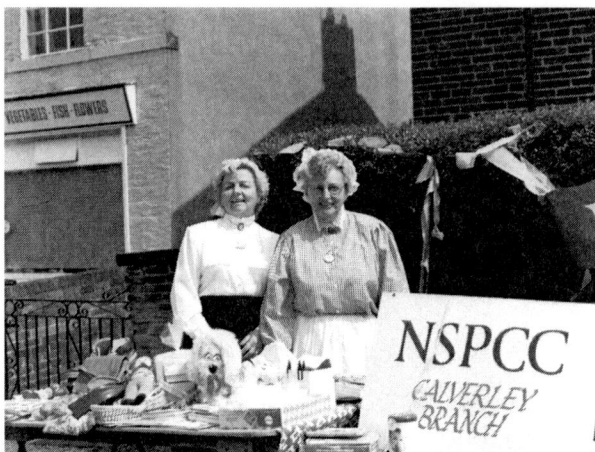

Pat and Neighbour, Olwyn, in Victorian dress fund raising for N.S.P.C.C.

Snapped at Sainsbury's.

Pat with Daughter's dog, Bella.

*That must have been a good one Ron!
Good Luck - Harry Worth*

Colin and I share a laugh with comedian, Harry Worth.

'Harry's Kingdom'
At the preview with Peter Vaughan, Jill Baker and Timothy West.

Charlie and The Missus

Charles Walls Advertising
Mr and Mrs Charles Walls, front centre, Ron (stripey tie), John
(bow tie, middle left) and Kenneth Wilkinson front, lower right.

30th June 1984 – the two of us with Kenneth and Winn.

Grand and Great Grandchildren

Grandad with future Inspector of police and Entrepreneur

Great grandchildren – Flynn and Florence – English style

Great grandson – Jarli – Australian style

Chapter 19: 1957
Charlie Winds Down

1957 was a momentous year. As previously mentioned we moved into Calverley but sadly this was the start of Charlie's inactive part in the business. From 1957 to 1960 four of the main clients gave him the heave ho. One sacked us, 2 kept us on the basis Charlie never had anything to do with their advertising and Charlie's best pal was sacked as the managing director of a business where the advertising was over budget and unsatisfactory. I felt so sorry for him but then I got a clue as to what might have been what I can only describe as an illness.

One day I jokily tried to put on his trilby. "It won't fit you Ron." It didn't. Like the proverbial pea on a drum, Charlie told me he was prematurely born without eyelashes, eyebrows, finger nails, toe nails and a very low weight and couldn't be breast fed. Could this explain something in his brain that caused him to take on the 'can't be wrong' complex?

Another day he came to the office in a bowler hat, bow tie, long overcoat and rolled umbrella. The bow tie suited him. "The Missus says I should develop a personality." Charlie came in every day like that until he retired at 60 in 1966 but there's a lot more water to flow under that bridge before that event.

I would not like to give the impression that May Walls was a dragon, just the opposite. She was a very pleasant woman who could smell a dud from a mile off. She was an above average bridge player, took some lessons on after dinner speaking and was quite good at it. She was doing her best to help an intensely shy man get over his problem. Charlie too was no mug. I was still at school in 1937 when he came up North but in 1950 the advertising scene was pretty bleak apart from the Walls/Barthel partnership.

Incidentally Arthur told me he'd had enough and was leaving before the crunch actually came.

Here was a very unreal situation. A client, a Managing Director and personal friend of Charlie's turns down a very expensive ad with five more people in the room. The decision is queried but the job goes ahead then three people are sent with the advertisement to the client who turns it down and sacks us. Once more I was told I was a lousy salesman. Perhaps the saddest point was that Charlie was Godfather to the client's son and a 20-year friendship was ended. Now that's an illness.

The Provincial Building Society's head office, were on the first three floors, we occupied the fourth. Charlie was on good terms with the society manager, liquid lunches were many. The Society's balance sheet went direct to the printer. At one such lunch Charlie—quite a good salesman—persuaded him to place this work with the agency. The printer was not best pleased.

Charlie insisted he would do this job from start to finish. The front cover was good and Charlie beamed… then…

> General Manager: "Something wrong here Charlie."
> Charlie: "Always willing to learn…".

I'll cut it short Charlie had specified a type called Garamond. You never 'spec' Garamond for tabulated matter (Pounds, shillings and pence). The reason, Garamond figures are based on an old alphabet with risers and descenders. Example: 1 is normal size. 2 has an ascender, 3 a descender and so on to 0 which like 1 is standard size.

Charlie blundered on and used a few technical terms like Quoins and Formes and said he would sort it.

In the lift:

> Charlie: "Here you are chum," putting the work on my chest.
> I explained, he insisted on doing this from start to finish.

He suggested several alternatives which told me he had little knowledge of how type was constructed. I suggested it was re-set in the ever reliable 'Times Roman'. It would cost us a couple of hundred quid but would save the day.

Charlie was out on a liquid lunch. My phone rings. It's the General Manager. I go down. This job has been printed with Garamond figures.

I said Charlie must have forgotten to alter it. The outcome: Well Ron you can keep our business as long as Mr Walls never enters our part of the building again.

Charlie's reaction: 'You wine and dine him, taken him and his Missus to dinner-dances and a four day stint in Brussels on our entry into the Common Market and he does this to you. Nice chap'. Poor Charlie, that's all you can say.

Around this time Charlie's best friend, the Managing Director of a Rain-coat Manufacturer was sacked after 30 years or more service. They always paid late and were now refusing to pay a bill of above £10,000, Charlie still went on writing 'ads' and eventually with two or three concessions I got the money.

Finally, Taylor and Parsons were a middle market department store, Charlie waited until a department manager went on holiday then sent in one of his 'specials' for a junior to approve. A board meeting was called to look at a short list of other agencies. I was to wait in an office for the outcome. We could keep the business as long as Charlie never stepped in any of their premises again. This sadly, was the last straw. I went back to the office and told Charlie.

> He said: 'Of course you agreed.'
> I said: 'I can't without your approval.'
> Charlie was in tears. He agreed.

And that's when I got my first car.

It was 1960. For the next 6 years he came in each day, read magazines, took reps out for liquid lunches and picked up the odd bits of business. One was from a man who wanted to sell fridges mail order. Don't ask. Then there was the London Fiasco, more later. This was when I took over the day-to-day running of the business. I was 35. In 1964 I became Managing Director. I felt sorry for Charlie. A thoroughly nice man who could never be wrong.

On a lighter note there were two 'T and P's' in Bradford, 'Taylor and Parsons' and 'Taylor and Pearson' (no relation).

> Taylor and Pearson sold 'pop'. On the back of their wagon was:
> 'Drink T and P table waters'.

The directors never saw the somewhat rude but very funny meaning that everybody in Bradford knew.

> A well-known toothpaste stated on their box:
> Remove cap and squeeze from the bottom.

Chapter 20:
An Actor's Life for Me

I joined the Calverley Players the day we moved in. In a career spanning almost fifty years I appeared in 116 plays or musicals and directed 30 or so more.

Help! He's an amdram. He's going to bore us senseless with 116 rave notices in the Bloggs Gazette and other pillars of truth. "Oh no I'm not" but as it played an important part in my life I think it's worth a few paragraphs.

Calverley Players saved my sanity. I helped building the sets, took over the publicity, Pat became treasurer and after two years, I got a medium-sized part in a medium sort of play. Pat said, "You're a different person." The answer was obvious. You rehearse three nights a week for six weeks then five nights then four performances. You can't be thinking about the firm.

On the Sunday after my debut a Bradford Playhouse scout rang me and offered me a part. The play was called '*The Immoralist'*. I've never heard of it since and rehearsals were to start the next evening. Five nights a week for a month, two dress rehearsals Sunday and a six-day run. I turned it down. I was to find out in later years that when the Playhouse ring you on Sunday to start rehearsals on Monday it's not that they want you, it's because they're desperate. Another factor was I had no car. In the next ten years I was to receive several offers from Bradford and a couple from Bingley Little Theatre but I was happy where I was.

Calverley Players were extremely well-organised and well-disciplined. There was a rule book. Nobody allowed front of house in costume or make-up; nobody allowed in the dressing room until after the show; no gifts or flowers to be handed up; no individual bows are a few of the things I remember.

Bradford Playhouse needs a book to itself. Billie Whitelaw, Dudley Foster, Tony Richardson, Edward Petherbridge, Rita Barlow, Duncan Preston, Gorden Kaye, Peter Firth and a good few more started their careers as humble amateurs at The Playhouse. On two occasions I was tempted to go professional but turned it down. Here's the scenario. I'd moved the business to a beautiful house in its own big gardens half a mile from our house. I walked to work in the fine weather. The business was booming. I got a good salary, a very good car and shared the profits with my partner. Would you swap that for a dodgy career as a middle-aged pro? No way.

Duncan Preston won the Youth Club Award at Bradford, before winning a scholarship to R.A.D.A. where he picked up the Olivier Award for his particular year. After several seasons at Stratford with the R.S.C. Duncan was a regular member of the Victoria Wood crew and latterly in 'Emmerdale'.

He once said to me, with open arms "Come and join us". I knew I was a good actor, but not that good. At 49 I might get a part of a murder victim or a shifty character with a couple of short scenes. Here in Bradford I got good parts, slept in my own bed every night and was "comfortably off". Kipping over a Chinese caff in Brixton while waiting for jobs did not really compare to my present situation. Duncan had to agree. He said, 'You've got a better track record than me'. Not quite true but it made the point.

In 1973 I appeared in my first musical at the Alhambra, Bradford, a wonderful experience in the very first amateur production of *Fiddler on the Roof*. Half a dozen more followed. I was a good actor, a reasonable singer and a lousy dancer. They hid me behind the scenery when they could. Only joking. Well, I was not very fleet with my feet.

Part of my success was accents – American, Geordie, Welsh, Irish, Scouser, Brummie, I did them all. Twice weekly visits to the 'Pavilion' from age 6 to 26, probably helped. When Bradford Playhouse went on the slide, now closed, I transferred to Ilkley Playhouse. A two-week run, usually to full houses and a very good standard. I also appeared regularly at Bingley Little Theatre and once at Keighley and many times in Ilkley Playhouse.

It only struck me when writing this I never had an acting lesson and only one nark in rehearsal. "Don't do that Ron, it's irritating." from the director. I'd been gardening and scratching my thumb where I'd caught it. That's it folks. Oh I forgot a cub reporter at the Pudsey News criticised my American accent and an American came into the dressing room and asked me how long I had lived in Brooklyn?

On the opening night of 'Close the Coalhouse Door', a Club comic came up to me in the bar and said 'Well done. But don't you ever go to Newcastle with that accent. They'll run you out of town'.

Man at Bar: 'Can I buy you a drink? I've come down from Newcastle to see this. You're the only true Geordie amongst the lot of 'em.' Ah well.

Not a word about the training film I appeared in for British Rail or the one for the British Sports Council. All over and done with.

The 1962 Advertising Conference was held in Pitlochry in Perthshire, three items stick in my memory:

1. It was Autumn and very, very cold. We were in The Blair Atholl Hotel which was on top of a hill. The bedrooms were icy cold. We put our overcoats and a rug on the bed.
2. Irishman, Charlie McConnell had several agencies in parts of the British Isles. Tall, grey-haired in a cream tuxedo, he was a real

146

charmer. Nellie Somerville of Somerville and Milne was a nicely rounded middle-aged lady with jewels.

Charlie: "Dance with me Nellie and O'Connell Street is yours."

3. Saturday night was free time. In the afternoon we strolled to the theatre to be told it was fully booked.

At the bottom of the street was a cinema showing a Bob Hope film. We settled for this as second best.

However, in the evening I made a final effort to get in the theatre. Two people from Carnoustie couldn't come. Hurray. But it was evening dress. We ran back to the hotel. Quick change. Everybody was piped in and announced. There were various titled people plus:

"Mr and Mrs Ron Pearson of Pudsey in the West Riding of Yorkshire."

There was a buzz in the auditorium and heads turned, the couple on either side of us were gracious and chatty. A lovely evening and experience.

The play was a Scottish comedy. I think the title was 'Man of the World'.

The leading character being: Sir Pertinax Mcsycophant, a truly memorable and again very lucky evening.

Chapter 21:
On the Move in Bradford and London

In the spring of 1957 the company moved into central Bradford, opposite the Town Hall, sorry City Hall. We were on the top floor of the Building Society who were also our clients. No windows for most of the offices but skylights. The offices were light and airy, a big improvement on the rabbit warren that was 35 Morley Street.

So, what's new pussycat? Commercial television, that's what's new. I think the first commercial was shown in 1955. If I'm wrong does it matter? I think it was for a toothpaste. I added tv space booking to my repertoire, nobody else wanted it. I didn't have a television. A client at Oakworth, far side of Keighley, invited me to his house with a few others to witness the event. The 'creepy' one would have entered in his diary "Went to Geoff's to see the first commercial. Had sardines on toast and lemon drizzle. A very nice evening."

Charlie did pick up quite a bit of television business. The T.V. channels would only accept work from established IPA agencies to minimise their losses. Commercials were of course black and white with 1½ seconds silence at the beginning and restricted sound levels. Everybody wanted to try it. Fifteen seconds, is that all you got for quite a few quid? Look at your watch for 15 seconds. It's longer than you think. You could buy 30 seconds or more but most local companies tried the 15 second slot. Of the national brands, Murray Mints—the too good to hurry mints—was a big success and Halifax produced Riley's toffee rolls were also a winner.

Charlie Walls, being a Londoner always had a yen for a London office. Charlie Gilbert was a long-time pal from London. I'd met him a few times and he seemed a thoroughly nice chap.

Charlie had been to Stavanger and picked up the Norway Prawns business. The 'Prawns' had come over and were guest at the Blighty Club armistice boozy do. They booked a stand at a London food exhibition. Our Charlie lumbered the other Charlie with designing the stand and manning it without payment. Charlie Gilbert had a bad leg, it could have been artificial. Our Charlie asked me to look in at the stand. The other Charlie was furious. It was the end of a very long friendship. When the boozy dos were over Norwegian prawns didn't last long with the agency.

We then had an arrangement with a chap called Ron Sharp. He was a little bit sharp but I liked him. He had a one-man business in one room on the fourth floor in Oxford Street. He came to Bradford several times and I met him in London a few times. One of his side-lines was collecting passengers from El Al Airlines and finding them a kip for the night. I'd occasionally stayed at the Hotel Russell where there is a very large ground floor lounge. When all the residents have gone to their rooms a hundred or more El Al customers settle down on mattresses for the night to be roused at 7am. A nice little earner for the other Ron.

An observant chap, he once said to me on Oxford Street, "How many brown cars do you see?" The answer is none. I wonder why? If you drive a brown car all I can tell you is they're still a rare sight in Pudsey.

I don't know what happened to Ron Sharp. He was no mug and gave talks on advertising. I attended one and it was both good and entertaining. Let's move on. 1961 was the turning point in the history of Charles Walls and Partners and also my life. It's quite a long story so I'll try to cut it sideways and spare you the gory details.

Charlie sent me down to the smoke for me to interview a London manager, another Tom. The first interview was in the agency where he worked which was strange. Was he already under notice? At his suggestion we next met at the Savoy, a bit posh that. I was having doubts. He was tall, good-looking, very affable etc. Charlie came down to the third meeting and he took us to the Talk of the Town cabaret. Charlie was convinced. I wasn't.

Many years later Charlie wrote a book in which I supplied the chapter headings. In it he says he was doubtful, I wasn't. I couldn't be bothered to change that and upset him.

We opened a small office near Baker Street with Tom, a very good secretary and a lad. Business started to come in, maybe I was wrong. Charlie and May met Tom and his young wife. I can't give her name as she may be still around. Everything was rosy.

One day in spring 1962 his secretary rang me. "Ron I'm very worried about Tom. He's very irrational. I'm frightened of him. His wife chucked him out of the house in Holland Park and there's a box of shirts and so on under his desk He's sleep in the offices." Guess who was down to sort this one out? I had the locks changed and put the clothes box in the hallway. It went.

Here's the story. Tom was a professional con man who'd done time for larceny, bigamy and you name it, he'd done it. He'd also worked the cattle boats to and from Canada to avoid the coppers. I got all this from the London solicitors I used to get this matter cleared up. There's more.

The young Mrs Tom asked me and our accountant Kenneth Wilkinson to a meeting in London. It turned out that she had the brass not Tom and she had 49% of the shares in CWP. If Charlie knew that I didn't know. Her words, "Every time Charlie comes down he gets Tom rolling drunk. For a while I chucked him out but left a mattress and some supper in the cellar which has an outside door. I don't know where he is now. There is no way I will let Charles Walls have my shares but you and Kenneth can have them for a peppercorn sum."

"I don't know where he is now." That's worth repeating. I did. Before he disappeared he was ill and asked me to meet him in a flat that was much nearer to the office. On the staircase I nodded to a woman coming down. It appeared she was the new love of his life. How do I know? She committed suicide and having met her I got this info from her solicitors.

Quite a saga isn't it? Nearly over. Come Monday, Charlie gets the letter from Mrs Tom setting out what she told us. Charlie calls us in, "You've sold me down the river you two have." I pointed out my options. "Mrs Tom wants rid of the shares and anything to do with the agency. If we persuade her to change her mind she gets 49% of the profits for evermore. I haven't put 13 years into this business to see that happen." Mild, quiet, Kenneth said, "I agree with Ron." We struck a deal. All the shares came to us with a rider that if we turned in a loss Charlie could come back in and take over. From 1963 to 1984 we never made a loss. However our London connection was not yet over.

Oh, go on. Surely two bright lads like you and KW aren't going to fall for another city slicker are you? No we are not but read on. Charlie still came in every day and read papers, made phone calls and went out to lunch with reps who sometimes passed bits of business to him. He also asked a bloke with a double-barrelled name and a very big dog to come up for an interview. The dog was wonderful. Charlie booked a few seats at the Alhambra. It was a show of bare-breasted African dancers in grass skirts. He didn't book for the dog. Well, it wasn't his sort of show. On the Alhambra steps Charlie gave KW, John B and me the thumbs up. We gave a thumbs down. I can only presume Charlie went to the Great Northern for a night cap or five. In the morning it was a done deal.

This bloke was always on the brink of doing a deal with Wembley Stadium, Flowers brewery, the Palladium, Rambler cars. After about a year he brought in one order, a £16 two-inch single column ad in Titbits. It was a bad debt.

Let's get a closure on this.

The drunk with a double-barrelled name living in a posh part of London couldn't possibly be a wrong 'un could he? He was a drunk, he got his correspondence mixed up. An engineering firm in Birmingham got another 'jam tomorrow' missive meant for us whilst we got this Birmingham letter. Here's an extract. "I'm still getting a decent wage from the mugs in Bradford…"

I left it for Charlie then went in to see him and explained what had happened. I said I'd sort it. I returned the letter with the key sentence underlined, told him I'd taken a copy and that the sixteen quid order was a no-no and he wouldn't be hearing from us again.

Then there was Steve, another of Charlies' 'finds'. I was to meet him in a pub in London. He'd brought a couple of mates along. I went to order drinks at the bar. "Not on my manor squire." were his remarks. I took an instant dislike to him.

Another oik took me on a long ride on the Tube to meet a man sprawled out in a coffee bar who yawned a lot but had loads of contacts. London was full of them and that, dear readers, was that. I had to tell Charlie that if we opened in London again I would be doing it with Kenneth's approval. So very sad but it had to be done. Jumping backwards a bit.

In 1960, I told you, I got a car I'm on wheels. Prior to this I was going by bus to see clients in Leeds, Halifax, Keighley, Barnsley, Batley, Wakefield etc. It was an Austin A35, my pride and joy. I had lessons in Leeds.

Just before I took my first driving test a client suggested a drive out to Morecombe one sunny, summers day. I'd driven about 3 miles when my companion, thinking I was taking a difficult bend at too wide an angle grabbed the steering wheel and the car crashed into a very sturdy bollard. I'd no sensation of moving forwards then back but my shirt had blood on it. I'd gone forwards, smacked my head into the driving mirror which had shattered.

Fortunately we were within a few hundred yards from a hospital and they patched me up. Several weeks later my forehead began to ache. The gash hadn't fully healed and I was able to prize a fairly large fragment of glass out or my forehead. How lucky can you get?

I took the first test. Towards the end of the test I was told to pull in and the examiner said, "I will bang my pad on the dashboard and you will do an emergency stop." We drove on. We were at a crossroads when a rag and bone man's pony broke its shafts and careered towards us. I did a left-hand turn and pulled to the curb, a bit shaken. I failed the test. I should have done an emergency stop in the middle of the crossroads.

I took a second test. Before we set off the lady driver in front of me reversed into me, twice. It was snowing. I did a three-point turn and hit the rear curb which was covered in snow, another failure.

I transferred to Bradford. What a difference. I almost got into a jam when the examiner shouted "Employ standard driving procedure." I passed. My next car was a Vauxhall Victor, not a popular car but Charlie 'knew a man'. They were generally known as a rust bucket, one of the reasons being the lower edges on the main body curved inwards. It took me a whole afternoon on my back with a blunt instrument to clean it out.

I can't leave the old VV without a story. I was in the habit of travelling to London there and back in a day by plane. On the a.m. trip I sat next to a client I knew vaguely, a very smart impeccably dressed quiet sort of man. He treated me to a G&T with ice and a slice. On the return journey he'd had two, three or six G&Ts and managed a couple more on the return journey.

He had to be assisted off the plane. I decided he was too far gone and would drive him home in the Vauxhall. He must have been able to mumble the address for I had no idea where he lived. Halfway there on the main road he shouted, "Where's my Merc? I'm getting out." This was the day well before seat belts. I think the Victor had an odd gear change by the steering wheel and a bench front seat. The door was open. I managed to get him back, close the door, change gear and drive at the same time. At his house he fell out of the car. It was raining. I managed to get this drunk, wet mess up to the door. A stony-faced woman said "Are you the police?" I explained. I got him upstairs, undressed him and got him into bed. She thanked me and took me into the kitchen for a coffee. She was a different woman. She cried and said "It's our daughter's 21st birthday and he promised he would stay sober". He was an alcoholic. He rang up next morning bright as a button to apologise. How very, very sad.

A few years later I saw him in town and he said "I can go for months without a drink then the first one after that is never ever the last." A few weeks later he rang me, "I want to spend £14,000 on a campaign. Can you pop in 10am tomorrow?"

I popped in, we shook hands, talked about the weather. "Could you excuse me Ron I've a rather important call to make." This happened three times. His office manager said "Forget it Ron. He's got a bottle of gin in his desk drawer and is swigging it neat." I never spoke or heard about him again.

My next car, I was now Managing Director, was a brand new Sunbeam Rapier in light blue metallic with white roof. Now that was a car.

Chapter 22:
1955-1965: A Review

Reading what I have written it gives the impression that I was the all-time wonderman that fixed everything in a very workmanlike manner. Not a bit of it. OK I was a director but I didn't feel like a director. I was a good production man doing his best to sort other things out. My London trips to sort out and eventually close down the offices sounds as though I breezed in and breezed out, job done. It wasn't like that. I was not happy with my efforts and lost a lot of sleep both before and after these events. Something I haven't mentioned is Charlie bought an agency in Halifax. An agency? One man, one girl and a poor artist. Halfway through the negotiations the man, a very affable man of Irish descent, died and his son in London took over.

The turnover was around £30,000 per annum. On average an agency hopes to make 2½-5% net profit. That's not much for wages, rent and supplies so how did a three-person business make out? By charging 33 1/3% on printing blocks, artwork and the rest. As I said, the owner was a very charming man and I can only presume his clients never bothered to check on prices but when this man died, there was another good agency in Halifax and a lot of the business went there. I was trying to rescue a poor set-up with two or three bus trips a week to sort out the business and visit the few remaining clients. The girl was very good and came to work in Bradford for a few months before getting another job in Halifax. The artist was not very good. Apparently the owner sacked him on average at least once a month and then took him back a few days later. He was a 'process white specialist', daubing the artwork to cover mistakes. According to the girl this sacking saved him giving the poor bloke a rise.

So getting back to the plot. Why didn't I feel like a director? I spent a lot of time on muddled thinking on this. Directors were well-dressed, knew how to order drinks, read a posh menu, at ease with a balance sheet, very good on the dance floor… wait a minute just there… I once ordered a made-to-measure dress suit plus a shirt, tie and black shoes and socks and cried off at the last moment with some silly excuse. Any dance I attended would need an ambulance in the car park. Years later, at a client's do, the Chairman's lovely daughter asked me to dance. She must have been told to do so. I came prepared. I bought an elastic knee bandage and slipped a folded hanky inside it and pulled up my trouser leg to show this. I then had to limp for the rest of the night. Next morning, I dispensed with the hanky but needed the bandage. I'd sprained my leg with the limping act.

I ramble a bit I know that. So will you when you write your autobiography at my age. I also miss a few things and then can't be bothered to include them. They can't be important.

Charlie seemed quite content to come in every day until he reached sixty. I made sure the *Yorkshire Post* and *Daily Mail* were on his desk with regular fresh tea on a tray. Every Tuesday his long-time friend and rep Harry Lomas came in and they had a long lunch. A pleasant man I'd known Harry since I was a lad when he worked for the *Yorkshire Evening News*. It folded. He then worked for *Fashions and Fabrics*. Next was *Drapery and Fashion Weekly* known in the biz as *Rapery and Passion Weekly*. Then the American magazine *Esquire* launched a British edition. Finally he saw his days out with *Leeds Graphic* a magazine full of pics of retirement dos, weddings and such like.

Why didn't I feel like a director? How did a director feel? There's a question that takes a lot of answering.

I was never much of a drinker. One client who agreed with me said "You can't drink and think Ron." I never forgot that. I was not easy with a posh menu. I could just about read a balance sheet with our accountant Ken Glover at my side, still can't. I didn't do small talk. Do I need any of these? No, no, no. I was an advertising man who knew his job. Then it dawned on me, two words; 'product' and 'client'. I laid awake one night repeating those two words until they dulled my brain but that was it, 'product' and 'client'. As the magazine articles used to say "now read on". If you're bored to tears it's your fault, you shouldn't have picked up the book in the first place. Product: It was OK. Is OK good enough?

Because the client likes it and we get on well.

These questions buzzed through my brain. The answer was always the same.

"No, No, No" in big letters. OK isn't good enough.

Then it dawned on me:

'Does it look good? Does it sell goods?'

John Bell was a wonderful artist but a one-man band. Artists and visualisers came and went. John was difficult to work with. That needed adjusting.

Production: getting a job ready to go into the studio. I needed help.
Creative work.
Charlie did it no more.
Arthur had gone.
I did the lot and often not as good as it should be.
Copywriting.
Charlie did it no more.
I did it. You know the answer.

So, I advertised for a production manager, a visualiser and a copywriter.

Production:

Donald Maud was a superb production man and above average artist; problem solved. Donald joined us in 1962 and retired the same day I did in 1984. Nothing to do with work but Donald was a talented trombonist with the Yorkshire Symphony Orchestra and a jazz group. Imagine all that talent in a very shy man. He made trombone noises when working, very amusing. The charging out of technical work was often charged exactly as invoiced in. I asked him to simplify this into readable language and the invoice queries virtually disappeared.

Visualiser:

I needed one. I took on two. Allan Hainsworth and Colin Harrison had worked together in another agency for ten years. Their thinking was fresh and different. Allan was with us about five years but Colin stayed a long time but that's another story.

Copywriter:

Not really a success there. We had two or three who all stayed a year or two with me still doing the majority.

Finally I coined a phrase, a very simple phrase:

"What is this advertisement for?"

So simple but so many ads were produced to satisfy the visualiser, the artist, the copywriter, the client but what were they there for? To sell goods in the majority of cases. Look at tv ads. Thousands are spent on them but ask yourself as you lie in bed, "How many do you remember?" If the answer is not a lot the ad has failed.

> Murray mints the too good to hurry mints.
> Riley's toffee rolls, was it? Soft and creamy. Delightfully dreamy.

People of that era didn't forget them. Simple so let's try and knock the client problem on the head. Clients come in all shapes and sizes. Bosses, managers, sales directors and the bloke who just sort of does it because nobody else does.

Live your own life. If the client's a liquid luncher, see him early morning with an excuse… another appointment at 11.30. Keep looking at your watch. If he gets off the point bring him back to it. Solicitors do this all the time and then send you a bill for it. These things work believe me but you knew that all the time didn't you?

John Bell had to go. Charlie was very good about this, "I set him on I'll tell him." I chickened out but added a rider, "I want to use him as a freelance." In the next couple of years he earned more as a freelance than he did at the agency. As he reached 63 it eased off and finally faded out but I still hadn't got a full team.

Chris Lear joined us and eventually took over as studio manager. Around 1966 John Oldfield joined us as a jack of all trades but he needs a whole storyline to himself.

Chapter 23:
Happenings on the Home Front

Pat's parents finally moved out. We've done that. My Mum died, not a very happy life. If there is a heaven which I very much doubt, spacemen have knocked that on the head, I would prefer to meet my Mum than my Dad. Let's face it, if I'm to meet my elders and they meet theirs right back to the Stone Age and that's before Adam and Eve would you believe it? We'd have an awful lot of hand shaking to do.

Dad and Eileen moved house to another Council house that was nowhere near as good as the one they left. My Father was 68 but determined to carry on working as a relief manager and I have to admit this house was more convenient for a couple of the cinemas. He never told me he'd officially retired. I found out by accident. I called to see him one Saturday after the Test Match. A new bloke there said he'd been 'retired' a year.

I called to see their new abode. The front door didn't open and there was no stairs carpet. We had some spare. I lugged two heavy rolls by bus and shank's pony. Move on "Don't you ever bring me anything like that again" (as if I was likely to). What a job that was. Bare stairs were obviously a better answer. Asked about a couple of Bridlington pictures in oak frames and a number of other of Mum's things. "We put them by the dustbin" was the reply. Ah well. I did manage to get a blue glass tumbler with a rather unusual rim. Cut to 1898 Granny Pearson and young son Harold were on an open top London tram for Queen Victoria's sixty glorious years. It was very windy. One of the illumination shades fell into Granny's lap. "Take it. It's of no interest to us", said Dad and that folks is all I got from the family bits and pieces.

Oh, I almost forgot…

When Mum and Dad got married a man where she worked made a small hexagonal table with black cotton bobbins on steel rods for legs. Made in 1920 it is now and antique I suppose. Not worth much but I look at it every day and it gives me pleasure.

Louise started school at Calverley St Wilfrid's primary school. If you're interested in cricket you might have heard of Jim Laker. He took 19 wickets in a Test Match. I think the captain shook his hand. None of the nonsense that goes on today. Well, Jim as a mixed infant went to that school.

The apple of my eye was not happy at school and often came home crying. Luckily the newly qualified teacher lived next door with her parents and discovered Lo couldn't read the blackboard, her writing was minute and it was affecting her whole way of life. She's worn glasses ever since and her writing has been larger than most peoples.

Let's talk about home life for a bit. I've mentioned earlier that Pat's Mum and Dad finally moved out in July 1957. We had the house to ourselves. Everybody liked Pat and she soon got herself involved in local issues. She became assistant then took over as treasurer and box office manager of "The Players" and this was a busy job. There were three, occasionally four plays a year running for four nights. The theatre held 199. 200 and the performing rights went up. As an aside the Bradford Playhouse held 299 for the same reason. The first night was on Saturday and was usually full plus a set of single seats down each side. The reason for a Saturday start was quite clever, (a) it was and still is the main going out night and (b) the church and the chapel were often full on Sundays and people talked about the play after the service. This practice was dropped by the new wave and sadly the seating capacity also dropped and became 150 then 100 then three nights then the scenery was burnt and a stab at theatre in the round then nothing. It was a similar story at Bradford Playhouse. On one occasion I was in a sparsely filled house when halfway through act 2 the chairman came in with a pint pot of beer, sat in one chair, put his legs over the chair in front, finished his beer and went out.

I was treasurer of the village cricket club and Pat helped in the tearoom. Our small garden at the front of Carr Road was pretty and Pat was often in this garden weeding, planting out and many passers-by stopped and introduced themselves.

The NSPCC was reformed with 12 lady members, Pat included. At first they held an annual jumble sale in Shipley open market. However the 'Pro' buyers were out waiting for the stalls to open and all the best stuff had gone within ten minutes of opening. From then on the jumbles were held in Calverley's Mechanics Institute. However the main source of income and donations came from members having lunch time or evening do's. 12 members, 12 husbands then children growing up then boyfriends and girl-friends. Our 'do' was usually Christmas Day morning. It was never advertised. People just turned up, usually well over 50, once we'd planned and had built Cliff Cottage.

Here's a fishy tale.

I was in North Shields for a meeting at 'Geordie' home brew and I usually saw Mr and Mrs Brewin, (great names for a home brew business) but on this occasion the boss Mrs P wanted to see me. Now it was known that the very likeable boss was partial to the odd nip or so of mothers ruin, she wasn't quite ready so I went for a stroll. I was watching some men in a small hut by the waterfront, one expertly cutting and cleaning, the other expertly packing fish into wooden boxes. "Fancy some?", asked one. "At a good price", said the other with a nod and a wink. "What is it?", I enquired.

"Halibut", came the reply. "Twenty quid a box. Cost you forty in a shop." Halibut was our favourite. Not thinking—a favourite pastime of mine—I said a boxful. We had the meeting, got home very proud of my bargain.

Pat: 'There's loads of pieces, what on earth can we do with it all? I think all 12 members of the Calverley NSPCC. Committee had halibut that night plus half a dozen friends and neighbours.' It was so wonderfully fresh 'Why did I marry you'? Was a familiar question on Pat's lips. I never did give a satisfactory answer to this very simple question.

It was Christmas, Benjamin Britten v Morecombe and Wise, no contest. Pat, Louise and I were Eric and Ernie fans. I can't remember Dad ever liking a comedian apart from himself. Eileen knew a man in the chorus of Mr Britten's platform performance of Noye's Flude. We watched Noyes Flude. He was spotted. "Could we watch MandW then?"

"Well, yes". It was then a continuous switch over to see if we could catch another second or two of Eileen's friend. I think the viewing figures for Morecambe and Wise was 28,000,000 plus a 100,000 or so. I'm guessing but I've put down 6 for Noye's Flude, that is presuming Benny Britt watched it. That's life kiddo. I've never understood Benjamin Britten or Pablo Picasso but they must be good at what they do to be so famous. Pat and I were disappointed. Poor daughter, aged about 10, went to bed almost in tears.

When she moved to Bradford Girls Grammar School and I worked in Bradford I became an official chauffeur to Lo and Jo and Dorothy and Elizabeth. I made a rod for my own back. I once told them a story about a bulldog called Wesley Gribblesdale and another one about the World's Custard Eating Championships. Each night in bed, I had to rack my brains to find another story for the following day. I found serials were the best bet, timing the final minutes with a cliff hanger incident. 'To be continued'. Such happy days in a lovely warm village atmosphere.

On one occasion somebody sped out of a filling station and gave my car a glancing blow. They caught him. He was 11 years of age and 'known to the Police'.

I've mentioned earlier about my move to Bradford Playhouse, one of the best amateur theatres in the country. I acted there for over twenty years but as the original hard-working member grew older and retired, I moved to Ilkley Playhouse with many happy memories appearing, directing and giving a helping hand at set building until the problem with my right leg forced me into retirement in 2015. My final role was an 89 year old Russian Jew, an ex-acrobat now a used furniture dealer in Arthur Miller's *The Price*. Miller said he often walked outside the theatre in New York just to hear the laughter. He couldn't believe it was so funny and it was.

Each night we got a big laugh and a round of applause on one line and didn't know why. We asked the director who came every night and he didn't know. The other actor figured it out and with permission from the director we kept it in.

I'm paying out money for the furniture sold. 'I'm giving you one hundred, two hundred, three hundred, four hundred, five hundred, six hundred, seven hundred'.

> His brother comes in for a short scene and exits.
> 'I'm giving you eight hundred'.
> Big laugh and round of applause.

My fellow actor worked out I never actually gave him the seventh hundred and therefore was in typical character twisting the buyer, out of a hundred. How sharp the audience was each night to pick up. A tip to budding Artistes. Never under-estimate audiences. They're smarter than you think.

Before the play I'd gone with the director to see *The Price* at the Alhambra with Warren Mitchell playing the furniture dealer. I wish I'd gone after our production just to see if Warren M picked up on this quite simple crowd pleaser.

Chapter 24:
New York, New York...
Chicago, Chicago

I made a trip to America. Charlie had wanted to take the ex-con Tom so I took his place. The air hostess started her routine, Charlie lit up, she spoke to him, "I'm sorry but I'm a chain smoker and haven't smoked since the signs lit up. Put me on the tarmac until you're ready to go."

"We can't do that sir." The end result was that Charlie was moved to a seat by a window and asked to turn to the window until take-off. Charlie often said I've a lot of sympathy for drug addicts 'cos I am one'.

My dream holiday. I'd been watching American films on a twice weekly basis since I was six. Most of them were of course made in Hollywood on the other side of USA. Quite a lot had Hollywood interiors and New York exteriors, Central Park, the Empire State Building, the docks and of course the speakeasies were regularly featured. All in all it was a wonderful week with just a hiccup or two. We did the Empire State Building and went to a small bar, 'The Drum' which was nearby. Almost empty apart from a man at the far end of the bar, hearing our British voices shouted "Hey fellas, whatever became of Jessie Matthews? Great kid she was." To younger readers Jessie Matthews was I suppose Britain's equivalent of Ginger Rogers. If you've never heard of Miss Rogers I'm sorry for you. She partnered Fred Astaire in a lot of big box office mainly black and white musical movies. Fred was a superb dancer. Famous quote from Miss Rogers, "I did everything Fred did but backwards in stiletto heels."

So back to the drunk at The Drum. I was able to tell him Jessie Matthews was still a big name in the UK and as she'd got older and filled out a bit, she now featured regularly on radio. I explained I'd used her once in a radio commercial. She said, "Darling I'm not interested in the money as long as I'm met at the station by a chauffeur driven Rolls Royce or Bentley."

The barman called Chuck whispered, "The drunk Louie (he just had to be Louie) slept in the bar when it finally closed for the night/morning." and that's why I'm writing this. It's a tiny bit of American life and a very good memory for me.

Later on we went to a bar where Cozy Cole and Gene Krupa took it in turns on the drum kit. I was entranced. This is what America was all about.

I could have stayed the night but Charlie wanted to move on. If you've heard of neither you should have and so the week went on.

Tuesday evening we dined at The Plaza. A wonderful big band with the McGuire Sisters as the star act. If you've never… forget it.

Wednesday lunch at an ad do, I was sitting next to a very affable American and during the conversation he said "Ever heard of Wharfedale Loudspeakers?"

> Me: "They're clients of mine."
> He: "Wow, wow, they are the world's best. I've got them. There's a guy who give talks…"
> Me: "Gilbert Briggs."
> Him: "That's the fella. You heard of him?"
> Me: "Had dinner with him last week."

He was speechless. Let's fantasize: If I'd told him an ancient relative of mine was a late starter at the Last Supper, it would have come a poor second to dining with Gilbert Briggs.

I explained that Gilbert Briggs was a woolman who had taken up coil winding for Yorkshire company Ambassador Radio during the depression. He then became a world authority on loudspeakers and every two years did a world tour and lectured at London's Festival Hall and other international venues. He had of course written several very good books full of Yorkshire wit about loudspeakers. I got a G&T with ice and a slice on that.

Now here's yet another funny thing. In the evening I was at the back of the hall listening to a very boring (yes folks even Americans can be boring) so I slipped away for a look around and ended up in the kitchen. The two chefs were from Lincoln and had come over in the early 30s to avoid the depression here and walked into the depression over there.

This is interesting – it was the prohibition era in the USA and they got jobs with the harbour police.

Each boat had a signal system; red, amber, green. The red you stopped as they were the beer boats. These were the barrels you saw being smashed up on newsreels. Amber: cheap wine, sherry, you stopped and did an easy search. Green, whisky, rum, brandy etc they got through. My phone tells me the famous Kennedy family were into bootlegging so they probably used this signalling system. Fancy that.

> Thursday: All I can remember is this. The phone rings.
> Voice: "Hi Ron. How are you doing?"
> Ron: "Is that Mike?"
> Voice: "Well it ain't Tony Coitis."

It was Mike Metzgar from McGregor Golf Clubs in Chicago. I'd met him a few times in the UK and we'd done some work for him. He had a very dry humour. Once in a Leeds hotel my client Paul Ziff had ordered tea and biscuits for three please. Metzgar grabs the phone and says: "Now that the ladies have ordered I'll have a double Jack Daniels with lots of ice and put it on his bill."

Back to New York in 1964. I was to catch a plane to Chicago Friday morning and spend the day there. Several wows, the spotty kid from Bramley, Leeds, West Riding of Yorkshire was going to hop a plane for a day in the Windy City. What a day. I think I flew from La Guardia. I knew I flew to O'Hare. Everybody was so kind and helpful. "Gee, what a tricky accent." said the girl giving me my ticket. I arrived. "Will Don Pearson please go to the main reception area, please. Don Pearson now, please, Mr Pearson." OK so they got my name wrong and I'd no idea where the main reception area was but I'd been paged at O'Hare Airport in the U.S. of A. Mike Metzgar's wife was there to meet me, a charming woman who drove me to the McGregor offices overlooking Lake Michigan. I got a round of applause on entry. All the staff were there to greet me. My accent was again cute but it was a lovely warm accent, so they said.

Then it was lunch at The Cart on State Street. I've still got the book matches. There was Yorkshire pudding on the menu. I declined. A chef came out with a big soup ladle and said, "Who's the guy that said no to my Yorkshire pudding?" Lot of laughter then I explained that Yorkshire pudding was always served as a separate course in Yorkshire with beef gravy. Londoners often had it with onion gravy but there you go. Oh and the sides should be three inches deep and crisp. "Get your coat off and come with me" said the big chef. "Gimme a phone, I'll get the wife." All good natured and great fun.

We had a tour of State Street and walked by Lake Michigan. I don't think there was a word about business then Mike took me to his flat in the famous circular twin towers whose name escapes me. They're probably not there anymore. His wife had prepared a buffet starting with anchovies on toast. We went out onto the balcony 30-odd stories high. My anchovy flew off the toast and descended. Mike said, "We've got the fattest damn cats down there."

They got me a taxi to take me to the airport with a very dry humoured taxi driver who refused a tip. "All been taken care of pal." We shook hands and I was New York bound.

Before the flight I was standing in a room with a rotating turntable. On it a gleaming white car, I think a Ford Mustang. A black man and his very young son were looking at it. I went over, "Would you like your Dad to have one of these?"

"Oh gee yes, I sure would." We chatted for a few minutes and they moved on. A big white man approached. "You're not local?"

"No, I'm from England."

"Well, be warned. We don't talk to people like that." He tapped me on the shoulder and was gone. This was 1964… Terrible.

What was it Hoagy Carmichael sang? Don't tell me you haven't heard of him. Well Hoagy and a chap called Mitchell Parish wrote the one song Paul McCartney wished he had written, 'Stardust'. Now you must have heard of McCartney. If not you must be living in a cave.

So what did Hoagy write in Hong Kong Blues?
"For a ticket to the land of the free.
Though he says his home's in Frisco where they send the rice.
But it's really in Tennessee."
Land of the free?
Or.
Louis Armstrong singing:
"My only sin is the colour of my skin.
That's why I'm black and blue."

On the plane I was sitting next to an elderly German man and we chatted about useless wars and all sorts of things. The air hostess came around with two free miniatures. I chose a Manhattan and a Canadian Club and put them in my pocket. He said, "You're not drinking?" Me "I'm taking them home as souvenirs."

"Then you're having one of mine," he said. I've still got mine and a couple of hundred or so others in a glass display case. People bring me them from all over the world and I haven't opened a single one of them. Goody two lips, that's me.

I don't know what Charlie did on Friday apart from a bus trip around the city including The Bronx which he said was awful with drunks and druggies lying in the street begging.

Now Saturday. This takes some telling so settle down with a mug of Yorkshire Tea and a couple of ginger biccies which is what I'm doing as I write this.

The buses to the World's Fair set off at 9am prompt. I got up at 7:15am, to wash and shave etc. Charlie sat up in bed for a smoke, I went down to breakfast, Charlie is still smoking. I went for a 'fresh of breath' before the trip to Yonkers. Driver: "OK folks we go in five minutes." No Charlie. Leslie Pickersgill said he was in the first coach. We travelled. Charlie didn't.

The World's Fair was very interesting but hard on the feet. I saw some people outside going past the World's Fair. I went out and asked some kids. "New York Mets v St Louis Cardinals". I had to be there. There was a large banner in the hotel foyer welcoming the St Louis Cardinals. I didn't see any of them. I can't remember the result. It was a double-header, i.e. another game in the evening. I had to go and missed the bus. I travelled on the A train. Hey man, I travelled on the 'A' train now you must have heard of Duke Ellington, probably the world's greatest jazz composer and piano player who with Billy Strayhorn wrote his Signature tune "Take the 'A' train".

I saw Duke and his orchestra at the Wakefield Theatre Club. Before the show the band went around introducing themselves. My pal Gordon and I got alto saxophonist Russell Procope, such a charming and polite man. After a few minutes conversation I said:

"Will you be giving us Mood Indigo tonight?"
Russell: "Who knows? We do what the man says and when the man says it, we do's it."

They did do Mood Indigo.

I've been to many jazz concerts: Stan Kenton, Woody Herman, Stan Getz, Illinois Jaquet, Dizzie Gillespie, Louis Armstrong and a few more but when Duke Ellington finished his waltz time solo of 'A' Train and the band came in with the proper beat it's the one and only time I felt shivers down my spine.

Oh he does go on doesn't he? Listen, you've paid your money. If you've read so far you're not going to get your brass back. If you've borrowed this from the library it's cost you nowt so don't moan and at 97 and a bit you might go on a bit.

Back to reality. What had Charlie done Saturday; breakfast, smoke, lunch, smoke, tea, smoke just about sums it up. He was very down. I told him my story with Pickersgill thinking he was on the first bus. "Ask him if you don't believe me."

"Where are you going tonight then?"

"I enjoyed the show at the Plaza Hotel and there's an intimate revue in another room. I thought we might try that."

"Both of us?"

"Yes, who else?"

"Ron that would be wonderful." There were tears in his eyes, such a lovely man at times like these.

We sat at a table, ordered a light snack and enjoyed a wonderful satirical show. I bought an EP of the songs from the show including a song about the Plaza.

Several years later I appeared in the Bradford Playhouse production of the Neil Simon comedy *Plaza Suite* and we used the *Plaza Suite* song to open. "How in the world did you get hold of that?" was a question often asked. Nobody knew except me and I stayed schtum.

Another diversion when I went to the New York Mets baseball game I bought a programme. When I was cast in Neil Simon's Odd Couple I wrote to the baggage master listed in the programme – I think his name was Casey Stenghal – and I sent £10 and asked him for a large (big headed) baseball cap. Baseball caps weren't readily available over here. The cap arrived with a very nice letter wishing me all the best in the production.

So Sunday in New York. We flew back. Sunday in London. We flew to Leeds Bradford. Bed. That's it folks.

The following Sunday I went to tell my Dad and Sister. They were not impressed.

Chapter 25:
A Milestone and a Few
Bits and Pieces

On 30 June 1964, the company's year-end, I was officially appointed Managing Director of Charles Walls and Partners Limited. Pat and Louise were very proud of me. I asked Lo "Where should we go for lunch?"

"Harry Ramsden's" was the immediate reply. We were very happy. I can't remember the response from Dad and Sister. I think it was similar to the American trip. As there were no partners left we became Charles Walls Advertising Limited. When the business moved to Calverley, I had a big sign put in the garden by the main road. That brought in a few bits of business. Good advertising: it told you what we did. And so simple.

When Lo became a teenager, we went to London. Looking in Hamley's window there was a tap on my shoulder. It was Bill Ellison, a client from the Wirral in Cheshire. He was there with his wife and daughter. That night we went to see the musical *Charlie Girl* which starred Joe Brown of The Bruvvers fame. We settled down in the circle. A tap on the shoulder, Bill Ellison, wife and daughter were in the three seats behind us again a wonderful coincidence.

We bought a few things in Hamleys, including a pack of trick cards. Dad always insisted conjurors could force a card on to an unsuspecting victim. "Takes years of practice," said Dad.

Here's the trick. You fan out the cards so the victim can see the fronts then you fan the cards to show the backs and the other person picks one.

> Me: (the conjuror) Closed eyes, concentrating. "I think it's a red card so hearts or diamonds. Diamonds. I don't think it's a picture card or an ace so it's got to be from 2 to 10. I'm going to go for the seven of diamonds."

Dad's flabber was completely gasted. He'd seen all the different cards, front and back, had a free choice on where to pick and I'd picked the exact card, just like proper magicians do after years of practising. The answer is so simple. I'm doing Hamleys a favour here. Buy yourself a pack with a folder explaining the trick and like the song says, "You too can be the life of the party." Simple.

Business was booming. Provincial Building Society, the sixth largest in the country had been with us since 1950 but the advertising spend about £16,000 per annum was very low for a company of that size. Suddenly in 1965 they decided to spend £14,000 in one month to announce they had reached assets of £100 million. It was a great success. The following year the budget was £100,000 per annum. We produced a series of ads on getting married, getting a mortgage, retirement etc and this was again successful. So it was £100,000 from now on. I had a cunning plan.

Quite a few of the upper echelons of Head Office men were in favour of a tabulated ad i.e. showing what you put in and how it increased year by year however Leeds Permanent Building Society, just above Provincial in the league table had been doing this for years and we needed something different and effective. I have to take credit for the headline and basic concept. The studio did a brilliant job. Come the day I would present three ideas; 1 similar to last year, 2 tabulated ads and 3 the surprise packet.

On the big day Pat was not well with some sort of tummy trouble. I was a bit worried but not overly so. My spiel was:

1. This is what we are running now. It's OK but there is a limit to how we can find new ideas for saving, getting married etc.
2. This is tabulated matter, similar to Leeds Permanent.
3. This is what you need. My headline was "Worth Saving with Provincial". Nothing special about that unless we feature top comedian Harry Worth in a series of odd costumes and humorous copy. For instance, Harry Worth in seaman's gear, first line: "My Uncle Herbert had a pleasure boat in Brighton, or was it Grimsby?"

I showed three ads and said Worth's agent wanted £15,000 per annum up front but I would not be taking a commission on this nor would I add anything. I'd done my bit, got a nice thank you and left the various projects with them and left.

When I got home it was serious. Our friend and doctor Keith Manchester was with Pat. She'd crawled to the phone and dialled him. Keith, "There's no time for an ambulance. I've called BRI." Park where it says "No Parking", they'll be ready for you. No registering, straight into the theatre. It could be peritonitis.

I got back about 3pm from the hospital when the phone rang. Oh no, please, no. Was it the hospital? No, it was Peter Clough from the Building Society.

"We've been trying to get you." I explained and Peter was very understanding then said, "You sold us on the Worth Saving Idea and if Harry Worth wants more than £15,000, we'll think about it." Then the hospital rang. Our friend Keith was right. There were minutes to spare and it was peritonitis. A big operation, no visiting today. Ring tomorrow.

How do you cope with good news and bad news in the same hour? I just sat down and cried my eyes out. Then I thought Pat was hopefully through the worst. Without Pat dialling and Keith coming straight away there would have been no chance. How would I have coped with that? Not very well, I'm afraid. So Pat came through and although she was fragile she was going to be OK and she was.

It was around this time that Charlie retired 5 May 1966. There was a very pleasant lunch and speeches. Now I often get laughs unintentionally. Everybody called him Charlie including one or two ex-employees. I was the last to speak, off the cuff. "Mr Walls, you only call him Charlie when you've left." Unbounded laughter. I can't remember another word of my speech but it was a very pleasant occasion.

Charlie still came in every day.

When Charlie went on holiday, I handled what little work arrived on his desk. When I went on holiday he delighted in handing over a pile of 'stuff' a foot or more height. 'There you are chum all yours', was his usual comment.

'Have you taken out the urgent....'

'All yours chum', big smile.

It was almost as he wanted the firm to fail now he had taken a back seat. A very strange man, had he lived a little longer his pension, drawn up by 'a pal', would have gone and he would have been left with his O.A.P. but that's another story.

On one occasion he stopped me in the car park and said "Ron, do you think the company could manage £500 so the 'missus' and I could move up a deck when we go on our next cruise." I managed "leave it with me". I was almost in tears, a good and decent man who had given me a break when I most needed it and now almost begging for what was a small amount compared to the profits we were making and which he knew about as he always attended the A.G.M.

I went straight into Kenneth's office; the cheque was signed and K. W. gave it to him within five minutes of asking. He was very grateful.

The business was developing fast and one of the problems was space. Charlie had a big room all to himself. Staying late and measuring up I realised we could get a boardroom and a reception area out of this big office. Moreover this meant the current reception could become another office. I then put this to Charlie and had to ask if he would mind moving into one of the smaller offices. He was very good about this but to me it was odd that the man with his name above the door, so to speak, was in one of the smallest units.

We then had to move the studio into another building nearby. It was all happening, something had to give. And it did. But there was quite a lot of water to go under the bridge before that happened.

Chapter 26:
Holidays

I know we went to Filey a time or two when Lo was little and, I think, Whitby. Before we left Bradford early 1957 we went to Cumberland. I can only put this holiday at 1956 when Lo was 2¾. I can therefore only presume Pat's Mum and Dad took her by car and Pat and I went by train. Another presumption and we'll move on. Pat's back went as we were walking through Lancaster so I think there must be two stations there. Our destination was a converted railway coach at a tiny little seaside place called Seascale. Poor Pat spent most of her time laid down. We found a local doctor and he did what he could and the return journey was difficult for her. The weather was indifferent and Lo couldn't paddle because the sea was full of plastic off-cuts from a factory in Whitehaven. Nevin D Hirst had a plastics client in Whitehaven. It's a small world.

1956 is 60 odd years ago and now we are in a plastics age. From schools to confectionary, we are surrounded by plastics. It makes you wonder what the sea is like now in Seascale and in fact the whole world; Examples: lemon cake slices, cardboard box, plastic sleeve, plastic tray for each individual slice; Chocolate bar, tin foil and paper is replaced by plastic and very difficult to open, all for our good health and hygiene but paper rots down, plastic doesn't. That can't be good, can it? Add plastic chairs, tables and a couple of dozen etcetera and it can't be doing the fish a lot of good either. Makes you think a bit does that.

Could the vast open spaces that were coal mines become plastic mines? Out of sight, out of mind and good riddance to the unsightly plastic mountain we have now. Worth another medal that.

Early in the 1960s we made our first trip abroad to Guernsey in the Channel Islands. I'd been on a plane before on business trips to London and once to Brussels. Pat was never easy on planes but Lo just took it in her stride. We loved Guernsey and Pat and I must have had 20 or more holidays there. It became our second home. Some of the shopkeepers and stalls in the market knew us and we were always blessed with good weather with just the odd shower. Mind you when it rains in Guernsey boy does it rain. We had a couple of holidays in Jersey which is much busier than quaint old-fashioned Guernsey.

On one of our many holidays in Guernsey we were sitting on a bench—as you do—and got talking to a very pleasant German couple, about our age. One thing led to another and I told my story about the Padre at the end of my army training period. If you've forgotten this it ended up something like: most of the men we'll be fighting will be innocent men like me, called up to kill innocent Germans…

He cut me off there and said 'I was also in the army and had exactly the same thoughts many, many, times'.

Next, he said 'Could we have dinner together tomorrow?' Sadly we were going home and they weren't available that evening. A really genuine, lovely couple and our similar thoughts on the futility of war gave us a real bonding moment it was very memorable and happy afternoon.

One time in Jersey we took Lo's friend Jo and I can't remember having laughed so much on a holiday. I ordered a drophead Morris Minor. It broke down and we managed to chug back to the hotel. It was replaced. We couldn't get the top down. It was replaced. It rained on and off every day for two weeks and every time we got the roof down it rained. It stopped. Roof down. It rained. We started laughing. It was infectious. On the final Friday we had gorgeous weather and I'd taken the car back. Good news. They charged me half price. Bad news. They flew us to Newcastle then bussed us to Leeds Bradford Airport. That's life. We had many other happy holidays with Lo, the last one being to Interlaken.

An amazing coincidence… not another?

Now, remember I said a chap at Castletown in Douglas I.O.M was getting up a Nucleous for Captain Napper? Of course, you don't. Well, you have read it earlier.

40 or more years on we were on a trip to Norway on a Postal Boat from Bergen to North Cape. Let's set the scene: on our table two very affable people from the Midlands. He worked for the 'Wolverhampton Express and Star'. I knew the Advertisement Manager.

Now I heard the chap on the next table say he wanted the Morse Code. I wrote it out for him. He'd already got it, from our friend Jack.

Jack said he was in the Signals… Special Operations.

Me: Were you in Castletown IOM ticking off a list to form a Nucleous for Captain Napper' He was.
Jack: "How did you remember that 40 years or so on."
Me: "I just did. Furthermore did you know there was an Advertising Agency in London called Napper, Stinton and Wooley and I'm fairly sure Mr Napper was Captain Napper in Special Operations."

We kept in touch with Jack and he invited me to attend a Special Ops dinner in London, I bought a Signal tie and sadly Jack died so I didn't go. The fifth member of our table was a lady in late middle age from Australia. This is going to be hard work I thought. How wrong was I. She was wonderful, so many laughs and good stories. On the final night we all had dinner in Bergen and it was one of the most memorable meals, lots of laughter and a few tearful goodbyes. We kept in touch with Mavis for many years and she sent us a lovely tapestry she had done which hangs on the bedroom wall. Sadly, Mavis died a few years ago but I'm still in contact with relatives Gai and Lance.

Chapter 27:
Stan, Ollie, Harry Worth,
Eric & Ernie

I'd seen Harry Worth's agent, Billy Marsh, in London. He was a tough cookie.

He was the front man for London Management, the top theatrical company set up by Lew and Leslie Grade. I think Leslie must have died but his son Michael was in the business and was to do me a big favour twenty years on.

A diversion. The stories about Lew Grade are legion. Like many of those attributed to Sam Goldwyn of MGM they are fables. Both Lew and Sam loved them. Here's my favourite.

Lew Grade goes through the pass door at the side of the stage to see one of his acts. The last turn on is a juggler packing up his stuff.

> Lew: 'Nice little act'.
> Juggler: 'Thank you, Mr Grade'.
> Lew: 'What are you on?'
> Juggler: '£14 a week, Mr Grade'.
> Lew: 'I could get you twenty. Who are you with?'
> Juggler: 'You, Mr Grade'.

Here's another attributed to Leslie Grade. You may guess the answer, but it's a good smile. Here's the gist.

The manager of the Walthamstow Palace rings Leslie late one Thursday.

> Manager: "The incoming show on Monday's folded. Can you help?"
> Leslie: "Here's some numbers to ring. Keep me informed. All the best."

Leslie's phone rings at 2.15am Leslie wakes up.

> Manager: "How do you think 'Good Night Vienna' will go down in Walthamstow?"

172

Leslie: 'About as good as "Good Night Walthamstow'll" go down in Vienna. Goodnight.'

Back to the Billy Marsh/Harry Worth Scenario. At our first meeting Marsh was very cagey. The media schedule was for provincial press, no nationals. Billy said the London Evening News wasn't provincial and to a degree he was right but it wasn't a national either. After a bit of to and fro I said 'OK, it's a national'. Get on the train and to go Liverpool, Birmingham, Manchester, Leeds, Newcastle and try to buy it. Billy loved a good argument and from now on it was Billy and Ron with not a bit of trouble. I know its corny but that's me folks, he became mellow in fact. "Marshmallow", Billy in his words had been a hoofer, a dancer to you and me and was full of show biz stories. Let's settle for one, the Harry Worth, Stan Laurel connection. I could write a hundred pages on the Laurel and Hardy team. I contributed a few items for a book on their British tours and got hold of a poster for their Bradford appearance.

Harry Worth was a middle of the bill ventriloquist on the Laurel and Hardy bill and was asked to introduce the comedians. Stan Laurel was the business end of the duo and Stan rang Billy one Tuesday.

> Stan: 'This vent on the bill, the one that introduces us is getting laughs. I'm giving him another thirty seconds'.
> Billy: 'How will you do that?'
> Stan: 'Trim a bit off our stuff'.
> Stan: 'Thursday I'm giving the vent a full minute and I'll tell you something he's not much of a vent. He's a very good comedian'.

So started Harry Worth's comedian career. One of his gags was to build up his intro to the world-famous L&H then fail to remember their names and look to see what he had written in the palm of his hand. If you think dealing in seconds is a bit fussy that's how a variety bill worked. Harry told me his first act was 4½ minutes twice nightly and the most boring job in the world. There was 15 minutes between houses and if you overran in the first house the manager would be knocking on your dressing room door. This happened to Dad's brother Charlie. He was a Sergeant in the North Nottinghamshire Regiment and his first date was at the Mansfield Empire. First house Monday was full including a lot of his old regiment. He couldn't go wrong. He over-ran, a knock on his dressing room door. The Manager, "Well done, Mr Pearson. Do that second house and you can pack your bags."

A couple more bits on L&H and we can move on. At the height of their fame in, I think, 1932 they toured Britain to promote their first full length feature film and appeared on the balcony of the Majestic Cinema in City Square, Leeds, (now Channel 4). they spoke and did some bits of typical Stan and Ollie comedy. Mum took Sister and self down. City Square was jam packed. I couldn't believe it was happening. Getting off the tram in Bramley, Mr Drake the greengrocer was clearing up outside his shop.

> Me: 'I've just seen Laurel and Hardy in City Square.'
> Mr Drake: 'Aye and my mother's Greta Garbo.'

A very tired little lad thought quite a lot about that before nodding off that night.

One more bit. I saw the famous duo at the Bradford Alhambra. Absolutely packed house. The film 'Stan and Ollie' gives the impression they were playing to The Wood Family, an old theatrical term for empty wooden seats. The Alhambra poster tells me it was the week commending Monday 28 July 1952 with an extra matinee on Saturday plus the quaint term "Free list entirely suspended" in other words nobody got in for nowt.

That's that out of the way.

Back track to 'Brum'.

Billy told me Harry was rehearsing for the panto at Birmingham and it was OK for me to meet him. Harry Worth, what a charming man and so conscientious. He was trying to remember the song "Lily the pink". "You see Mr Pearson in the first week or so there's no money but now I'm on salary so it'll have to be quick." I pointed out I'd travelled 100 miles for the meeting and not to go through with what I had come for would be letting him down. I looked at my watch. 'Give me 45 minutes and I'm Ron.' It worked like a charm and he was Harry. The copy on the ads made him chuckle and he loved the various costumes. He chuckled at lot. In 45 minutes we were through and I arranged another day, meeting in Birmingham to do some routine photography.

Harry was an ex-coal miner, performing and improving his act in India and getting near demob asked his Mother to put a small ad in The Stage "Harry Worth new style ventriloquist available Whit week onwards" plus his Mum's phone number. On getting home he got an offer to appear at a small venue in Bradford. I think it was the Mechanic's Institute, not easy to find at the bottom of Bradford surrounded by shops. Eric Martin who did the booking for this small venue had been in trouble a few times during the war for breaking the Lord's Day Observance Society rules on Sunday concerts. Ladies were expected to wear High-necked and to the floor evening dresses and men dress suits, no funny hats or odd make-up. Eric sailed close to the wind.

Band call in the major variety theatres was usually around 11 to 11.30am so Harry travelled by bus from Barnsley, found the venue, at 10.30am tried the doors, all locked. A cup of tea at 11am still closed. Finally at 2pm with a 2.30pm Whit Monday matinee the doors were opened by a typical Bradfordian. "I'm Harry Worth. I'm the ventriloquist on the bill. Could you point me to my dressing room please?"

"Aye, there's one for lasses and one for lads back there and if you're wanting lavs there's one for men and one for lasses but don't pull the string if there's owt quiet on." Harry: "Thank you. Now I've brought my band parts…"

"No band here lad, George on piano and Colin on drums."

It was a blazing hot day and Harry was to be second turn on following a couple of local girl dancers. There was a thunderstorm. Mums and Dads taking their kids to the parks thronged in.

"Can I have an ice cream Mam?"
"Mum I want a wee."
"Can I have summat to drink?"
and the endless replies. "No you can't. Sit down and listen to the funny man." Etc., etc., etc. A lot of noise.

Harry came off and said to the stage manager, the one who'd let him in. "I need to speak to Mr Martin at once."

"He's out front in the box office" Harry went. "Mr Martin, I must object in the strongest possible terms. Nobody heard a word of my performance." Eric Martin is counting the take, LSD in neat piles and without looking up said, "Aye lad and I hope it'll be the same every bloody night this week." That's show business Harry.

I then asked Billy Marsh if he could get Harry at the Alhambra in Bradford next Christmas. He did. The panto, "Merry King Cole". It was a great success; Harry would not allow the proper title Old King Cole. I don't think there was much of a storyline to the panto. I remember a teddy bears picnic, a ballet sequence and a number of variety acts unconnected to the Merry King Harry did a pie-making scene with "Merry Queen Cole", Peter Butterworth. Harry popped on every so often before his very amusing ventriloquist act just before the walk down. Surprisingly, he ended his act with a summersault. I believe this panto broke box office records at the Alhambra but times were a changing.

The next time Harry came up to Bradford for the more complicated photography and we were off. The ads were a great success however the general manager at The Provincial retired and the new man wanted more building society and less Harry Worth and even less still in the third year. In the autumn of year two I received a very odd call from Billy Marsh. "Harry'll do another year at half price." One can only presume Harry's career was on the slide. I said no it'll be ok but I would like to take 15 percent off his take for our commission. Deal done.

Variety was now a dead duck. Summer shows were not what they were and Harry had been in a couple of tv series without a live audience.

Back to the plot, I took the ads for Harry's approval between shows. He introduced me to Peter Butterworth who appeared in a number of Carry On films. Peter told me this. "They were casting a film about POWs tunnelling out of a camp. I read the script and one of the characters in the script was me under a different name. I auditioned but didn't get the part."

Harry Worth meets Harry Worth

Harry Worth was a well-known Pudsey politician when Pudsey had a Mayor. I think this Harry had been Deputy Mayor or even maybe the full job.

Now Harry Worth, the comedian was about 5'8", dark haired and wore dark rimmed glasses.

Harry Worth, the Pudsey man was about 5'8", dark haired, somewhat slimmer, dark rimmed glasses and bore a resemblance to the well-known comedy star. So, a photo shoot was arranged around 1968. Sadly, I don't have a picture of this.

In 1987 when my T.V. play 'Harry's Kingdom' was shown one of the many callers was the Pudsey Harry Worth. He'd enjoyed the play and once again thanked me for bringing the two Harry Worth's together.

The comedian's real name was Illingsworth. I think he was one of ten and worked as a miner before call-up. I seem to remember comedian, Jimmy Cricket, (surely not his real name), unveiled a plaque on the house where Harry spent his early years.

Harry had a very quirky sense of humour and once said:

'Ron, have you ever noticed that all jugglers are round shouldered?'
I said: 'Never having met a juggler, this thought had never occurred to me.'
Harry: 'Well you see they rehearse leaning over the bed so that when they drop a club it falls on the bed and it's easier to pick up.'

Harry kept asking me about parts he could play and I suggested Henry Ormonroyd, the tipsy photographer in JB Priestley's wonderful Victorian comedy 'When we are married'. I took him the script. I'd played Albert Parker, another good part but Ormonroyd is the plum. It's not a big part, about two pages in act 1, 4 in act 2 and 10 in act three. Harry read it. "I don't think Auntie would approve of me playing a drunk.", Auntie being the BBC. Later in his career he took the lead in Harvey the somewhat dated American comedy about an alcoholic whose best friend is an invisible six foot rabbit called Harvey.

Harry rang me, "Ron, Billy's booked me to do a one-man show at The Crucible in Sheffield." Me: "How wonderful. On your home ground so to speak." Harry said, "Ron I've got a fourteen minute act and a few bits and pieces I could string out to half an hour or so. What the hell am I to do?" Things weren't good. I never heard what happened at The Crucible.

During this very busy period I had a breakdown.

We'd had a very pleasant holiday in Edinburgh and saw the dress rehearsal for the Tattoo. Monday am at home I was putting on my socks and said "I'm not going to work anymore." and started to cry. I was having a breakdown. From being appointed a director in 1952 I'd worked my socks off for Charlies. When you're in your twenties, thirties and early forties you think you're indestructible. You're not or I wasn't.

I sat on the stairs, unable to go in the living room or kitchen with Pat and not wanting to give in and go into the bedroom. About 11 without speaking I took the dog for a long walk. When I returned our dear friend Dr Keith Manchester was in the drawing room with Pat. Here's the gist.

"Ron you think you've had a major breakdown. You haven't. I've seen much worse. Pat was truly frightened. She thought you'd gone out to commit suicide. I eased her mind by telling her you wouldn't have taken the dog if that was the case. I know from experience you never stop. You must. You're not irreplaceable. Nobody is. A month off then I'll see you again. You do nothing."

Keith was right. I was to take Valium and I think Aventyl and after a month gardening, dog walking and all sorts of things to take my mind off the business Keith told me to go in each morning for another month and never to bring work home. I started to delegate. Some mornings I drove in and had to get the bus home. I got the shakes.

From September to December this was my life. In January I was off the tablets and working full time with differences, I'd always done the interviews for staff. Kenneth took this on. I'd done the charging out. Donald Maud took over plus other bits and pieces. I was told never to bring work home. I didn't. It was damn hard. John Oldfield became my assistant and did a wonderful job doing a lot of the client visits and writing reports. I was back in the business I loved with one proviso – I was not indispensable.

Thanks to a very good friend and doctor Keith Manchester, a very understanding and helpful wife, not forgetting a very young John Oldfield who did a man's job handling a load of work meant for me with regular visits to my home.

Almost forgot.

After years of dithering I joined Bradford Playhouse. I'd been acting for getting on for 10 years but I still had to audition. I chose two longish pieces from plays I'd been in and then an American bit from a book full of pieces for auditionees. That went down well and in spring I got a card offering me a smallish but good part in a George Bernard Shaw saga. That's enough of that.

On 2 January 1971 two days after his contract with Provincial, Harry rang me "Happy New Year Ron etc. Tell me is there anything doing at your place where we did the photography?" I pointed out it was amateur theatre. "Yes, I know but I thought there might be something I could slip into." As what and what could we pay him? He was obviously desperate to save his career and earn a few quid, few being the operative word. What a difference, three or four years can make.

When I first met Billy he told me Harry was on £75,000 a year. Harry always said 75,000 sixpences after tax. Not quite true. So why didn't Harry control his career? I don't know what the outcome was but he rang me again asking me if I had any scripts for him. He'd been in another flop in London and things weren't looking good. He was appearing in a panto at Leeds Grand when he rang me. "Don't come to the show. It's terrible. See me between shows and bring some scripts with you." I brought '*See how they run*' a British farce and said he should play the Bishop. I also told him John Osborne writing in *Plays and Players* said the funniest line in British comedy was the Bishop's but it was a slightly different line in the play copy. I'd played the Bishop and did the John Osborne version of this line and it got a massive laugh and a big round of applause every night. I altered the line on my copy and showed Harry this.

Come on Ron. What was the funniest line in British comedy? You need to know it was a farce that included a couple of vicars, a curate and an army Sergeant. The dog collars are dashing about the stage, the Sergeant arrives, the bishop says, "Halt. Sergeant, arrest several of these vicars." Each night when I went down to the bar after the show I was asked what was the line that stopped the show.

Harry got a part in '*See how they run*'. The curate who, as I remember it, came on in the middle of act two and was usually played by a younger man. I also gave him '*The wind in the branches of the sassafras trees*'. What a title. It's a send up of how Rockefeller discovered oil, written by a Frenchman René de Obaldia.

We were to run it at the Playhouse with me playing Rockefeller. Just before the start of rehearsals the director, Denis Linford rang me. "Ron the 'Sassafras play' has been withdrawn from amateur production. I've got hold of an adaptation written for Frankie Howerd that lasted one night. It's not good. Can you come to my house this afternoon and we'll try and cobble something together." It wasn't the greatest comedy script but it played to very good houses with the house full signs out on the final Saturday.

Harry Worth did play in this but which version I know not. I saw a picture of him in it somewhere. Harry was the politest man I've ever met. One night on the Terry Wogan show he was asked "Well Harry, what's next?"

"Well your lot don't want me" was the curt reply. How sad. I believe Harry spent his last years of his life in a wheelchair. I wrote to his wife when he died and got a lovely response including "He never really new why so many people loved him."

A showbiz memory that may interest you.

Talent show were very popular on the variety circuit and one of these was 'Youth Takes a Bow' featuring aspiring comedians, dancers etc. These shows took up most the second half of the bill. On one visit, the first act on was a gormless, not very funny man who sang a not very funny song "I'm Not All There". Last act Top-of-the-Bill was a very slick dancer in dress suit and straw hat singing 'Putting' on the Ritz'. This was how Morecambe and Wise met. Eric, with an outsize lollipop, early on, and Ernie – a seasoned veteran from the age of eight, had appeared with his Dad in local venues as 'Carson and Kid', so I was there before Mr. Morecambe teamed up with Mr. Wise.

Eric Morecambe and Harry Worth were big friends, both living in Hertfordshire, Eric in Harpenden, which I knew well from my army days on a nearby posting. Harry's home was also in Hertfordshire, not too far away.

> Harry: 'We, with our wives, would visit each other and after a good meal move from living room to drawing room. When we were the visitors, Eric would show endless MandW clips laughing all the time. You got the feeling Eric was the most conceited man in show business.' But it wasn't so. He'd say, 'Look at this bit, he comes in stumbles and nearly knocks that vase over then a few minutes later another incident.' Harry said, 'He was two people, the chap on screen and the chap watching'. He was full of praise for Ernie Wise 'Look how he sets this up for me'. 'I come in.' More laughter.

Eric Morecambe, or to give him his original name Eric Bartholomew was Morecambe born and bred. Ernie Wise or Ernest Wiseman was born in Leeds.

When not rehearsing and boy, did they rehearse, every moment was rehearsed, they did not see much of each other, Ernie moved from Leeds to Peterborough. Always the best of friends, things occasionally went wrong, just watch Ernie's face when this happens, full of laughter and admiration for a true friend. They were, without question, Britain's best and most loved double act.

Did you notice the curtain that usually started the show: a zig-zag 'M' on Eric's side: a zig-zag 'W' for Mr Wise? Smart that.

Just after the war the first half closing act at The Empire was listed as 'They're Out' and featured three 'hopefuls.' First up was Max Bygraves at the piano with a few jokes. In a couple of years, he became a 'Bill Topper'. Sunny Rogers was next, a 'Peppy' singer and dancer who never really made the high spots but was very watchable. Third on, another aspiring comedian. This is the one and only time I cried in the theatre, with laughter. I had to turn away, tears rolling down my face. This man sang 'Three Little Fishes', a song with lots of silly words 'oops oops, diddy doddy, wallop, oops', comes to mind and the facial expressions and delivery of the words were what made me cry. In one month, this man was 'Top of the Bill'. His name, Frankie Howerd.

Chapter 28:
Celebs

Whilst I'm name dropping why not do it properly? Prince Charles, Princess Margaret, Marlene Dietrich, George Raft, Brian Glover aka Leon Arras, Sir Ralph Richardson, Jim Laker, Sir Bernard Miles, George Best, Jackie Charlton and one or two more including a non-celebrity London taxi driver with a very interesting story to tell.

A very young Prince Charles was to open the new Yorkshire Post building, now the old Yorkshire Post building for I believe they have recently moved again. I was invited to the opening. We were split up into threes and my two companions were the very affable Chief Rabbi of Leeds and a very horrible Jimmy Savile. I'd met Savile a few times previously. A client often asked him to attend meetings and he was usually accompanied by a plain clothes detective Sergeant. Always brash and smoking in a small room with no windows or daylight, he brought nothing of any use to the meetings and usually left after fifteen minutes or so. To use a well-known phrase of the time half of Leeds knew he was "as bent as a nine bob note". On one occasion I had to attend Leeds General Infirmary. I was barred from entry. Savile arrived in his Rolls Royce and was handed a white coat. A patient was wheeled out, the photographer snapped, white coat off, into the Roller, five minutes at most. That night's YEP carried the pic with the caption "Jimmy lends a hand at LGI".

On another occasion I, with several others were in a room at Radio Leeds waiting to go on air when Savile burst in through the door, "Hi friends, can't stop. Behave yourselves. Tarrah."

A lady said, "Jimmy never married did he?" and one of Yorkshire's MPs said, "I think you'll find his interests lie elsewhere."

Setting the scene for the YEP opening ceremony.

> Savile was wearing a Leeds University blazer. We were the first to be spoken to.
> Prince Charles: "Are you eligible to wear that jacket?"
> Savile: "Who's askin', sunshine?"

The Prince's stay with us was brief. When he had moved on Savile said, "I've just had two weeks on the Royal Yacht. They're all at it like rabbits and the Queen Mother's permanently pickled in gin." What a thoroughly disgusting man and a blatant liar too. I suggested to the Chief Rabbi that we should mingle. He readily agreed. After lunch I went up to the Prince and thanked him for being here and said I'd like to apologise for Mr Savile's brashness. We had name badges. Mine said Ron Pearson plus details. He looked at the badge and said, "Thank you Mr Pearson. It's part of our world. We get used to it." or as playwright Arthur Mills said, "It goes with the territory."

On another occasion this client rang. "I want you over here now." It was 4:30pm. I arrived to a room full of yes men, smoke and Savile plus minder. "We're launching a football boot it has to be different over to you." In this business you have to think quick. I said, "Wicketkeeper's gloves have always been brown leather until Kent and England Wicketkeeper Godfrey Evans...", client interrupting "We're here to talk football boots Ron."

"Then let me finish... John Arlott on the BBC... and this ball goes safely into the blood red palms of Godfrey Evans." Every stumper had to wear blood red gloves. "Give the man a toffee apple", was Savile's comment. "Must go" and he and his detective minder went.

A side fastening boot was developed and George Best, Manchester United's charismatic player was signed to wear them. Brilliant move. A minor snag. To the best of my knowledge Best never wore them. Best was a quiet, shy sort of chap until he and his henchmen got near a drink. On one occasion I was to meet him at Old Trafford. He didn't turn up. Bobby Charlton suggested I try the training facility at The Rock, the old Broughton Rangers Rugby League ground. He wasn't there either. Eventually he turned up, put the boots on for some pics and then we went to lunch. He ate very little, drank quite a lot and said his life was a mess.

Now we're in Paris with a lot of retailers plus Best and a few of his mates. One night we went to The Lido floor show, excellent but with a few very tall models wearing feathers and not much else. George was missing. One of his pals found him backstage with 'les girls'.

In later life George had a liver transplant but his abstinence didn't last long. A wonderful talent wasted and such a nice polite charming Irishman when he was dry.

Marlene Dietrich, who? Surely somebody reading this book must have heard of her? OK, here we go. German born, she was big in German movies, went to Hollywood, was big in American movies. In the late 30s, her career dipped a bit and then she played in a Western film "Destry Rides Again" singing in a flat guttural voice.

"See what the boys in the back room'll have?"
"And tell them that I'll have the same."

She was big again then eased off a bit. *Where's all this* getting – *you may well ask?* Just be patient, I'm setting the scene.

I'd been to the theatre in London and walking through the side streets to my hotel, there's a rush of people around me including Ms Dietrich leaving the stage door after her one woman show.

"Sign here Miss Dietrich."
"Sign my programme Miss Dietrich."
We are now by the main road with Miss Dietrich next to me.
Marlene: "Oh dear. I have nowhere to rest the paper."
Ron: "Use the car."
Marlene: "What a good idea."
Marlene signs a dozen or so autographs and her chauffeur driven Rolls draws up.
Marlene: "Now I must leave you and thank you for the use of your car."
Ron: "Oh it's not my car."
Big laugh from everybody including Miss D. She walks a few paces then points, and said, "You are a very naughty man." and blows me a kiss. I caught the imaginary kiss and clutched to my chest and said, "It will stay in my heart forever." Another quick wave and blown kiss then she was off.

It made my night. What play did I see that night. I've absolutely no idea but whatever I paid it was worth it for me to meet and have a laugh with Marlene and I didn't mean it for laugh, I was just stating the truth.

Not a celeb but an unusual happening in a theatre. Kenneth and I were in London tying up a few loose ends after the somewhat swift departure of Tom the Con. We went to see Maggie Smith in *Mary Mary*. We got there early, three or four rows back in the circle. Two men centre circle. One of the men stood up and moved to the far left, and the far right for no apparent reason. The play started. After about 20 minutes this man was now back at the far left. A lone actor, Timothy West's Dad, Lockwood West was alone on stage and went to the bookshelves and picked out a book.

Man: 'Come on Dearie, pacey pacey. Get a move on'.
A commissionaire was there quick time to escort this bloke out.
Man: 'Don't manhandle me. I know my way out. Come on Gerald, we're not wanted here'.
Commissionaire: 'That's the lady's lavatory Sir'.

Big laugh in the circle but of course those in the stalls knew nothing about this. Very strange and very amusing. Poor Gerald.

Before we move on here's another amusing incident at the Stephen Joseph Theatre in Scarborough. On the way there I developed a very bad nosebleed. So there I was in the gents toilet furiously stuffing toilet paper into each nostril when the last call came to take your seats. It was some years ago and we were in the front row and had to cross the acting area to get there. Pat stifled a laugh and said, "You look like Michael Palin in *a Fish called Wanda* with a chip up each nostril." The play started.

Our area of the stage was in darkness but a few feet from us was a girl lying on a camp bed. The action swung towards her and an actor Gawn Grainger walked to the bed. I was in full glare. The people on the opposite side started to laugh. It wasn't a long scene but I believe Mr Grainger caught sight of me and stifled a smile. Thankfully that was the only scene in that area until the interval and with Pat's assistance we went outside and made a few adjustments. Why do these things happen to me?

Not a celeb I met apart from putting my hand on his shoulder and saying "well done." A very young Michael Palin was a member of an amateur dramatic society in Sheffield, it had a very long title like: "The Dore and Totley Co-operative Amateur Dramatic Society of Sheffield". Each year the Bradford drama group held competitions at the Bradford Playhouse with prizes for the best junior group, the best general group and the best visiting group. The Sheffield group presented a farce called "The Tricolor Suite" and Michael Palin won the Best Actor Award. Now Margaret Clough, the stage manager for this festival, did not take prisoners. On the clearing up Sunday, she told me, "Y'know, that lad who's won from Sheffield, well, we'd run out of best actor shields so we gave him something else and told him not to look down and we would replace it later."

"What did he get then Margaret?"—"Darts"—I'd love to know whether he got the best actor shield or whether he still treasured the one for the oche game?

So who's next on the name dropping list? Brian Glover aka Leon Arras. Never heard of him? Well, all Yorkshire has. OK so all Barnsley has and there's a couple or three good stories so read on dear reader and I'll take it in easy stages for this multi-talented Yorkshireman.

I first met Brian at the Bradford Alhambra one Friday evening. A number of extracts from Shakespeare plays. One member of the cast was our hero. At halftime there were some barrels of beer at the rear of the stage and the audience were invited up for a drink. I went up, Brian was serving at one barrel. After a few opening remarks Brian said, "This closes tomorrow."

> Me: "What next?"
> Brian: "Leeds Town Hall Monday."
> Me: "You mean wrestling?"
> Brian: "I do. Got to keep the brass coming in."

I had a motive for going up.

> Me: "I do the advertising for Fisherman's Friend. Would you be interested in some tv work."

Brian: "Always interested."
Me, getting out business card: "Who's your agent?"
Brian: "Let's leave him out of it. I'll ring you Monday. And that dear reader is how I signed up Brian G for TV ads for Fisherman's Friend."

His fee was £150 in notes, for each commercial. Each time I handed over the cash in a plain envelope just like baddies do on the screen.

The commercials were videoed in London. Brian never stopped. He was on the first few episodes of *Porridge*, fronted a show of interesting general items for Yorkshire Television, the other names being Magnus Pike and Miriam Stoppard. Brian told me he bought two jokes in case of a breakdown. There was a breakdown. He told his jokes. More breakdowns, so he got the camera to pan the audience, and to stop at me. "Hi Ron. This is Ron Pearson who wrote and directed me in *The Fisherman's Friend* tv adverts." A round of applause. I must have been on tv for all of ten seconds. Every single person in the village saw it. People I'd nodded to for years stopped and said "Now then Ron, I saw you on the telly. Right good it was." Fame at last.

One of the FF commercials had Brian in a Fleetwood fisherman's jersey with a backdrop of high waves on a screen with Brian talking direct to the audience. We went into a separate room whilst they were setting up and Brian was a very quick line learner. On to the set.

Take 1: A lady presses a switch and a blue screen lights up with the words.
Brian: Fluffs it.
Take 2: Another fluff.
Take 3: Another fluff.
Brian: "The screen's putting me off. Ron's been through it with me a few times and we've got it as he wants it. I'd like the screen off."

A conference.

The outcome: Union rules state the machine must be on.
The answer: A middle aged lady was knitting a garment for her first grandchild so she would sit in front of the screen and on the words "Take 4" would take one hand off the knitting and put it behind her back and switch it on.
Take 4: Perfect

Brian became a good friend and told me a couple of good tales about wrestling. 'The Ghoul' a wrestler dressed from neck to feet in black with a white mask, was supposed to be a doctor who suffered terrible face injuries in Italy during the 39-45 war.

Brian, 'Not a bit of it. He was Harry Bates a boxer out of Manchester who never quite made it'. The Ghoul always won by a rabbit punch to the neck, the opponent in great agony. At first The Ghoul refused to help but being 'a doctor' always relented and gently eased the agony.

The next story involves The Royal Shakespeare Company in Stratford upon Avon where Brian was a regular actor. I've forgotten the play. I know it was Shakespeare and I'm not sure I've got the right forename but at the beginning of act one George the wrestler (Brian) is wrestling the King. Off stage he gets a message "Can you get to Leamington Spa? A bloke's cried off." So still in his George the wrestler outfit Brian gets in his VW drives like mad and does the four rounds as Leon Arras then gets back to Stratford in time for the evening performance.

Finally, he was appearing at the Whitehall Theatre in London in the Joe Orton play '*What the butler saw*' and I went to see it. Having a drink in a pub opposite he said "Yarmouth pier Sunday." I said "Wrestling?" Brian "Yes indeed. Money in the till Ron lad." I said, "I'm surprised a London management would allow…" He cut me off. 'Ron there's more chance of me being hurt over the road than there is on Yarmouth pier.'

This is how it all started:

> Brian was a P.T instructor at a school in Barnsley. The phone rings.
> His Father ran the wrestling in Barnsley.
> Brian's Dad: "We're in a bit of bother for tonight."
> Brian: "What?"
> Dad: "One of the wrestlers has cried off."
> Brian: "Who?"
> Dad: "Leon Arras a Belgian lad, can you step in?"
> Brian: "Who am I in with?"
> Dad: "Primo Carnera."
> Brian: "Bloody 'ell fire."
> Dad: "You'll be alright. You know the game."
> Brian: "Yeah. Does he know the game?"

This went on for a while and Brian finally agreed. For the uninitiated Primo Carnera was a 6'5¾" Italian known as the Ambling Alp. The story goes that Adolf Hitler had a European boxing champion in Max Schmelling so Benito Mussolini had to have a champ and sent his scouts out to find one. They discovered Primo Carnera, a tree feller, not a man who lived in a tree but a fellow who cut them down. A few weeks training, a few fixed fights and Primo was ready for the real thing and became European champion. Musso wanted more. Primo went to the States and after a few bouts became World Heavyweight Champion in June 1933 to June 1934. Brian wouldn't know this but at the time Carnera knocked out more opponents than any other heavyweight boxer and one suffered a brain haemorrhage.

185

He beat Ernie Schaaf for the title and I believe American born Max Baer took the title from him in a very one-sided contest. Many people believed all his previous fights were fixed. Why did he become a wrestler? What else could he do? Back to Barnsley and the plot.

All the wrestlers change in the same room except Primo who also had a manager. Enter the manager a squat man in a cream suit and Stetson and big cigar.

> Manager: "Who's fighting the champ?"
> Brian's hand goes up. "Me."
> Manager: "OK fella. You gotta full house. They've come to see him not you. So round one, even Steven, round two you win, round three the Champ wins, round four it's all over you lose. OK so the champ got a gammy right arm. Don't touch it and he don't like 'beeling' (hitting his stomach)".

Brian was introduced as Leon Arras and kept that name throughout his wrestling career. Why am I prattling on about this? Read on cos it's interesting, that's why.

> Round 1: OK.
> Round 2: Arras (Brian) takes the round
> Round 3: Primo starts hurting his opponent who says "steady on mate that hurt."
> Primo's reply, "Don't gimme that s… t." Primo continues hurting our hero quite badly.
> Round 4: Brian grabs Primo's dodgy arm and gives it some humpy.
> Primo: Hey that hurt.
> Brian: Don't give me etc., etc.
> Brian: Took a gentle fall and stayed there.

What happened to the real Leon Arras I have no idea. "Ask him now ref" was Brian's catchphrase.

What a character. Brian was also a scriptwriter in his spare time. I believe he died of a brain tumour.

Then there was Shirley Crabtree, better known as Big Daddy. One of his regular opponents was Malcolm 'King Kong' Kirk who started his sporting career as a front row forward with Doncaster R.L.F.C.

Big Daddy's speciality was a belly flop onto a prone opponent. Accidents happen. A belly flop on to 'King Kong Kirk' went wrong, so wrestlers do, on rare occasions get hurt this time with fatal consequences. R.I.P.K.K.K.

Another bit of wrestling memorabilia and a very pleasant occasion for me was travelling by train from London to Bradford. I was in a single seat alongside the four seats opposite me. I recognised one of the men opposite me as Edwin Richfield, a well-known actor with a wonderful voice.

ER: "Would you care to join us in a glass of wine?"
I did and thanked him.

We toasted.

> ER: How far are you going?
> Me: Where you're going.
> ER: To Bradford?
> Me: No, all the way to Calverley.

Now let me explain. Calverley was the setting the *Champion House* a black and white television drama mainly set in a big house in Clara Drive, Calverley the family home of mill owner Francis Garnett who was for many years president of Calverley Players. I kept quiet about my acting career. I think Honor Blackman was also in the cast and half the village was used as non-speaking extras walking down the streets of the village. After the meal and a very good chat I offered to return the favour with brandies all around but Edwin wouldn't hear of it. "There are four of us to one of you." We split the bill.

What's all this to do with wrestling? Hang on we're there now.

Now the fourth member of their party was Jackie (Mr TV) Pallo, a wrestler, a jovial man. He had the full menu – soup, fish, main course, sweet, cheese and biscuits, a glass or three of wine, coffee and a brandy… Coming into Doncaster there was a thick fog and the train was crawling.

Pallo grabbed the ticket inspector, "Look I've got to get out and make a phone call, just a couple of minutes, ok?" Pallo got out and in again and explained, "I've rung St Georges in Bradford and asked them to keep the lads going until I turn up. I'll have to be in and out quick, I'm on the sleeper tonight cos I'm down at Brighton tomorrow afternoon." So that's the dangerous sport of wrestling. You do it on a full stomach and 2 bouts in about 18 hours. Pallo said he always carried a razor blade with him and nicked himself before he went in the ring, dried it off then in the fourth round opened up the small wound because the audience loved blood.

Here's a good smile. To celebrate the Centenary or something, St. George's Hall in Bradford decided to have a one-night stand with a number of well-known celebrities, plus half-a-dozen Bradford Playhouse actors, giving a brief potted history of the venue.

Playhouse Chairman, Geoff Bryson, got together a cast, nothing to learn, as we would all had clipboards to read from. We would be in Victorian dress going round in a circle doing our bit when we were facing front. Bryson's good friend, Peter Walker, was in the cast…

Then he wasn't. He'd hopped on a plane to America on business. We rehearsed Tuesday and Thursday with Geoff taking over Peter's bit. Come

Friday, we were having a noggin in the Great Northern when Walker walks in.

One of the musicians is running late so we rushed to St. George's, got into our Victorian gear with minutes to spare. Walker said he hadn't a name to say on the final walk round, so he pinched mine, Sir John Barbirolli.

As I was last to speak, he said, 'You'll think of somebody.' Everything was going well. It was my turn in the spotlight. My mind was a blank. Then a thought. 'Mr. Jackie Pallo'. A big laugh. We were through. Geoff B. was furious. 'Trust you to louse it up', or more colourful words to that effect. I explained to no avail.

Cut to Saturday's 'Yorkshire Post'. It went something like this... Tops for me were the comedians from Bradford Playhouse, with a potting history of the Hall. They got the biggest laugh of the night with a sly reference to wrestler, Mr. Jackie Pallo, a regular at St. George's.

The 'phone rings.' It's Geoff, full of praise and apologies for his harshness. A true gentleman.

Edwin Richfield was a very pleasant man. I was able to tell him a little of the history of the village including the fact that a chap called William Shakespeare had, allegedly written a play about the infamous Calverley family called 'A Yorkshire Tragedy'. Another sort of fact is that 'Under the spreading chestnut tree' might refer to Calverley as the blacksmith in Calverley, was indeed under a chestnut tree. The house in Clara Drive is still called Champion House and is now a Cheshire Home.

Now George Raft. I hope you're enjoying this. I am, and it's really testing my memory.

Mr Raft was a Hollywood actor in the 30s 40s 50s but with many strings to his bow. Born George Ranft, he became a superb dancer, particularly in the bolero and that sort of dance. He worked as a dancer and then in the early hours rode shotgun on the booze wagons during prohibition for Chicago gang boss Owney Madden. Madden was born in Armley, Leeds. *'Oh come off it Ron'*. But it's true. Madden emigrated to America, never lost his Yorkshire accent, got several bullets in his body and eventually moved to Las Vegas where he continued with his criminal activities. He was played by Bob Hoskins in the film 'Cotton Club', but not with an Armley accent.

Back to Raft. He played in many gangster pics and in *Scarface* played a coin tossing baddie who came to a sticky end. In *'Some like it hot'* that wonderful film with Marilyn Monroe, Tony Curtis and Jack Lemmon in the leads, the oldies turned out. Pat O'Brien, George Raft, Joe E Brown. In Scarface Raft tosses a coin in every scene he is in. In *Some like it hot* there's a small part for a coin tossing young actor. Was it Edward G Robinson Junior? Raft approaches him and in a movie buff's magic moment catches the coin and says, "Where did you pick up that cheap trick?"

So how did I come to meet Mr Raft? Remember the con man Tom in our London office? Well, he sent in a bill for a £112 for dinner for two at the Colony Club. In 1962 that was a lot of dinner. Strolling in London one evening I saw the Colony Club sign in the distance. I walked over to see if there was a menu displayed. There was. The electric doors opened and there was George Raft in dark trousers, dark green velvet jacket and dark grey toupee. "Good evening Sir, will you be joining us tonight?" In the familiar throaty voice. "Maybe a bit later" in my usual Yorkshire voice. "Then I look forward to seeing you later." I thanked him, we shook hands and I moved on. One great line of his was, when holed up in a shootout with a younger mobster at his side, "What's the matter kid, you wanna live forever?"

Raft became famous for turning down star parts including Rick in 'Casablanca' superbly played by a late choice Humphrey Bogart. If you've never seen 'Casablanca' do, it has loads of one liners and is a very well-produced film. When it came to the final frames they couldn't hire a plane and made a small plane out of cardboard and "stuff" and used midgets as porters. Incidentally the piano player in 'Casablanca' couldn't play a note. Dooley Wilson was a session drummer and the ease with which he was able to push the Joanna from table to table was a clue to its lack of inner workings. Dooley was perfect casting for the part of Sam and like many movie myths Bogart never said, "Play it again Sam." I think he said "You played it for her now play it for me."

Oh no Ron, a big head like you could never be wrong Next you'll be telling us Mickey Mouse is a potbellied chap with thin legs in a mouse suit who once turned out for Cleckheckmonfax United.

Sir Ralph Richardson, actor and eccentric. My father-in-law took me on a Northern Cricket Society trip to the Oval and Lords. At the Oval Jim Laker was the welcomer. I mentioned Calverley St Wilfrid's mixed infants school and he confirmed that he was one. Obviously his 19 wickets in a Test Match was mentioned and he told me a good story. On his way home he stopped for a drink and the pub was jam packed with people watching a re-run of his remarkable feat. Standing at the back a bloke nudged me and said, "This fella just taken 19 wickets in a Test Match. Unbelievable innit?" Not looking at each other Jim replied, "It certainly is" and finishing his half pint moved off.

Where does this thesp Sir Ralph come in? The impatience of some people. We have to get to Lords first haven't we? So we're at Lords and after a look around, somebody started a fairly boring talk. I tend to sit at the back and if I'm not listening tend to drift off, no not sleeping but quietly walking out as I did in the New York trip where I met the two gentlemen from Lincoln. On this occasion I found myself on a sort of veranda overlooking an indoor tennis court. The chap next to me said, "Do you understand what's going on?" I said "Well it's some sort of tennis but they serve onto the low roof at one side." He explained it was Real Tennis and explained how the game worked. He noticed my accent and we chatted about Yorkshire of which he was most knowledgeable then said, "Look I'm on in five minutes. How very interesting meeting you." You've guessed the answer, if you've read this far.

A commissionaire came up to me and said, "Do you know who that was?" I said, "No." He said, "Sir Ralph Richardson." and behold there he was on court.

That's not quite the end. Two weeks later I'm walking down Jermyn Street, as you do and Sir Ralph is walking towards me. "Good morning. Beautiful weather, lovely to see you." I almost had my hand out for a handshake and he walked right past me. "Good morning. Beautiful weather, lovely to see you." to the couple behind me. He was an eccentric still riding his motorbike at an advanced age to attend a film shoot and on occasions forgetting his teeth. However on stage or screen he was a perfectionist.

Nicky Henson, the one with the open to the waist shirt and the dangly chains in *Fawlty Towers* was in a stage play with Sir. Every night on the pre-West End tour Henson got a big laugh and a round of applause on a certain line. In London the line got a murmur. Richardson saw Henson going out for a breather between matinee and evening performances and shouted, 'You're missing out an "and".'

"Silly old buffer." thought Henson but looking at the play copy he was indeed missing out an "and". He put it in, at the evening performance… got a big laugh and round of applause. That, my friends, is comedy timing. As one noted actor Sir Henry Irving pointed out, "Tragedy's hard but comedy's harder." Fancy an eccentric like Sir Ralph knowing another person's part and why he was missing a big laugh on one word.

If you find all this a bit tedious and would prefer to watch *Strictly come dancing* or *Match of the day* I'd skip the next bit about another actor, Sir Bernard Miles because if you're not really interested in thespians and never miss *Strictly* or MOTD… It won't make much sense to you. Here's a diversion. Pat and I went to a New Year's Eve party. Where's Frank? In the other room watching a recording of "Match". Frank was the host but what he loved most and never ever missed was his late night footie. So New Year's Eve came second.

Who's he on about now? Dear friend it's another ramble. Here we go:

One of my clients, sold suede and sheepskin coats and we found advertising in London theatre programmes very profitable. I think there was a tag line in the ad about bringing the programme with you for a discount. The manager of a fairly new theatre *The Mermaid* said, "When you're next in town come in for a chat and a look around." This I did. Now Sir Bernard Miles founded, ran and often appeared at The Mermaid and the manager asked if I would like to meet him. I think he was auditioning that day for the manager said, "This is Ron Pearson." Sir B: "Sit down. What are you going to do?" He thought I was an actor. I explained who I was and why I was there and he was fairly curt and held out his hand and said, "Nice meeting you." I then said, "I believe Sir Bernard you married a Bramley girl." *Here we go again. He just has to get Yorkshire in it somehow.* But it's true. Before he became dubbed he married Josephine Hinchcliffe who was from the Hinchcliffe family who were involved with the world famous Binns church organ works in Bramley, living in Hough Lane (pronounce Huff) a few hundred yards from where I lived before marriage. Hinchclife wasn't an actressy name so she became Josephine Wilson and helped to run *The Mermaid* and appeared in many of the productions there.

Sir Bernard was a different person and when I told him I'd seen his variety act where he rolled a very big cartwheel on the stage of the Bradford Alhambra then folded his arms and leaned on the wheel to tell his delightful rustic jokes, including the NHS teeth routine where the man's pals dipped them in their beer before passing them around. He laughed his head off. I said, "Was Terry-Thomas also on the bill?" We just went on until the manager knocked and peered around the door and said, "There are still a few actors waiting to audition."

So that's about it. Oh, a prince from Denmark, not the lad himself Hamlet wanted to launch an air purifier in the UK. One of my staff arranged for us to meet him and his product at a launch do in London. We did a bit of research and it was a crowded market. His retailing cost was too high and it was nice meeting him. That night "our 'enry Cooper" was in a televised fight and it was not surprising that the room thinned out as the fight time neared.

We'll come to Princess Margaret at the right time, someway away.

Finally, I almost met Sammy Davis Junior. It takes a bit of getting into but it's worth a read. The wise cracking Mike Metzgar starts this episode but doesn't finish it. "Hi Ron." You've guessed it, it's Sunday morning. "I sent you some dope on Tommy Armour who won the open in 1900 and something. We've got Tommy with us and we're at the Midland Hotel in Manchester on Thursday. I want you to knock up some sort of display and don't let me down. This could be big bucks for you. Caio."

I didn't speak! That's unusual. I called a couple of the lads in on Sunday morning. They worked like mad to get something that would flatpack for the trip to the rainy city on Wednesday. I addressed the pack to Mike Metzgar. The Tommy Armour presentation, McGregor Golf, Midland Hotel, Manchester. The Southern TV rep called to see me. He was based in Manchester and had a roof rack and it was delivered on time.

Come Friday I received a phone call from the Midland. We've got a parcel. It was never even opened. I asked the hotel to bin it. I put a fair but large profit margin on that item.

A few weeks later I got a call from Tall Tom in the London office. "Hi Ron. We've booked you in at the Mayfair in London for next Wednesday. We want you to display a few ads Wednesday afternoon and give a talk to some golfers. OK?" I turned up on the Wednesday afternoon and the man I met said the classic phrase, "It's Wednesday I must be in London." He was on a World tour and had another half dozen or so countries still to go. He loved the ads and the set-up for tomorrow. I asked about Metzgar to be told "He's not with us on this trip." He signed the space bookings schedule and that was all I did on day 1. Day 2, 9am I went down to the room to set up my stuff. It was a mess. A man came in. Here's the story.

The man was Sammy Davis' manager. Sammy was appearing at the Palladium twice nightly. He then got the hotel manager to round up an audience for a late night show to help him unwind. This ended at 4am hence the mess, the drinks and Sammy's props. I helped him clean up and he helped me set up. Nice guy. I told him my Sammy Davis joke. It's a bit rude so if you're of a sensitive nature avert your gaze now and move down to the wider writing.

> A teacher is giving a lesson on modern history. One question, "Who was the first to cross the Atlantic east to west?"
> Kid: 'Amy Johnson Sir'.
> Teacher: 'Wrong'.
> Another kid: 'Jim Mollison Sir'.
> Teacher: 'Wrong'.
> Cheeky kid: 'Sammy Davis Junior Sir'.
> Teacher: 'I'm watching you lad'.
> Now for the answers.
> First to cross the Atlantic East to West, Alcock and Brown.
> Cheeky kid to his pal: "What did I tell you, Sammy Davis Junior."

He had to sit down after that then said, "Can Sammy use it?" I said I didn't write it. As a matter of interest who wrote any joke? "Why did the chicken cross the road?" Who wrote that? Here's a different take on that. Why did the chicken stop in the middle of the road? Cos it was a Rhode Island Red. Another big laugh from the manager. "Can he use that too?"

Cut to the lunch. I gave my spiel, went down well and we had lunch. Several of Britain's best golfers were present. They told some good jokes. I chipped in with a couple. It was a very happy sometimes boozy event then Tall Tom put thirty or forty golf clubs, slightly sloping against a wall and the golfers were asked to keep the clubs they liked stood up and the others tipped on the floor. The golfers said goodbye. The man who flew in said "Jeezuz" and then "That was just amazing. You see all the upright clubs were made in America. The others on the floor were made in Canada where the tariffs are cheaper."

I was checking out with my bag and stuff when the Sammy Davis manager came in the room and said "Sammy's still in bed and when I left him just now was still laughing and sent me down to say thank you. Do you want tickets for tonight? I waved my cases." So I almost met SDJ and it was quite a good memory to recall.

The McGregor story is almost over but not quite. It's November. Tall Tom rings. "Look Ron. I want you down here tonight. It's very important."

The gist is he'll meet me at Heathrow to tell me the story. It was the village Cricket Club AGM and as treasurer I had to give a report. I usually looked at the balance sheet and did it off the cuff. I got the President to stand in for me. The Leeds Bradford airport was not what it is today and neither was the small plane. It was a stomach churning flight. The chap next to me was a yachtsman. He loved it. I didn't and had to get back the same night. It's not hard to pick out Tall Tom. He bought me a coffee and showed me a very short letter. "You are unauthorised personnel to sanction the magazine stages booked by the Charles Walls Agency. Please cancel."

Now he could have told me that on the phone. I then told him all our schedules have to be signed by the client and all our space order copies were sent to Chicago before the man on the move returned with the signed schedule. Apart from another awful flight back that was that. I never got another call from Metzgar and I can only presume the McGregor golf clubs did not click over here for I never heard from them again, apart from the cheque.

Here's a nice little story with once again a surprising coincidence. I was going by train to the big city. A pal of mine gave me *Talking Heads* to read. If you've never heard of Talking Heads I can only presume you live in Pernambuco or Oswaldtwistle. If you're an Oswaldtonian reading this book, I hope you'll forgive me. Anyhow it's by Alan Bennett. I didn't like to tell my friend Randall I had already read this but it was nice to flip through and re-read some instalments. Particularly moving was the play featuring Thora Hird, one of A.B's favourite actresses. I believe they're actors these days. So is a duchess now a duke and a princess a prince? *Come on sunshine get on with it.*

Here's the coincidence. Of all the theatres in London my writing colleague booked to see a couple of Alan Bennett plays. Sound familiar? 'Of all the gin joints' is a classic phrase from the lips of Bogart in Casablanca, but you knew that didn't you? This is beginning to sound like the smaller Ronnie in his new pullover in his chair telling one of his hilarious monologues. This isn't hilarious, just interesting, I hope.

After the plays which were very entertaining we retired to the bar where lo and behold Mr Bennett joined our party. He strolled in just like an ordinary human being carrying a plastic bag full of "stuff". After the handshakes it was mentioned I was born in Bramley. The others were out of it.

AB was born in the next neighbouring bit of Leeds known as Armley. Remember Armley, where gangster Owney Madden first breathed a breath? So the conversation carried on with all sorts of happy memories. It was coming up to my friend Randall's birthday so I pulled out Talking Heads and asked if he would sign it? More than that, he asked for the correct spelling of Randall then wrote "Happy birthday Randall Alan Bennett" then drew a little cartoon of himself. How wonderful for one of the world's top playwrights.

Bennett loved odd stories and so I chipped in with one. Here goes.

Pat and I were making our way to the very interesting Piece Hall in Halifax when we heard the following:

'How's your Ethel?'

'Well she's had it all taken away down there but she managed to get on the day trip to Llandudno.'

Alan roared with laughter 'I like that, very funny' were his comments.

Back home Randall came to visit. I handed over the book and said "Just check it to make sure I haven't folded over a page or something."

"No, I'm sure it'll be ok." I tried three times to get him to open the damn thing before eventually opening it myself. Dour Randall "Have you done this?"

"No." I explained the story. He was absolutely chuffed. Hope you enjoyed it.

This is the sort of thing that just sort of happens to me. Not a celeb but a London taxi driver though I've dropped in a well-known lady at the end.

> Driver: Where to mate?
> Me: Cumberland Hotel Marble Arch.
> Him: 'Where from'?
> Me: 'Leeds'.
> Him: 'Oh yes, string of beads... Whereabouts in Leeds'.
> Eventually it got to I was born in Bramley.
> Him: 'Know Town End'?
> Me: 'Yes'.
> Him: 'Oh my gawd. The tram sheds?'
> Me: 'Yes'
> Him: 'Oh my giddy gawd'.

Here's the story. It turns out he was a trumpeter in Harry Roy's band. Apart from Mr Roy's slightly off key playing on the liquorice stick, 'clarinet' to you and his slightly off key singing they were a very good band. I asked if he was Tommy Balderstone who did a terrific solo break on 'Struttin with some barbeque'. Yes. That's the correct title. "Originally written as Struttin, with some barbaric". They who make the rules altered the last word without changing "with" to "at". Just another bit of useless knowledge that flipped into my brain.

"No I'm not Tommy. He's a Lancashire lad still around. We were playing the Empire Leeds. Every night the girls were at the stage door. I got friendly with a Bramley lass and took her home on the tram. Saturday night I had my wicked way with her at the tram sheds. A few weeks later we're at Newcastle and at band call there's a letter for me. She's up the duff. Now I know it was wrong of me but I was just a lad and I panicked. I went to see Harry at his hotel, told him the story. "Leave it with me." First house Monday Harry, "You're on a boat from Liverpool tomorrow am. You're playing with Ray Noble in New York. OK?"

"What about you?"

"It's fixed. Get out of my sight and play your socks off tonight." *Ray Noble* was a very posh speaking Englishman who made it big in USA largely due to his very, very English voice. He would often say a few words in the middle of a song.

Taxi drivers love to chat. "Gracie Fields, heard of her? Every Christmas Gracie rings me, asks me to get a small group together and we fly over to Capri. Gracie pays for the lot." Gracie's third husband was Boris Alperovici. The taxi driver said it was an anagram of 'I love Capri', and amazingly it is. Not the most enlightening of stories but another instance that happened to me.

Another big attraction was trumpet player Nat Gonella and his Georgians. Nat was a Londoner but somebody told me he now lived in Leyland, Lancashire. I tracked him down. Bingley Little Theatre had lots of fund-raising events. Their theatre was being knocked down and a new more expensive theatre was built. I rang Nat. He came to Bingley. No fee. We paid his fare and a room for the night at a good hotel. He liked to keep his hand, or his mouth in and in the evening was a sell-out success.

Louis Armstrong, you must have heard of him, on hearing Nat said with his mischievous chuckle. "Gee man this cat can play, I thought it was me."

The big bands are of course no more. They were a big hit in variety theatres, now gone and their 78's were big business.

Here's a micro meeting, 30 seconds with the Queen Mother. We were having a day out in Alderney, C.I. Suddenly a rush of people. the Queen Mum was opening something. HRH and Lady-in-waiting plus chauffeur crossed the road and flowers were presented and passed to the chauffer and Lady-in-waiting, when the Queen Mum had had enough she crossed the road to make for the car. I was next to the car, nipped round and opened the car door.

> HRH: Thank you very much indeed
> Me: My pleasure Ma'am.

Nothing silly from me-that's a relief – but another indication of how I always seem to be in the right place at the right time.

Back to 1939, standing in a queue at Leeds General Post Office and standing in front of me was George Formby. From the mid-thirties to the mid-forties he was the highest paid entertainer in the British Isles.

Formby bought a book of stamps and said I "Thank you very much. Do you know what a Lancashire Cocktail is?" Everybody, including me said 'No'. Formby, 'It's a pint of best bitter with a celery stick in it'. Laughter all round and he was gone.

He was appearing at the Empire Theatre, Leeds in a panto at a reported £1,000 a week plus a percentage. It was a sell-out. I had to stand at the back of the 'Gods' – the Gallery.

Formby couldn't tune a Ukulele and had half-a-dozen different ones on a settee at the back of the stage. He always insisted they were Banjoleles.

He made 2 or 3 films a year at £25,000 a time, add long summer and pantomime seasons plus a stint at the London Palladium. His 'bill matter' was simple 'George Formby and his Uke' was all that was needed. He seldom, if ever, told jokes and it's hard to believe that this apparently gormless man with the high pitched Lancashire accent was a sell-out wherever he appeared.

It was, of course, the 'cheeky' songs, expertly timed that made him the star.

His records and song sheets sold in their millions. I read somewhere that Queen Elizabeth II knew quite a few. Now that would've been a sell-out recording.

Think of it – £1,000 a year man was on a very good salary, Formby must have pocketed £200,000 a year and counting. In the final fade-out of his films he always got the girl but never kissed her. Mrs Beryl Formby was a former champion clog dancer. You don't argue with that.

Towards the end of his act an old-fashioned gas lamp was pushed on stage. It got a round of applause. Formby, "I can never get off without singing this." The song: "Leaning on a Lamp Post" was a pleasant lively sort of song. No cheeky bits. So this ramble started with George buying some stamps and the 14 year old me standing behind him. What did Perry Como sing?

"Memories are Made of This."

Was it or Wasn't it? I was looking at a David Hockney Exhibition at Salts Mill in Saltaire when a memorable voice to my left said:

"D'you think he'll make out then?"

I turned and the familiar white cap was some feet away, with his back to me, waved and was gone.

Now I can't honestly say I met Mr Hockney, but if not, it was a very good impersonation.

Chapter 29:
Business Simply Rolled In

The move to Calverley was a good one, a lovely building, a lovely garden and most of all a lovely car park.

Reps found car parking very difficult in Leeds, Bradford and all big cities. We made sure there was ample car parking and reps loved to see us and reps gave tips on new enterprises and established companies looking for a new agent. I never gave kickbacks on the principal that if you're working on narrow margins, 5% given to a rep almost certainly resulted in a loss on the business. Most of the reps came from Manchester and if a tip proved fruitful on his next visit I would stand him a lunch, made sure he went on our Christmas list and include his publication on our schedule, pointing out that the client had the last say on which publications made up the final schedule. It worked.

Sir Giles Shaw was the Pudsey M.P. and I'd met him several times at various do's in the village. On one occasion he asked if he could look round The Agency, prior to becoming our M.P. He'd been Sales Director at Rowntree's in York.

We had a superb cook, in Kath, and she often provided 3-course lunches.

Sir Giles was impressed by The Agency and enjoyed meeting key personnel at the lunch. He also arranged for me to meet Jack Laycock, the very likeable Advertisement Manager. The Rowntree's Agency was J. Walter Thompson, then the biggest in the world but we picked up some very profitable design work.

On one occasion we were asked to redesign the Twiglets box which we did and produced the finished artwork. Always genial, Jack asked me if I would like to see the Twiglets set up on the factory floor. It wasn't there. Just a metal plate in the floor fixed by four big bolts. It wasn't anywhere else either. It was tracked down to Norwich where Rowntree's had another factory but nobody had bothered to tell Jack or amend the blueprint of the factory floor. Sadly, Jack died shortly after this.

On another occasion the phone rings at 5pm. 'Be here at 6pm. and bring your Art Director with you.' Ah, big business methinks. There were about ten of us at the Boardroom table when a slender youth entered with a very large envelope. Silence as he, very ceremoniously, emptied the contents of the XL envelope onto a large white plate. One Smartie. Apparently, this was the new 'Purple' colour for this popular delicacy. That was it, Finito Benito. 6.15pm time to saddle up and go back to the ranch.

I had a good team working for the agency. Of course we lost business. Geordie Home Brew, based in North Shields were building up very nicely when they sold out to Ovaltine. After one year where I signed Jackie Charlton to promote their products the account moved south. Jackie must have lived fairly near the agency. One morning he came in. "Ron, where can I buy some sloes?" He wanted to make sloe gin at home. An excellent after dinner speaker, Ovaltine held a big do at Sutton Coldfield. There was a club comic, just about okay then the President. Everybody laughs at the President's weak jokes. Jackie, was an absolute riot. One of his gags was "Norman Hunter came off with a bad leg. Trouble was we didn't know whose leg it was." Sadly Jackie died recently of dementia. I have read that heading the ball in a long career could be the reason for this yet it is part of the game and it is difficult to see this part of the game being dropped.

One of my new additions was Willeys wallpaper and paint stores. Doesn't sound much but it proved to be a very good client and I made a dear friend in Jack Morris.

Jack was Jewish, didn't look Jewish but like me loved Jewish humour. On more than one occasion he would tell me some Jewish jokes then invite me to a Jewish gathering. He said I looked more Jewish than he did and told the jokes better.

At his Christmas party, yes I'm right Jack did have a Christmas party, Pat, my wife was stuck with Uncle Louie (Who else but Uncle Louie) who placed his walking stick on her foot. Pat managed a pleasant smile and never let on.

The wallpaper business had a sort of friendly mafia. I hope I've got this right and don't get an ominous knock on the door. Willeys were in the Bradford area plus Manchester. I think it was an unrelated Morris in Leeds. In Leicester it was Cherry and Co. Ellisons, owned by Willeys, did the Wirral but not Liverpool. Willeys sometimes known as Blakeys were in London and also Bristol. It was somewhat complicated but seemed to work.

Jack was a dynamo. Once, with me driving he jumped out of the car at traffic lights in Manchester to re-arrange the pavement display at one of his shops. Chaos.

I was in hospital, gall bladder, no TV so Jack brings his TV to my room and we watch *Rising Damp* and other sitcoms. Arnold Morris ran London and Ernie ran Bristol. One day Arnold's son rang me and asked me to handle the promotion of a West End revue he had invested in. A charming man. The show folded. Arnold's lad went to live in America. I never got paid. You win some you lose some. I'm not quite sure why this happened but the whole set up became Decormecca. They had a big do in London where I had to give a talk on the advertising strategy. However it was very light-hearted with Roy Castle as the main event. A very talented and likeable chap and Huddersfield born. He too was a workhorse telling me that he and his trio had already done the act once that night and had another venue after this one. At £700 a time in the seventies, this wasn't bad going.

Jack M was not with the company anymore. He opened a shop in Skipton and one in York. He was getting older but couldn't slow down. He had a heart attack in the York shop and luckily for him the manageress had some medical training and got him on his feet but that didn't stop him and sadly shortly afterwards he had another heart attack which proved fatal.

Pat and I went to the funeral. Let's have a smile. At a funeral? 'Jack often said I looked more Jewish than he did'. We were ushered into a small side room where the nearest relations prayed. This involved reciting something in Hebrew from the prayer book and swaying forwards and backwards all the time. Pat almost got the giggles. It went on for quite a while. I mumbled rubbish. Jack would have loved it.

It is often said that Jewish people are tight-fisted. Not so. They are wonderful wheeler dealers. Jack took me to a couple of wallpaper manu-facturers, one in Darwen in Lancashire and one near London. Apparently, the wallpaper trade demanded new designs every Spring. They all knew Jack and it was very jolly. A paper that sold for £2 a roll Jack would offer 10½p. Everybody laughed but Jack knew and they knew the shelves had to be cleared for new stock the alternative being pulping the old stock so eventually a very low price would be agreed for a large number of rolls. Jack would often buy the complete stock for say 25p a roll to stop his rivals buying them. This is where the Jewish sense of craftiness comes in. He could advertise a £2 retail roll at 50% off which is true and gives him a good profit, having bought at a very low price.

As for generosity, Jack took Pat and me and two of his friends to see Louis Armstrong at the Batley Variety Club, everything on him. There were many other over-generous gestures, including a day trip to Amsterdam by this all-action never stopping man.

Jack's nephew was Philip Morris who launched the Suedecraft shops. Pat and I were invited to the Lancashire Christmas do plus 40 or 50 staff at the Palace Manchester pantomime starring Harry Secombe and Roy Castle. Another, really generous man. Sadly he too died recently.

Paul Ziff, now here's a character. Often charming, often raging, one of several brothers and cousins part of the Stylo Shoe chain of shops. Arnold, a very clever quiet man moved out early on in his career and founded Town Centre Securities, a listed and very profitable property company. Neville Ziff I know little of as he went to America early in his career. Alan and Alwyn ran the shoe side of the business whilst Paul was responsible for the very successful Stylo Matchmaker golf shoe range. I learnt how to handle Paul when another client invited me to watch an excellent training film featuring a young John Cleese. In the first half the other bloke blows his top and Cleese joins in. In the second half Cleese sits calmly until the other man says something like this, "Look mate, I'm sorry. It's been a hell of a day etc." Try it. It really works. Paul hated artwork charges and always knocked them down. I had John Oldfield to help me and he often did the leg work on the Stylo Matchmaker account. We evolved a cunning plan on a big pad with columns; in, up, and out. In the first column we entered the correct studio charge. Second column an inflated charge out price, and third column blank for Paul's knockdown price. For instance Studio price £30, next column £40, estimated knockdown £35 extra profit five quid. It worked and more often than not we came out top. Although he was younger than me, I called him Uncle Paul and the name stuck.

In the 1960s Stylo bought the Barratt chain of shops, famous for their tag line "Walk the Barratt way". They had hundreds of shops including one in Oxford Street, London. I was called to a lunch and development meeting in Knaresborough and pleaded with them to utilise this slogan and re-name both the Stylo and Barratt shops as Stylo/Barratt or keep "walk the Barratt way" or add on "walk the Stylo way". These were off the cuff suggestions. I was never really involved with the shop chains and after I retired I believe both chains ceased trading. Incidentally Stylo never made a shoe, they were all bought in. Our offices were very close to the Stylo warehouse, now houses, and one day Paul came to see me. He was completely deflated. "What's wrong?" I asked. "I've been asked to take over the retail chains. I've turned it down. They're going nowhere." How right he was.

Here's a very unusual business meeting in a... I'm not going to tell you, you'll have to read on. I can't remember how we got this business but I've often said some business just walks in the door. The other type, the harder you try the less likely it becomes and you finally give up.

I think I must have been given a tip to a petrol company in Ashby, the far side of Scunthorpe. The little-known brand names were Globe in England and Wales, Golden in Scotland owned by Tenneco in America. My first job was to find a poster sites as near to their petrol stations as possible. This wasn't easy however yet again Lady Luck held out a helping hand. Sheldons were the poster company in Leeds. I'd used them for the Gateshead opening while at Nevins. Their rep had been the office boy at Heslock and really did his best for me. Globe had about two hundred sites in England and 100 or Golden outlets or so in Scotland. I tried many times to try and amalgamate the sites under one brand name with no success. The poster contained too many elements which made them too messy. There was only one poster site in Calverley, next door to us at the village Post Office. I couldn't avoid it and it didn't please me. The nearest Globe pumps were three miles away with several other petrol stations before you got to theirs. They held a competition for the best dealers, North, South, East, West and Scotland. I attended the Congleton one but the Rotherham one was truly mirthful. It took place in the Mayor's parlour.

> The Mayor: "Now then everybody. Who'll have a drink? I've never drank bottled stuff in my life so I've had barrelled beer and a pump installed."

Everybody had a drink. It was very convivial. I went to the loo.
The Mayor: "What do you think of it then, that toilet seat in royal
velvet? We 'ad the Queen 'ere and thought we'd splash out a bit.
Every day lad my bum 'as touched royal velvet.
Not many can say that."

Here's a couple more Globe stories. The man I worked with was Jay Lee
Lammons, a younger version of Mike Metzgar. "The one thing you've gotta
watch is somebody dropping something nasty and sticky in your pocket."
was one of his favourite sayings. Not as crisp as Mr Metzgar but there
you go. Sorry, I've rambled again. Here's the funny meeting place. One
day, my birthday, I got a call to be there "pronto tonto" for an important
meeting. When I got there I was told to go to Scunthorpe Hospital where
his wife was about to have a child. So Jay Lee and I start the meeting at the
bedside and Mrs Jay Lee goes into labour and is whisked out of the ward.
The meeting continued. It wasn't very important, let's say trivial.

Me: "The gimmicks have been for adults. Why not have a gimmick
for the kids? Gee Dad free mint rock, can I have some?"

So I had to find a manufacturer of small sticks of mint rock. Buy as a wholesaler, sell to Globe with a retail mark-up and deliver them by the cartload.
Wagons ho! A nice little earner, that was. What about Jay Lee Junior. He
arrived during the meeting. Jay Lee senior went in, kissed the baby's head
and we continued for another hour or so with all kinds of bits and pieces.
The matron bought us coffee and Jaffa cakes. They seemed to have no
contacts in this country so I got all sorts of jobs including printing visiting
cards for reps. One such was OK Jones III. I met him. Here's the story:
His grandpappy was born. "Looks ok to me" said the doctor. So OK
Jones he became. OK Jones II was pop and so the tradition continued with
OK III. Why didn't I think of that? *You're not a slick talking American Ron,
that's why?* What if he'd then had a daughter? Simple was the answer, O.
Kay Jones IV. Globe/Golden was part of the Tenneco empire in Tennessee.
The Globe and Golden brands were bought by another American giant
Connaco and I believe phased out.
Pat and I had a little ceremony. Every time we passed a Globe or Golden
station which was very rare, I said in a kid's voice, "Gee Mommy, mint
rock. Can I have some?" Pat replied, "No you can't Junior, drive on."
One Saturday a.m. I was paying my coal bill at Stanley Goldsboroughs
and he said, 'Would you be interested in doing some work for the Yorkshire
end of the N.C.B.' My answer was in the affirmative.
Come Monday, a Bradford man rang – a meeting arranged, it wasn't
big business but it was definitely worth having. We decided posters – from
memory, 16 sheet and 11" × 4" columns Ads in Newspapers. We used
real coalmen with real coal sacks on their backs, a fairly straightforward

somewhat humorous message, in bold type. The Ads were a big success. There were a number 'wide' boys plundering the slagheaps and flogging poor quality stuff with a lot of slate in it.

Here's a pen portrait of one of the coalmen – Ken from Keighley. In addition to humping sacks of coal he was physio for Keighley R.L.F.C. He was also a Musical Director of some repute and occasionally appeared in musicals with a very listenable tenor voice.

We got to know each other when we both appeared in 'Guys and Dolls'. He played 'Nicely, Nicely Johnson', not a big part, but he sings the show stopping 'Sit down, you're Rockin' the Boat'. Ask anybody who's seen 'Guys and Dolls' and it's fairly certain this song will crop up. *Stop rabbiting on Ron.*

One Day my Coal Board friend said to me, 'Go to "The… (I've forgotten the name) in Carpaby, North Yorkshire, mention my name and you won't be disappointed." The mixed grill was overwhelmingly good – and it was on the house.'

He had a number of other interests – a sort of northern 'Arthur Daley'. Now you must've heard… played by George Cole in 'Minder'.

In fact, my friend and Mr Daley gave me the idea for 'Errand Boys', my TV scripts that almost won the 'Radio Times Drama Awards'. Still in the 'in tray' hoping for the 'out tray'. More later.

My Coal Board chum, 'Would you be interested in running the Coal Board full Northern set-up? It could lead to you getting the lot.'

One day he rang and said:

'Right. 2.30pm Queens Hotel, Leeds, be there.'

A London Agency presented a pleasantly cheerful 30second commercial, featuring a bouncy male singer.

Coalman: "Who the xxxx was that?"

I was to learn coalman don't mince their words.

Apparently he was the very well-known somebody or other.

Coalman: "Well I've never 'eard of 'im".

That was the general consensus of opinion.

We didn't get the national business.

We didn't get the northern business.

We hung on to the Yorkshire business, but only for a while. The coal business was deader than a duplicity of Dodo's.

One day my Bradford pal told me this: 'Quite a few Bradford men go to Morecambe on a summer's evening.'

It's true. Morecambe is often referred to a as Bradford by-the-sea. So he was strolling along the prom one evening when a chap approached, 'You have an interest in the theatre here'. 'Yes'. 'Well I'm running the show and I can't pay the nudes. Could you lend me a 100 quid and I'll pay you back, next week, same day, same time'. A hundred quid changed hands. The following week this man was conspicuous by his absence. A stroll to the theatre, the padlocks were on. The show had folded. This man became very rich millionaire presenting 'Girlie' shows in London.

On a serious note, it was known as the 'Scargill Strike' after Arthur Scargill, Leader of the N.U.M. I was driving to Hertford in Hertfordshire, when I was pulled over by two serious looking men. One asked where I was going, the other had a club hammer on the windscreen. I showed the Ads, I was taking to the meeting. They waved me through. I can't remember whether this was before or after my Coal Board work but you don't argue in those situations.

Remember Tom the con man in our London office? If you don't I do. A Greek shipping line owed us £7,000 and a few hundred and I went down to collect it. Who should be sitting in the chairman's office but Tom the Con. "Hello Ron. How lovely to see you." Big handshake. What was he doing here? Did he work here? Not beyond the bounds of credibility. I never found out. The Greek guy was a wheeler dealer. "I offer you £7,000 pounds."

"You owe me £7,000 three hundred and twenty pounds 15 shillings. You've owed it for almost a year. I should be charging you interest."

"OK £7,300 deal done."

"If you can afford £7,300 you can afford fifteen bob." He changed. "Where are you from?"

"I'm a Yorkshireman and all I want is a fair deal on a long outstanding account."

"You are a very difficult man to deal with." The cheque book was out and the full amount paid. "Do you have any children Mr Pearson?" I'll cut it short. He got out a large envelope and big bag of foreign stamps and poured half of them into the envelope. "For your daughter and if you ever open up in London again give me a call." I don't think tricky Tom spoke apart from another big handshake and "good bye". Why was he there?

You may remember I mention Wharfedale Loudspeakers in my American bit. Here's how it happened. Fred Dawson a printer's rep and very good friend of the agency told me they were not too happy with their London agency who visited them in April and October. I went to see them. They arranged for me to see Gilbert Briggs the brains behind Wharfedale's success story. He was somewhat testy, asked me to leave the room, came back, I'd got the business, mainly full pages in trade magazines. I called twice a week on my way home and all sorts of business cropped up. Our first job was to re-design the Wharfedale logo. It was in an old-fashioned Gothic typeface. Gilbert Briggs approved then wanted some 'exploded' artwork where you see the inside of a loudspeaker and I found a man in Hull who did this at very reasonable cost. Then I had to spend a day with my photographer re-taking all their speakers as the existing pics were not to scale. We produced a series of booklets in the form of record sleeves.

Gilbert Briggs proved to be a very clever man with a dry sense of humour. He lectured all over the British Isles and abroad including the Festival Hall in London where he had a small orchestra and some loudspeakers. The packed audience was asked to close their eyes and put their hands up when the orchestra stopped and the speakers started. No hands went up. The speakers won every time. He also raised a smile with this. Take an industrial drainpipe about 12" across, cover this with a marble effect wallpaper, wire up a loudspeaker and put the speaker in the top of the drainpipe and it produces an above average sound. Gilbert Briggs was about to retire. He sold out to the Rank organisation. We got even more business and Gilbert moved to a small office in Ilkley where he lived and promoted and sold his books. Another nice little earner for the agency.

The new Managing Director they sent up was having a bungalow built and spending money on all sorts of things. We did graphs for meeting. I was there two or three times a week, twice in London. After a late session at the Audio Fair at the Russell Hotel he took half a dozen of us to Quaglinos one of London's top restaurants. On one occasion on a Friday one bloke, a Catholic ordered fish. As it struck midnight he dashed into the kitchen and changed to steak. Someone pointed out it was British summertime so it was still officially just after 11 so he dashed back in to re-order. They chucked him out so he just ate the veg. Give the man triple Brownie points and a bagful of 'Hail Mary's'.

Gilbert Briggs once asked me where I stayed in London. I said "Where I could get." He said, "I stay at the Great Northern at King's Cross." I thought it would be a bit noisy and a bit smoky. "Not a bit of it," said GB and "You don't need a taxi to get you there. You can always get a cab to get to meetings and one to get you back to Kings Cross." I took his advice and each time he treated me to dinner and every time I went to see him in Ilkley he took me to lunch. It couldn't last. It didn't last. G.B. went down the night before to be at the meetings promptly. The new M.D. travelled in the morning. On one occasion we worked till midnight producing graphs for a meeting. The morning plane ran late. Oh dear.

One Christmas Eve I was called down to a studio in Armley, Leeds to supervise some shots of a completely new innovation for Wharfedale; a complete cabinet unit containing speakers, radio, turntable. An inside back cover in Reader's Digest was booked for September. Nine months later the boffins from Rank never got around to making it. Over 4,000 enquiries in the first week. We were sacked and so a few of the Rank insiders at Rank Wharfedale became Rank outsiders.

Three of Wharfedale's top men moved out and opened Castle Loud-speakers in Skipton and appointed us as agents. A much smaller operation but something is always better than nothing.

Now a bit about trade unions.

When Webb Offset came in it changed newspaper and magazine printing forever. Loads of artists were made redundant which meant trade union membership suffered so the unions decided that Advertising Agencies should be unionised. In our case they even wanted the receptionist to be a union member.

The two unions involved were Slade and NGA. There is or was a Slade

College of Art but this Slade stood for The Society of Lithographic Artists, Designers and Engravers. Now I'd been in the business for a quarter of a century. I'd seen a litho stone but I'd never seen an artist working on one. Designers ok on that one. Engravers? They're the men who transfer an image onto sheet metal and through an etching process using the much loved 'dragons blood' to stop the process, produced a printing block. NGA I'm not sure. I think it stands for National Graphical Association or something similar.

Switch now to the IPA President's committee. I don't know how I became to be involved in this but I was. I'd been on the Northern committee in Manchester for years and I'd run Bill Metson, secretary of the IPA around a bit to various newspapers. He couldn't get over the fact that—in good weather—I walked to work, walked to lunch and walked home.

The first thing I did on the President's committee was to have the time of the meetings changed from 10:30am to 2:30pm on the basis that members living in Leeds, Manchester etc could get there and back in a day.

London agencies handling big national and international concerns had 85% of their business on TV. The opposite applied in broad terms to provincial agencies. Now Frank Lowe, who usually wore a cricket sweater to meetings when everybody else was more formally attired, was a key man in a big agency. His hand went up, "Mr Chairman if you think I'm going to lose any sleep cos a piddling little agency in Pudsey is in trouble with the print unions think again."

Opportunities like this are very rare. My hand went up. "Yes, Ron?"

"I am the Managing Director of a piddling little agency in Pudsey (uproar) and I would remind Frank and everybody around this table that piddling little agencies make up the bulk of the membership of this Institute. Moreover if it wasn't for piddling little agencies there wouldn't be I.P.A." Applause. Frank Lowe got up, held out his hand and said, "Ron you've made your point. I'd like to withdraw my remarks and help in any way I can." These may not be the actual minuted words but this was the gist of the matter.

The upshot of this was that Mr Bigmouth, yours truly, was asked to be the negotiator for the Yorkshire region, the main job being meeting and arguing the toss with the two union leaders.

Now here's another funny thing. Let's set the scene. The phone rings.

Telephonist: "It's Charlie Farnsbarns (not his real name) from the NGA to see you."
Me: "Send him in."
CF: "Hello Ron. How you're doing? Nice day. Everything ok?"
Me: "Fine, absolutely fine."
CF: "What a night last night. Took the bloke from Design for a night out. Went to Heppy's in Huddersfield. Took a couple of girls. Y'know a good night out." (Nod Nod Wink Wink).

This surprised me as to the best of my knowledge the man from Design was a lay preacher and why go to Huddersfield when there were half a dozen or more clubs in Leeds?

CF: "Anyhow when we got there the drummer failed to turn up. I know a bit about drumming so I stood in until they got a replacement. So back to business."

Me: "Are you a member of the Musicians Union then?"

CF: "Oh look Ron. I was helping out see. I don't want any trouble with the MU. Let's forget I ever said it."

That made dealing with this oik a lot easier. I did get a number of small but important concessions. I can only remember this one.

Subscription to political party.

Me: "Which party?"

CF: "Does it matter?"

Me: "Well is it the National Front or Communist or Raving Loony?"

CF: "Oh look Ron. It's obvious it's the Labour Party. Let's move on."

Me: "Is it optional?"

CF: "Well yes I suppose so."

Me: "So let's have this altered to optional subscription to the Labour Party."

CF: "You'll never get that through London."

Me: "So we rule out with pen the current wording and add my wording. Do you send the forms to London?"

CF: "No."

Me: "Job done."

That wasn't the last of it. The house had some stabling undeveloped. We developed it into a studio complex and started a new business *Elmwood Studios* and so avoided the agency, including the receptionist being unionised.

This move had an extra bonus in that the studio built up their own list of clients, all money in the till. I'd a few trips to other towns and cities to talk them through the minor concession and wangles but eventually all agencies in Yorkshire signed up.

The following gives you an idea of how strong the unions were. In London having a chat and a Kit-Kat with the MD at the *Daily Express* he showed me a key. "This is the key to the room where we have recently installed a million pounds worth of Web Offset equipment." The 'Father of the Chapel', a quaint name for the union head honcho, also has a key. It's a complicated lock. One can't get in without the other. So the new investment remains idle. There was a lot of friction and I believe the print staff at *The Observer* printed Saturday night, went on strike. Eventually the seas were calmer and we came off rather better than we went in except about six or seven weeks later the studio boss came to see me.

We had a car account. Standard top and bottom. List of cars in the middle – most of the ad. The YEP were in the habit of stripping out our typesetting and to keep their artists busy re-setting this using their own NGA staff. There had been a few mistakes and we got a lower price for this. However the agency had been waiting for a union stamp with our number on it for a couple of months. Now the Father of the Chapel was 'Blacking' all our artwork because it wasn't stamped. What to do?

I'd met Malcolm Barker the editor of *The Yorkshire Post* several times, a very likeable man. I rang him with the problem.

> Malcolm: "As you know Ron editorial and advertising do not mix."
> Ron: "My next call will be to the editor of the *Sunday Times* feature department. I'm sure…"
> Malcolm: "Give me ten minutes."

Always be wary of men you've never met being over friendly and with a smile in their voice.

> Father of the Chapel: "Hello Mr Pearson, Ron. There's no problem. We'll get your union number to you. No need to get upset."
> Me: "I want that stamp by 9am tomorrow."

To cut a long story sideways I told him that Johnsons Engravers in Trinity Street would do it in time. It arrived, job done and not another word of complaint from either side. When everything settled down I was made a Fellow of the Institute. No brass in it but it looked good on the letterhead. Then, I don't know why, I became a Dip. Cam. Looks as though I got a diploma of Cambridge. Not a bit of it. In the army men who got medals that everybody else got, the bits you put on your uniform were known as toffee wrappers. I think the Dip. Cam. Stood for Diploma in Communications and Marketing. It was a 'toffee wrapper' but again it looked good on the notepaper.

Re-reading this it gives the impression I never miss a trick. Far from it, for instance I'm rubbish with a balance sheet and always got the auditor in early to brief me before the AGM.

One little point I cottoned onto was printer's quotes. After twenty years or so I turned one over and found loads of disclaimers to protect the printers. They were often set in very small, 6 point type in a pale colour. One clause stated they could deliver ten per cent over or ten per cent under. I added this full page in difficult to read type on the back of our quotes, just in case. As time went on things were a'changing and there were many times when I was a little bit out of step with modern methods.

Chapter 30:
Back to the Home Front

After my breakdown in 1968 I took things a little easier and John Oldfield was a great help. Quite a talented artist in his own right he soon grasped the business side of advertising and with a few hiccups we worked well together. He would be in his early twenties but had a very good head on his shoulders.

It was Dad's 80th birthday – I sent a card and a cheque for £80. Dad was very upset. He didn't want reminding he was eighty and it was then I found he'd never had a bank account. My Sister managed to get it paid into her account and withdrew eighty pounds in cash. There was no thank you. A sad and sometimes difficult to understand man. But he was still my Dad and we remained good friends.

In 1972 my Father died. He'd not been too good for a week or so. It was difficult to say what was wrong with him as his doctor was difficult for me to understand and as my Father was virtually stone deaf and refused to wear a hearing aid and indeed refused to wear a buttoned cardigan on the basis that both the aid and a cardigan were for old people. He was 82. I was in a position where I could slip up most afternoons as he only lived about three miles away. He was usually smoking and coughing and using the standard phrase of heavy smokers "But I've cut down a lot".

By Saturday afternoon it was serious. I came home had some tea and went back. Pat had very kindly made him some beef tea as he hadn't been able to keep anything down. He wouldn't even try it. The doctor came for the second time that day. I made out the word "hospital" and managed to get it through to him. He refused. I conned him into going by shouting to give Eileen a rest for a couple of days. He went. Eileen and I went about 9pm. He was in bed with an oxygen mask which he repeatedly tried to take off. I realise nurses have to follow a set procedure but all I could get out of the Matron is that he was seriously ill. That I knew. I brought Sister home for the night and she surprised me by saying, "I think we've seen the last of the old boy, don't you?" He died early Sunday morning.

So what sort of Dad was he? The best Dad in the world until I reached the age of fourteen. We were never enemies but he never understood why I walked out of the parcel packing job. The answer to that was simple. I didn't want to spend the next 51 years packing parcels and I still pack a mean parcel. I never saw myself as director material although when at Nevins an older rep from the Bradford T&A said to me "Your next move is running your own business." To me that was a million miles away. Dad didn't exactly disapprove of my further moves but didn't approve either and when I became Managing Director and major shareholder and moved the offices to the village where I lived, a beautiful Victorian house set in its own grounds, I don't think there was a murmur. He disliked what he called "fellers who have got on" so that was it. What really hurt more than anything is that up until he died I was an actor for over 12 years and he never came once.

There were a handful of people at the funeral. Eileen had the snack afterwards at their home. There were four of us, Eileen, Pat, me and Cousin Eric who'd travelled up from the West Country and needed a quick snack before the long journey home. No friends, neighbours or other relatives.

I've always wondered what made people tick, particularly my Dad. He'd had an above average education leaving at sixteen. His career at Royal London would have eventually given him a good job with an above-average salary and pension. He moved to a night job playing the piano in a closed down Methodist Chapel converted to a Silent Cinema. Then a day job and playing the piano at nights. Then running the concert party at nights and billiards several nights a week. Then the six days and nights running the cinema. On spare afternoons he would play billiards, dominoes, table tennis at the Methodist Institute and in the summer play bowls at the local park. From this you will see home didn't play an important part in his life. He had no interest in the house or its mishmash of contents. My mother often said "The only thing he cared about was the piano." I've mentioned earlier Dad could have toured the variety theatres with his slapstick distempering the living room ceiling routine. He also hated and ignored the sizeable garden. My Mum and I did most of it. I don't ever remember a man friend ever calling at the house. Similarly I only remember one woman coming when we moved from the Westovers to Stanningley Road. That was Joe's Mum, Mrs Lawrence who came but the once.

Mum had a cousin, Auntie Hilda, who lived in Pudsey. She walked down with her Airedale dog, Jack. Her own three Sisters came to see us often with tailoring jobs. My Father's family never came except to take us to Christmas parties.

Dad died with the money he had in his pocket. A year or so later an insurance policy paid out. I think it was £179 which my Sister wanted to split with me. However, she'd looked after him for almost 15 years, so I was happy for her to keep the lot. So endeth the life of Harold Nelson Pearson. No wallet, no bank account and a very small insurance policy. A good man in many ways though his attitude to life and mine were quite different. Who's to say which is right and which is wrong? Probably neither.

So now we're on family history, what about Mum? I have a photograph taken in her teens or when she was 21 and she was a beauty with dark naturally wavy hair. I'm going off on a tangent here. She was still attractive but much heavier, after childbirth. Cinema had a lot to do with it. Up until 1927, that's an odd date to slip in, well that's when talkies arrived and glamour came in. This is purely my theory and you may dismiss it as a load of old cobblers but hear me out. Up until talkies came in, millions of women produced kids, didn't wear make-up or fashionable clothes. It was one dress Monday to Saturday and one for church on Sunday.

> Another drift. Eddie Reindeer, "the wise crackpot", to my mind, a
> not very funny comedian usually had two spots on a bill and on his
> second appearance tottered on as an elderly fairy and sang:
> "No one loves a fairy when she's forty;"
> "No one loves a fairy when she's old".
> And that about sums it up. When you were forty you were past it.

In films particularly Hollywood films, heaven forbid women had plucked eyebrows, permanent waves, lipstick, painted fingernails and corsets, suspenders, directoire knickers, lisle stockings, flat heeled shoes were out. To millions of women including Mum these were also out. You had kids, you put on weight but not lipstick. Mum dabbed a powder puff on her face and went out. She went to the hairdresser twice a year. Before the annual holiday and at Christmas. Women who had plucked eyebrows, lipstick, painted fingernails were of easy virtues and to be avoided and divorce was a dirty word no matter what the circumstances were. I loved my Mum and still do but Mum and Dad just didn't get on. Sadly Mum was largely to blame. She egged Dad on to start an argument about his smoking, being out all the time, not wanting to make any improvements to the house or doing any gardening, knowing it would end in tears.

One evening I came home to the usual moan "We've had another row. He went out banging the door and lighting up the second he was out." I said I'd had enough of this. The next evening Mum said, "We had a long talk and both cried." Sadly it didn't last. At the outbreak of World War Two, Dad's Brother, my Uncle Charlie, his wife, Auntie Louie died. I think it was a brain tumour and my cousin Bobbie became his constant companion. Dad often said how wonderful that was. "It's marvellous y'know. They go everywhere together, holidays, cricket, theatre, like brother and Sister. Wonderful." Mum often said to me, "That's what he wants, me dead and out of the way so he can take Peggy everywhere." and that was unfortunately true. Mum died a few days after her 68th birthday and Dad got his wish. So very sad.

So what about my Sister and what about me? I'll do me first, it's quicker. Big headed, loud mouthed, never wrong. So that's me out of the way. There must be some plus points but I'm too shy to mention them off the top of my head… also can't think of any.

So what about "my Sister, Eileen". I've put it in quotes because there was a film of that name in the 1940s. Sister Peggy was my best friend for many years. She was my big Sister and it was a happy time. I'd always had lads in to play games but my Sister was and still is on her own admittance a loner, always content with her own company, never really at ease with other people. When we were kids we did lots of things together. One of the happiest times was on Saturday afternoons. We would go to the 'twopenny rush' at Dad's cinema then in Dad's tiny office we would have tea. Mrs Gaunt one of the cleaners would bring over a jog of over-sweetened tea and we would finish off with choc ice. Weather permitting it would be a walk around the nearby park and back to the Pav for the evening show. A short walk home, tea and biscuits then bed. I had a double bed, Eileen a single so she would come into my bed and make up stories about the film stars we had seen on the silver screen before Mum would shout, "That's it for now." and Eileen went into her own room. This routine ended when I discovered Rugby League and a bit later girls and stomach ache every time I took one out.

Back to childhood. Someone must have told big Sister about a chip shop down Bell Lane with a special offer for kids. If you bought a penny bag of chips, the owner popped on a small piece of battered fish 'on the house'.

> Sister: "Three penny bags of chips with a piece of fish on top please".
> Mr Wood: "Three?"
> Sister: "For our friend Elsie" (Mum)… not really a lie.
> Mr Wood: "And where is this Elsie?"
> Sister: "By the main road." Another half-truth.

The three bags of chips were prepared plus fish wrapped in white paper and newspaper and we ran home with our treats.

Mum had the plates warming, with salt and vinegar at the ready. What a treat for a penny a piece. I'm sure Mr Wood knew we were up to something, but it's a sign of the times that three whole pennies could make 2 kids and a Mum so happy. I think this would be just before we moved house, for I don't think it happened again.

At about the same time I became addicted to Rugby League my Sister had her fist mothercraft lesson at school, i.e. how babies were born. It was not for her and I seem to remember she fainted and from then on had to sit outside the classroom. There was no similar instruction for boys and my Dad never said a word to me on the subject. My knowledge came from lads in my class having lasses in my Sister's class who passed on the basic details. Motherhood was not my Sister's scene.

After leaving school she had several jobs before settling down as a very competent shorthand typist with a cloth merchant. I was called up in January 1943, she in December 1943. Being in the WAAF did her a lot of good. She was much brighter in her outlook. Back in civvy street she had a number of jobs before settling down as the secretary to the Leeds Coroner with a well-respected solicitors. And of course, in June 1957 she became Dad's companion and seemed very happy in that position.

Another odd memory comes to mind. A memory of yesteryear.

Poor little Lo age 10. We'd gone to pick up Dad and Eileen from Blackpool. Lo had had a couple of goes on an automatic machine and won.

> Dad: "Well done. Keep on, your luck's in."
> Me: "It's your choice love. Keep going and you'll almost certainly end up losing or you can treat yourself to an ice cream with your own money from that kiosk on the end."
> Lo opted for an ice cream with a few trimmings.
> Dad under his breath: "I'd've bought the kid an ice cream."
> Me: "But you didn't did you? She had a choice and is very happy. You keep on and always lose in the end. That's the name of the game Dad." or something like that.
> As Dad was settling up, outside the guest house my Sister said, "They're all after him in there but he belongs to me and nobody's taking him from me." She then repeated this phrase to Dad and even Dad seemed taken aback with this and replied, "Aye, I suppose so, yes."
> Just before bedtime Lo looked worried and asked, "Are Granddad Pearson and Auntie Peggy married?" It was easily explained away and no harm was done but my Sister not being a children person didn't see any harm to it.

Pat, daughter and I settled nicely into village life. It was and still is a lovely place to live. Before the three or four mills were built it was a textile village. A few of the older houses still have walled up windows where the hand spinning wheel workers sat, working in daylight, long before gas and electricity. Mills and any other factory based businesses produce communities and friendly rivalry. If you worked for Garnetts or Grimshaws or Harpers or the one I've forgotten you were proud of what you produced and friendly rivalry and banter played a part of life.

A very old church, a couple of chapels, a dramatic society, the allotments, a cricket club, a football club, a bowling green, a village park, not much different to anywhere else I suppose but they do give the area a sort of personality of its own, a proud personality.

We moved into Calverley before the nearby supermarkets. There were thirty or more shops, 2 fish and chip shops, two butchers, two bakers, shoe repairer, haberdasher etc and they were locally owned and run, now down to half a dozen or so. Supermarkets and other big shops are wonderful ways of quick fix shopping and life is much faster these days. An example:

I was going to a house when the woman next door was locking up. We were on nodding terms.

She: "I can't stop. I have to get to the chemists in town."
Me: "There's one in the village."
She: "Where?"
Me: "Thornhill Street."
She: "Where's that?"
Me: "The main street over there."
She: "I've lived here two years and never knew that."

Of course the two pubs (now three) had their own friendly rivalry.

With our work for the Cricket Club and Dramatic Society and Pat being a regular churchgoer and cleaner and a member of the recently formed NSPCC committee, we were soon accepted. Kids made friends at school. The three Garnett children lived a field away from us. I made a stile over our garden wall and "I'm going over the field to see the girls" or "the girls are coming over" were constant words. Despite the pressures of running a very successful business with a great deal of help we were happy. Everybody loved Pat, a smiling face, she got on with everybody, particularly the village characters who stopped by for a chat when she was in the front garden.

I wasn't a regular churchgoer. I liked the Easter and Christmas services and never missed when Louise started Sunday School. Gordon Lane, the long serving vicar at the time accepted this and we became good friends. He could use a few choice words strictly between ourselves. On one occasion I was helping Pat to decorate the church for a special festival and got talking to another helper, a young rather serious chap. Here's the gist.

Him: "I was at a rally on Woodhouse Moor and things weren't going well for me." God tapped me on the shoulder and said, "Don't worry everything will be OK." And it was.
Me: "In English?"
Him: "Sorry?"
Me: "Did God speak in English?"
Him: "Well yes."

We moved apart. Rev. Gordon Lane approached. "I've see you've been talking to the nutter."

More recently a friend of mine from 50 years or more ago died. I sent a card and something for the collection. His son and wife were attending a band concert in the park one Sunday. They came to see us, very religious; church am, couldn't stay long, church p.m. For no apparent reason she said, "Stop. God's talking to me."

Pat stifled a grin and went into the kitchen. Several minutes—a long time for God on his busiest day—she said, "Thank you." I posed the same question, "In English?" They were nice people and promised to pray for my leg at the evening service. As I said, it was open all hours for him. Is

God a him? Nobody knows, do they? Nobody's ever seen him have they? Maybe they have. *Stop rabbiting on Ron, get on with the story.*

Would you like to hear about my gall bladder operation? Now it's micro surgery, then it wasn't. I was in a week or more. On Sunday my PA came in with a load of work. Pat came in. PA left. Pat: "If you're going to do a runner do it with her, she's wonderful." She was. We went everywhere. After a long journey she always gave me a little kiss. It was lovely. She got pregnant, not guilty. She was very organised. George arrived. Pat: "In two weeks that kid'll be potty trained." They moved to York.

Monday I got a phone call from the Playhouse. They were in a jam. Someone had dropped out of the play going into rehearsal that night. Couldn't I help out? I explained I had a big slit in my stomach and a catheter. "Yes but we are desperate and it's only in Act Three." I'm not joking, this actually happened.

The specialist came in with my gallstones in a plastic bag. "How do I know they're mine? Bet you've got a big glass jar like a sweetie jar and you just dip in for a handful."

"Ron you're a cynic." Then he doubled up with mirth and said, "I'll remember that and tell it whenever I can." It didn't help a lot. I was born a worrier and a worrier I will stay. Fortunately I have a sense of humour which I hope I'm passing on to you.

Pat's Mum was diagnosed with pancreatic cancer in the summer of 1971. No treatment. By Christmas it was really bad. Yellow complexion, couldn't get her teeth in, couldn't eat. Pat's Father loved Christmas. Paper hat, ate everything, full Christmas dinner, pudding, sugared almonds, dates, figs, crystallised fruits, nuts then supper. He sang consistently the title of a silly song 'On the good ship Yaki Hiki Doola'. He was a really happy man. In late January early February I met my close friend Dr Gordon Edgar coming away from their house. We had stayed with our friend Dr Keith Manchester in Bradford. Gordon said, "I think I'll be writing the certificate within a day or two." I went to the house. Pat's Father was his usual happy self. He'd moved out to another bedroom but this didn't dampen his spirits. I went upstairs. Gordon was right. "Ron, could you move that heater nearer the bed. I don't think Douglas could manage it. I'm a damn nuisance, aren't I?" I move the heater saying, "Yes you are."

"Oh Ron don't make me laugh it's so painful!" I kissed her on the forehead and said what I always said to her, "Behave yourself."

I went back home and told Pat who spent Friday through to Saturday with her Mum. Her Mum died in the early hours of Sunday morning. Pat came home very distressed. I made tea and toast and she went to bed. About 10:30 the doorbell rang. "I'll never forgive my daughter for what she's done to me, not telling me my good lady was in that condition." I got him inside. More tea. I let fly. "Good God man she was bright yellow at Christmas, couldn't eat. You're sleeping in a separate bed. Pat hasn't slept for 48 hours."

It made no difference. "Never forgive, never." I've always been interested in what makes people tick. I think I got the key to it. His Father not recognising him on the train, forcing him into the business when he wanted to be an organist, serving petrol, swilling the frontage, parking cars, talking to customers, lighting the taxi drivers fire, getting under old cars and mending them with all sorts of bits and pieces. Booking his holidays and forgetting to include "my good lady". Didn't know her birthday and on and on and singing that ridiculous song. They were all body armour to ward off the realities of life.

There was a parallel in Charles Walls who in order to ward off criticism by never being wrong no matter how wrong he was. I was in tears writing this, they were both very nice men and I was very lucky to be running a successful advertising agency and living in a lovely house with a happy wife and daughter and so on.

After the funeral, like the rest of his problems, I don't think he ever mentioned 'my good lady' again. That's that out of the way. It needed to be said to reveal two very different but similar men, good men who couldn't face life's realities.

Here's another good smile, well really a belly laugh.

We decided to spend a few days in Windsor for our Silver Wedding Anniversary. We'd been there on several occasions. It's an interesting town with an excellent theatre and a short train ride into London if I needed to go on business. I'd recently bought a new suit in light brown plus cream shirt and posh tie. Pat looked absolutely lovely in a navy velvety dress and a few trimmings. We ordered turkey for our celebration, Saturday evening dinner. The elderly waiter came in with two plates of food under silver covers. He tripped, the silver tops fell to the floor with a din. We were the centre of attention. He stumbled across the floor. I had an early dinner, turkey and all the trimmings in my face, on my suit, dripping from my tie. Victoria Wood's sketch '*Two soups please*', wasn't a patch on this. In Oliver Hardy mode I moved some gravy from my eyes and Pat stifled a laugh. The other diners were in shock.

The hotel was marvellous. I went upstairs and changed and the suit was dry cleaned, the shirt washed and pressed, the tie cleaned as best they could plus a new tie and no charge for the meal plus a new bottle of wine although we'd hardly started on the original one. For this to happen on a Saturday night and all done and dusted by Sunday noon was superb. In the commotion Pat must have mentioned it was our silver wedding and when we got to our room there was a big box of hand-made choccies on our bed with a very big "with compliments" card. Why do these things happen to me? Some people live a very grey life. Mine is often in glorious Technicolor with a few awkward moments. I know which I'd choose.

On the home front Pat's Father moved out of the small house into retirement accommodation in the village. A living room, kitchen, bathroom, bedroom, a far cry from the big house with servants he'd known before his marriage. As always he seemed happy enough.

Chapter 31:
Fisherman's Friend + a Million Quid Walks in the Door

I'd built up a few clients in West Lancashire starting with Somic in Preston. Back in 1954 Arthur Barthel took me over and they took us out to a very good lunch and when Arthur left I took over until they were bought out in the late sixties. They made everything out of paper or rather wood pulp, mainly flooring mats but also chairs and string for the horticultural trade. It was a tedious train trip with a change and a long wait at Todmorden. The Blackburn family ran the business and one of them had married a girl who had lived in Roundhay, Leeds where Pat had lived. One Friday evening they were driving to Leeds so took me home and their daughter and mine had a really happy couple of hours together, with the doll's house I had made and Pat bought the furniture. Pat and Mrs Blackburn shared many Roundhay memories. From then on it was always a happy trip particularly when I got the Austin A35.

It became increasingly obvious to me that making friends with clients was a lot better than liquid lunches, dinner parties and all sorts of other boozy pastimes. On one occasion in London Somic's London man Stan Lucas said, "What are you doing tonight?" I said, "I want to see a musical called '*Most happy fella*' which had got good reviews."

"Would you mind if my wife and I went with you?" It was a very good evening at the theatre, my treat. Afterwards they took me to dinner, his treat. Two lovely people and no hangovers.

Other clients in West Lancashire included Long Playing Record Library in the old railway station at Squires Gate. Not a big spender but with full pages in *The Gramophone* and *Wireless World* it was a no trouble account which gave Donald Maud our classical/jazz musician a lot of pleasure.

GIC Pools Company in Blackpool (never heard of them), neither had I but they were a smallish football pools company who took small ads in all the national dailies at a decent profit and always insisted in taking me out to lunch.

Here's the rags to riches story. Well, not really rags but absolutely certainly riches.

I was in a local shop and seeing Fisherman's Friend were made in

Fleetwood bought a packet, went to see them. Doreen and Tom Lofthouse were in a cavernous building. I think they were the old tram sheds. The back story was the Lofthouse family had a chemist's shop in the High Street and a relation, I think it was an uncle, had a hand press and made the tablets in the back room. In the summer months they had a little kiosk on the sea front. They were interested in my pitch but had no money to spend on advertising.

A few months later the phone rang. "It's Doreen Lofthouse here. We've £200 to spend on advertising. Are you interested?" In my head "No". The profit on this would be 5 quid but if I added it to my other clients in the area so it would cost very little in petrol and worth a try. This account grew and so did FF. They moved into brand new premises by the harbour. For many years they were one of our most profitable pieces of business. When we had a bit of a do in our new premises they both turned up in Rolls Royce's. The agency could do no wrong. We even designed and had produced a mirror using the famous packet and of course the tv commercials featuring Brian Glover. They decided to launch a mint called *Mariner's mints*. I'd done quite a bit of work for Rowntree's in York and my contact there told me mint was a very tricky product to work with. I also tried to get them to give Fisherman's Friend a bigger image, i.e. Mariner's Mints by Fisherman's Friend in bold type. I queried the marketing strategy and apparently they'd got some trade telephone directories for Scotland and sent a postcard to every wholesaler. Was that enough?

I was very concerned that the product hardly feature the very well-known Fisherman's Friend brand and that a postcard to wholesalers would not have much effect. Pat and I were on holiday in Pitlochry in Scotland. I went into a well-stocked shop with a rather odd order. "I'd like a packet of every mint you sell and the list of the prices plus a packet of Fisherman's Friend." Doreen told me the mints would have the same number of mints per packet as the Friends. Pat was mystified. I asked the shopkeeper what was the most popular brand. Without thinking she said, "Kemps". They were a Scottish brand and like big Mint Imperials.

Back at the hotel, I emptied all the different packets on the bed and counted the contents and worked out the price per mint. Kemps were far and away the best value for money. Mariners were far and away the worst. In Scotland that matters. We made the commercial, at £17,000, the most expensive we'd ever made. We booked the slots on Scottish TV around £25,000, and fast forward to the January launch. Doreen and Tom went on holiday. Duncan their son rings me.

Duncan: "Ron the Mariners launch is next week. Mum and Dad are away and we've absolutely no retail coverage in Scotland. I suggested you could hire the Scottish Television sales team for a week at a £1,000, and give them a pep talk, show the commercial and hope for the best." It was snowing. Duncan hired a van, stocked it with MMs and off we drive to Glasgow. From memory I think coverage was around 3 or 4 percent before this sales drive and around 70% after. I can only presume this was a failure. The mints didn't sell. We got the sack. Some years later Tom and Doreen Lofthouse made the Sunday Times rich list. Duncan tried his best to get me back in to no avail.

Postscript.

1987 my play *Harry's Kingdom* went out Sunday 9pm BBC 1. I got a letter from Doreen. "We saw your play and enjoyed it immensely. Recognised you immediately but why didn't you give yourself a bigger part?" I wasn't in it. So endeth the parable of the Fisherman who became a Mariner and drowned in the choppy waters of Bonny Scotland.

I can't leave the Fisherman's Friend episode without mentioning a gory story with a very odd ending.

I was driving to Fleetwood when my car conked out. For many years I'd driven Rovers but at the time to change there weren't any. Bradford 9 months wait, Leeds, Harrogate, Ripon 12 months wait. You couldn't spec colour or engine size or anything else. That was the British car industry that was.

Where's all this getting? Some people… just be patient.

So I bought a second hand Merc 250 Coupe in green metallic my pride and joy. One fault, it kept cutting out completely then started again. Each time this happened I drove it to Charles Sidney's in Bradford for their highly skilled German mechanic to look at it. Nothing wrong with it they said. This time it broke down well on the way to Fleetwood. From memory I think I was approaching the A666 Swinton junction if you're familiar with that area.

Here we go, two men running up the steep embankment to the motorway, both ghastly white.

> One said: 'See that.'
> Me: 'See what?'
> Man: 'Down there.'

I looked, there was a railway line parallel to the motorway. A red bloody head by the track.

The two men ran across the busy motorway and disappeared. It so happened there was one of the little black Police phone boxes a foot away. I rang in and told them the story and asked them if they could ring the National Breakdown (now Green Flag) to get me home.

A few minutes later a Police car arrives, one man carrying a plastic orange bag, they go down the embankment, popped the crimson head into the bag. The usual questions:

Police 'Did you witness the event? Etc., etc and they were off. I then used the phone again and rang Doreen Lofthouse and she was very under-standing when I cancelled the appointment and was towed home.'

There's another bit to the story. I told my friend Randall this event he was never topped and said:

"Aye well there was a similar event a few months ago a few miles from here?"

He went into detail, mentioned a surname. It would appear this head belonged to the husband of one of my ex-girlfriends. Lucky Ron.

This may raise a smile. It did for me.

Is there a living person who has not heard of KFC? Their British base was originally in two rooms in St Annes on Sea. Worth a call methinks. I called more than once. The chap running it promised to spend £14,000 on advertising. It never altered. It never happened. It was then known as Kentucky Fried Chicken featuring the easily recognisable mug of Colonel Sanders who perfected the 'secret ingredient'. One day I called and there were a dozen or more Colonel Sanders, tall ones, small ones, thin ones, fat ones but all with the colonel type glasses, string tie and white suit. They were, I found out, KFC reps at an annual conference. Whether they wore these outfits on their daily sales trips I never found out. They moved their two room operation to a purpose built unit in London. Worth a call. They asked me to re-design a big 48 sheet poster. We had to lay the pieces on the ground and photograph from the attic to get an image of what we were altering. They loved it. Correction a 20 plus something oik loved it then he wasn't there. I never got to wear a white suit at their annual conference.

How about this? A million quid walked in the door, well sort of. The Yorkshire local manager of Anglian Double Glazing wanted the agency to handle his advertising. Now this takes a bit of explaining. You see the area manager for Yorkshire lived in Leamington Spa. His half back lived in Poole, Dorset. Now the Birmingham area was run from Newmarket and a bloke from London was responsible for Scotland or Wales or somewhere. The company was based in Norwich and the sales director lived in South-ampton. I had a bit of a problem with the man in Wood Green and I never did know which area he represented. It could have been Wood Green. No that would be stretching things too far. Let me explain.

All the reps were on commission only deals. A top rep could earn £40,000 PA, big money in the seventies. When an opportunity arose they were promoted to area manager and the regional manager also had a cut.

So I had to go to Head Office in Norwich, swing these men over and the annual spend would be a cool million. Our next biggest client was a hundred thousand. I took Suzanne, the gorgeous Suzanne with me. I put her case in the boot, she got in the car holding a brown paper bag. "What's in there then?"

"Peas." Nothing suspicious there then, and who knows a brown paper bag full of peas could be the deciding factor in swinging a million pound contract.

There is an explanation. It was a favour for her husband. Apparently, he's a mastermind in the podded pea set-up and his wonderful wife was taking a brown paper bag of this delicacy to a man in Norwich in the hope of swinging a big deal in the flat country.

Apparently all the decent hotels in Norwich were full up. The one we got was not exactly a flop house. I think it was a stop-over for HGV men. We'd looked at many options on which to hang on the Anglian brand and Studio Director, Mike Davies, came up with the word "trust". It proved to be a winner in every sense of the word. Apparently while Chairman, George Williams, was sexing chickens... yes, that's what he did... he'd had some double glazing installed in his then modest abode. It was rubbish and by all accounts the firm had done a runner. So Trust was a key word in George Williams mind. Most of the area managers were against me. One or two got a kickback from their local newspaper. I'd prepared a folder with some of the existing homemade ads and opposite each one an agency equivalent. The word "trust" was quite small but used as a tag alongside the Anglian nameplate. George Williams approved, head office men approved, the area managers approved. We were home and dry. I didn't want to be invoicing individual areas at several thousand a month and being paid when they got around to it. How to tackle this? Head on.

I asked if I could invoice direct to head office with individual branch accounts and could I be paid 90% on receipt of invoice plus 10% for any queries. We never had any trouble over this and I don't think there were any queries on the remaining 10%. There was a hell of a lot of details to work out but we were through. A million quid for a piddling little Pudsey agency.

Bill Hancock, John Keyser and John Mordecai Mason were the big hitters at head office. Matt Hancock MP was the spitting image of Bill Hancock and both lived in the same area. John Keyser couldn't have been more helpful. John M Mason was a stumbling block. At big 18st Welshman he threw his weight about a bit but once the ads started to work and the system was put in place he became a really good friend. We talked Rugby Union and Rugby League and he was a wonderful help to me when a personal tragedy struck. More later.

John Hart the sales director based at Southampton took Suzanne and I to a very good dinner but warned us it would be a bumpy ride. "These boys are up to every dodge in the book so watch it." My answer was simple, "If the ads worked and brought them more business they should be happy." As an afterthought no double glazing salesman is ever really happy. Tomorrow, probably evening, they have to close on yet another deal or there's no extra money going into the bank.

At last we were alone. We'd an hour or more work to before we called it a day. Suzanne gave me the usual goodnight kiss, our eyes met. How corny can you get? Well they did so there. The bed was a foot away. It was a temptation. We didn't but Suzanne really was my best friend. We laughed a lot, travelled the country by car and occasionally by plane. She was a lousy shorthand typist and said so at the interview. I knew she was the helper I needed. Simple answer, get a good shorthand typist. With a million quid bonus coming into the bank we could afford that. Suzanne was tall, blonde and had a lovely mellow voice. Diane was tiny, dark and very bubbly and giggled a lot. She became Diddy Di and I like to think we were a very good team for the agency and for me.

I'm glad I got this over without being too mushy. Time to put the kettle on and dip into the biscuit barrel for a couple of Jaffa cakes. Now here's a bit of useless knowledge. Did you know some of Europe's top brains sat around a big table for a considerable time, munching and trying to decide whether what they were eating were cakes, buns or biscuits? After much brain searching, they reached a momentous decision, Jaffa cakes were… wait for it… Jaffa cakes. Phew. They'd need a long holiday in the sun after that ordeal.

Now then. I liked wine gums as a lad, different shades with Bordeaux, Claret, Sherry etc stamped on them. They tasted of orange, lemon, liquorice and nail polish, not a hint of wine. No problem there then. I believe they are still made by Lions.

Lions also made fireworks in Huddersfield. Amazing what animals can do with a little kindness. Ok it's a smile but let's get serious.

What about cotton wool? Is it cotton? Is it wool or a bit of both? Don't tell the lads in Brussels I've mentioned this. It could have global consequences. Are manhole covers now personhole covers? We should be told. Sorry, I forgot we're not in the E.U. anymore but it's a good smile.

So where are we? *If you don't know Ron we're sunk.* Here we go. Yet another funny thing.

John MM invited me to a regional bun fight on bonfire night. There was no Anglian bonfire. That's not the funny thing. The minute I walked into the room John, 6'3" and big with it, lifted me high in the air. That's not the funny thing but an indication that I was well in with JMM.

Here's the funny thing.

I was having a quiet GT with ice and slice when a vaguely familiar face approached me. "Ron mate." Who was he? He was a regional manager. "I've invited my girlfriend to this do but the wife's decided to come. Can you take the girlfriend off my hands and give her a good time. She's over there and understands my predicament." I had no option but to do what the man said. It was 8pm, lights out at midnight.

Now I have given you a hint about my dancing skills. They're non-existent. She was a very pleasant 20 something. We had a chat, we had some grub, things were going nicely. 8:0pm, another 3½ hours and we're home and dry. Now I gave her a hint of my dancing skills. They played a waltz. I was dragged onto the floor. I did alright, she didn't. It was going to be a long night. Salvation, there was an hotel bonfire outside. Coats on, we went. Baked potatoes in paper serviettes with butter and salt, bonfire toffee and all sorts of snacks. She bravely went in for the last waltz and I helped her limp into a taxi. Never spoke to my mate the regional manager again but it gives you an idea of the shenanigans that go on at double glazing do's.

Anglian grew and grew, quite a few problems. A bloke in Southend said he'd come up and punch me if I didn't do it his way. I didn't. My way worked. We became good mates.

The head of Anglian Double Glazing was George Williams, the richest man I've ever met. He told me about being a bootlegger, ex chicken sexer, and was now one of the country's richest men. You can look up a lot of this on your clever phone but there will be a few more bits that will add a little more colour to the picture. If I didn't know it I couldn't write about it.

On my first visit to George William's house, on my right was a lake full of flamingos, not just half a dozen but a fleet of them. Sounds good that, a fleet of flamingos. Have I coined a new collective noun? I understood that a nearby trout stream had been diverted through the grounds. A nine-hole golf course was another plus point. I was told there were indoor and outdoor pools. I met George in the billiards room where the delicious Tanqueray Gin was in plentiful supply. I think what impressed me most was a small item, a current copy of the *Geographica* magazine in the gent's lavatory. Outside there was a fleet of vehicles and a helicopter and this wasn't his sole abode. I had more than one meeting with him at his mews house in London and there's more. His second wife was Cornish and I was told he bought a dis-used monastery in Cornwall and had it 'done up' for her. His third wife was I believe a West Indian beauty queen. A charming, very ordinary man we often talked about our humble beginnings. We spent lots of holidays in Guernsey. George knew the resort well and it was always a pleasure to meet this most likeable man.

Now, I had the most awful day of my life, so far. I'd flown down to Anglian. Their main offices were within walking distance of the airport. About 11am I received a call from Keith, the man who would replace Kenneth Wilkinson but then did a bunk. Here are the exact words. "Hello Mr Pearson. Your wife's not dead but she's been in a serious road accident and is in Leeds General Infirmary. No visitors allowed except you. Can you get back fairly quickly?"

The opening few words I'll never forget. John Mordecai Mason was with me when I took the call. He was brilliant, made a call, drove me back to the Williams house where a helicopter and pilot were waiting to take me to Leeds Bradford Airport. Suzanne had left the company to have her baby but new secretary Margaret wouldn't allow me to drive my own car. She drove me to the hospital.

Pat was in Intensive Care in a single room. She was drowsy and said, "Hello love. I thought you were in Norwich today." I was given 10 minutes with her, the nurse not leaving the room. Pat just managed a smile. Her eyes closed. That was it.

Apparently she was coming out of our drive to go to the supermarket in her Mini when she was hit by a big Volvo, the driver having assisted driving controls. The Sister who was with her throughout my visit said she'd dislocated or sprained almost every bone in her upper body. As soon as I got home I was in tears. My neighbours were wonderful. One looked after our dog until I got home. Another cooked me a meal and each night I was invited to a different house for dinner. I had a further problem. It was February 1982 and our first grandchild was due in June. Her husband coped very well. I told him Pat had had a bump. They were keeping her in hospital for a few days and there was no need to come up from Leicester.

Pat was in LGI for about two weeks. I collected her and brought her home with strict instructions as to what she could do, virtually nothing. Our good friend and doctor for over 20 years Keith Manchester visited several times. Pat's right shoulder was down, Pat thought, down a lot but it was down but if you didn't point it out if wouldn't be noticeable. Pat couldn't dress her upper body and her good friend, Sheila took a few of my more colourful shirts, slit them down the back and added tapes so I could dress Pat that way. Vicar Gordon Lane was a regular visitor as a friend not in his prayer mode although Pat was a regular churchgoer.

The police arrived, a very understanding man and woman. They were almost in tears but had to explain that Pat was the guilty party coming out of a drive onto a main road and causing the crash. The man was unharmed but there was a fair sized bump on his passenger door. Pat would have penalty points on her licence but no further action.

The next few weeks were difficult but I couldn't believe how helpful people were. Everybody loved Pat. Women in general are a lot braver than men. Pat didn't make a complete recovery but was soon out and about and driving again.

On one of our first shopping outings to Ilkley we saw a little glass ornament of a rugby ball on a plinth. Pat sent it with a thank you card to John Mason and he wrote a lovely letter in return. Incidentally he told me the basic materials for a standard double glazing fitting were 13% of the overall cost. I said, "What 30%." He said, "No 13%." So why didn't some bright spark sell them cheaper? Because once you've added made to measure manufacturing costs, delivery and fitting costs and a percentage for the salesman, a percentage for the area manager, the regional manager, the sales director and the big boss and a healthy profit mark-up that's your offer price. It's also a bulk business. Little companies often don't last long because you need a big turnover to create a decent profit margin. There's quite a bit more to it than I have explained but I've told you Anglian was certainly a busy account.

Here's a beauty. Due to other commitments, I set off at 3:30am, I repeat 3.30am, one Wednesday with our media man by road to Southampton to give an advertising talk at 10:30am. Quick lunch and we're on again at 2:30. Sales director John Hart took us on a round trip of local branches. 5:30pm to 8pm free time. John and his wife then took us to dinner. At 11pm we set off for Bath. At 2am I got a room with a loud cylinder noise. Finally bed at

3am. twenty four hours plus without sleep. 10:30am talk in Bath, 2:30pm talk in Bristol, 4:30pm drive home, me at the wheel for the full round trip. I took Friday off and made a good profit out of this effort. Each week I got the sales reports from all the areas and they were on the up week after week. They decided on a TV campaign using a big London agency. I met the London Agency team, we got on a treat. I was invited to Slough for the TV launch. In the theatre they'd done a sort of replica of windows, doors etc used in the commercial plus people dressed in monkey suits running in and out the doors. I can't remember whether their faces were covered or made up like monkeys but George William's current wife was a monkey. They also hired well known character actor Harry Fowler for the gig but whether he was in a monkey suit I can't remember. Nothing to do with double glazing but ventriloquist Bob Carolgees did his act. Then a real mish mash of various bits and pieces. Fred Hodges had started helping me on the account, I said to Fred, "There's a play there y'know." More about that and Harry Fowler later.

At 7:30pm that night I was on stage at Ilkley Playhouse. Here's how. I think Fred must have had a mobile. He'd left his car at my house. Friday traffic very slow. I got home at 7:05pm, Pat handed me a packet of crisps and a Kit Kat, I told her to ring Ilkley with the problem and have someone ready to park my car. It was a mammoth part in the Neil Simon comedy *Last of the red hot lovers*. Never off stage. I think there must have been an announcement. 7:25 in dressing room, shirt, suit, tie laid out for me. No make-up. 7:30 on stage. I got a round of applause before a word was spoken. I always go through a role on the day of the performance. No time for that. It went like a bomb. When I got home I didn't need any coaxing to take the wooden stairs to Bedfordshire.

Now here's another funny thing.

The piddling little agency from Pudsey was asked to make the next Anglian TV commercial and book screen time. Not London. I called a meeting and laid down the principal ingredient, namc, name, name. Commercials costing mammoth amounts of money fail because they look good but in 30 second fail to ram home the product or service offered. I turned down half a dozen efforts but an idea was forming in my head and this was the result.

Six foot or higher plastic letters A...N...G...L...I...A...N.

A girl by each letter. "Gimme an A. Letter lights up. Gimme a N, gimme a 'G.L.I.A.N'."

"Then you've got Anglian." I forget the rest but it was a good jingle with a pay off line about trust.

We shot it on one of the biggest sound stages in Europe. I was hoisted up in the crane viewer 40 ft up on my own, absolutely terrifying.

We started the auditions for the girls at 10:30am and finished the shoot at 3:30am. The afternoon before a singing group and a small band recorded the song. The girls on the set mimed the words. A couple of weeks later I took George Williams and half a dozen top men to a private viewing and lunch at Wheelers famous fish restaurant. The commercial was very good and slammed home the two key points, Anglian and trust. The commercial went out on all major channels in early autumn. I was down at my daughter's one day and saw an Anglian van at the end of the street. I strolled over. They'd seen the commercial and liked it and business had been on the up for week after week. My weekly figures confirmed this. We never did another TV campaign for them.

Another area manager invited me to stay at his house for the night. We met in his office about 3:30pm. He said he wasn't much of a drinker but would I like a drink? Yes please. He produced a bottle of gin from a deep drawer in his desk and poured two generous slurps of neat gin. Fancy another? No thank you. The bottle goes in the drawer. There's a clink. The bottle has a least one companion.

We get to his house, gold taps etc, swimming pool, everything you could think of. I had a shower, correction I got in the shower. The gold taps didn't work, had a good wash, the gold taps just about worked. Went across the road for an excellent evening meal, came back. I noticed my companions appeared to be shorter. They didn't wear shoes in the house. The wife and I sat down. He lay on the floor, no he didn't die, he had a bad back. His wife got out lots of coins, maps and other things from, I think, the Franklin Mint. Very interesting but they were still in their inner wrappings and tucked away. Quite a pleasant evening except she thought wrestling was for real and I knew to the contrary.

Eight wrestlers appearing in Leeds Sunday afternoon then to Manchester, in taxis for that evening. Then the same routines says it all. She accepted the situation and we laughed about it. Home again and a few weeks later I got the sad news that the regional manager's wife had died. I sent a letter of condolence. Couple or three weeks later the regional manager's deputy called in to see me as his boss was off work. Here we go.

A few days after the funeral he goes to the house, knocks on the door and the wife answers it. He apparently went chalk white and sat on a wall. Have you guessed it? The wife had an identical twin and they always dressed alike. Geddit?

A few months later I'm at yet another do and this regional manager introduces me to his new companion, a pretty young thing 25 going on 18 I guessed. "Say good evening to the gentleman and shake hands." was his instruction. She did. I moved on.

Back on home territory John M.M. decided to come to the office and for the 'copter' to land in the farmer's field opposite the agency. Half the village turned up for the landing. I got Fred Hodges to take the pilot to lunch and I took John to Harry Ramsden's. Cracks were appearing in the relationship. Although they had record weeks with the TV campaign too many managers wanted to do their own thing. Incidentally TV stations would only take bookings from accredited IPA agency and I held the copyright for the jingle

I had composed for the commercial. Believe me managers run this business. I met with Bill Hancock and apparently they all got on with Fred and I took a back seat. I was almost at retirement. A few months after I retired they moved the majority of the business out of the agency and left us with the Want Ads. A million quid goes, a few thousand stays. It was nice while it lasted.

Chapter 32:
Retirement

Now I had to start thinking about retirement. I didn't want to but it had to be done. Colin Harrison joined the company in 1959, John Oldfield in the mid 60s. Colin was the more experienced but didn't always get on with certain clients, one threatening to move the business if he visited them again. Kenneth Wilkinson would retire the same day as me and had an accountant waiting to step into his shoes. That didn't quite work out for the meek and mild contender left his wife and left the company so we had to recruit. John Oldfield could be brash at times but he got my vote because I'd worked with him for many years and he'd been a tower of strength during my breakdown. Colin Harrison was only a few years younger than me.

I called Colin into my office one late Friday afternoon and told him I'd come to a difficult decision regarding my successor, it would be John Oldfield etc. Colin cut me short, "Oh well, that's it then. You can have my notice right now and I'll confirm in writing first thing Monday morning. I'll set up on my own." He'd done this several times. Being an actor helped, long pause, normal voice. "Fair enough Colin. I'll talk to KW this weekend and…"

> Colin: "Oh well look…"
> Me: "You've held us to ransom a time or two in the past but I've just accepted your notice and I'll call Kenneth tomorrow am and we'll work out a deal for you."

There were one or two "I know but" and that was it. On Monday I called him in.

"You get a month's salary and it's up to you whether you work or not. You get a generous goodwill bonus and there are a couple of smaller clients you handle and one of mine can go with you. If you place artwork with the Studio we'll charge you at trade rates and the same applies to printing blocks from us." Colin couldn't have been happier. Ron couldn't have been happier. A deal well done from both sides. I was sorry to see Colin go but it was the best of two very close alternatives.

John Oldfield was now a director. It produced many advantages and quite a few problems. Chris Lear had joined us as an above average artist,

227

became studio manager. We put him in a car and he handled a few clients. John wanted him on the board. Ken Glover our accountant was called in and wanted things to settle. John didn't. Chris was on the board. John wanted him off the board. Now there were extenuating circumstances but these were hinted at before Chris was promoted.

Mike Davies, never an artist but a very good, somewhat vociferous studio manager and director of Elmwood Studios. John wanted him on the board. Ken Glover 'Not again John'. Mike joined the board. John wanted Mike off. Mike left the company. All these took a number of years but you get the general pattern and I have to admit John became a driving force in the agency.

Kenneth and I plus the ever faithful Donald Maud retired on 30 June 1984. There was a bit of a do. I'd taken on the role of chairman and was semi-retired only attending key meetings and occasional work at home.

Pat said, "You've turned down a lot of parts in the past due to business commitments now take all that's offered." Did she regret it? I appeared in four and directed three. I had Sunday nights at home and that was about it but daytime was the difficult time. I have a big garden and bought another piece so that kept me fairly busy. I went for long walks, often in the rain. We had the fittest dog in the village. We went out to lunch twice a week. *Aw come on, it wasn't a hardship was it?* It took me a year or so to settle down into comfortable retirement and of course there was the writing... more later.

In the run-up to retirement we began house hunting as we realised our biggish house on Carr Road would eventually be too big for us and too many stairs and it was getting noisy with traffic. We looked all over and where did we end up? In our own back garden. How lucky can you get? Our long time neighbour and village post master Peter Foulds said, "You know your garden's building land?" We didn't know and on enquiring found out it was about to run out so we had a bungalow built in our own garden, quiet, out of the way and built to our own design. We watched every stone go into that house.

Probably a Saturday in July we had a bit of a do for the NSPCC and mentioned we would be selling 40 Carr Road. Sunday a.m., a phone call, "My name is John Rusbatch. We know Barbara Hugill on the N.S.P.C.C Committee. Can my wife and I come and look at your house?" There was a bit more than that but you don't need to know anymore, do you? A deal was done on a handshake and that side of the deal was absolutely trouble fee. However, there's always a however isn't there? We were told by the builder we'd be in by Christmas. I had my doubts so told John and Monica to work on February 1.

One Christmas Eve we went to the carol service at our wonderful parish church, came down to the bungalow with coffee, mince pies, cheese and a packet of crisps each. We certainly knew how to celebrate big time. I lit the Baxi fire with bits of wood and shavings plus a few pieces of coal. Pat brought down a very small Christmas tree to put on the window sill. We sat on upturned crates and smiled at each other. This was ours. It was such a wonderful and simple evening and so full of happiness. There were problems. There always is.

We moved out and in on Valentine's Day in a blizzard. The drive was flooded with a broken drain plus a foot of snow so a van couldn't get down. With the help of our good friends Ann and Randall Paine we moved everything down the snow filled garden, not easy. We had to get out as John and Monica had to get out of their flat that day to make way for new tenants. We were tired. We were in and of course moving in on a special day you never forget it.

14 February 1979 until June 2017 were wonderful years and John and Monica perfect neighbours. Nothing lasts forever but we had 38 marvellous years plus a few upsets in Cliff Cottage so named because 40 Carr Road was Cliffe Holme. Both are in stone, the rather twee Cliffe Holme on the gate pillars. Cliff Cottage on the bungalow wall hopefully for many, many years to come.

We were always busy and for many years went out on Tuesday and Thursday up into the Dales for lunch. I recently found the diary Pat kept with all the pub names in, that brought a tear to my eye. We continued holidaying in Guernsey for a year or two. I continued acting but eventually we had to accept that I wasn't going to recover. When Pat was in hospital with the hip job I bumped into the specialist who'd done my hamstring op. He saw me four times and didn't send a bill. That tells you something. Instead he sent me to a specialist in London who sent me a bill for £190 and recommended Cortisone injections of which I'd had many times with minimal success.

He was Italian and Martyn Speight's surname gave him some trouble.

Dr Martyn Spa-heg-hetti was how it came out.

229

Chapter 33:
Harry's Kingdom and Emmerdale

I'd fancied myself as an author for quite a while. I was always good at composition at school. So, I wrote a 1 act play about an old actor and a young actress. No he didn't try anything on. A friend suggested I take it to Louie Senior a well-known actress, director and writer. I did. She invited me for a chat. "This Ron is a load of rubbish. An overdone theme with a lot of misplaced sentimentality. However there is a hint of something better. Find an original storyline, build your characters but stick to the plot and end when it ends. Leave them wanting more."

I wrote a full length T.V. play about an American jazz trumpeter who dies during a recording session and his life, how he was pressured into too many appearances and recording sessions had caused the demise told in flashback. I was working with actor, writer, wrestler Brian Glover at the time and asked him to read it.

"Ron it's a brilliant idea but you don't know enough about the American jazz scene. They don't talk like that. It's too gentle and get the lingo right. They have elevators not lifts and leave the director something to do." I read it again and binned it.

Hey what did I say to Fred Hodges on the Slough gig? "There's a play in this somewhere." and there was but not too fast. I joined a writing group in Leeds.

Twenty-four of us Thursday afternoon, week 2 eighteen of us, week 3 a dozen. The tutor was a playwright from Lancaster. We wrote, he criticised and you could have a few minutes one to one after the session. Week 2 he stressed "I hope to see a completed play by the end of the course." Two or three had just come into shelter from the rain in other words they'd done the other courses so why not do this one?

My theme was a double glazing prize giving night. "You don't start a play with a big scene like that but you did and it works." I over wrote a scene or two, he put me right on quite a few bits and pieces, for instance, "Cut the dialogue. Any good actress can do this without words." He didn't write a single word but I looked forward to Thursday afternoons and always a 10 minute face to face. On one of these he said to me, "You should enter this into the Radio Times Drama Awards." I did.

One small problem, one big problem. I don't type. Went to see John

Oldfield, told him I was writing a play about double glazing to enter into the Radio Times Drama Awards and I needed Margaret to type it for me. I asked John to read it and said I wouldn't enter it if he didn't want me to. John also had a job for me. Before I'd left I'd introduced a system of keeping a folder on each client updated as needed. The system was in a complete mess. He'd pay me to sort it out. Game plan, "Don't pay me but I want my play to be treated as proper work not just typed when Margaret had a few spare minutes." It worked a treat. One bijou problemette, I hadn't bothered with a title. I came up with *The Rainbow Chasers*. Andy the tutor didn't care for that. He came up with *A roller next year*. It went off with a recommendation from Radio Leeds. This was a stipulation. It had to be read by an independent body connected with the arts.

I think there were three letters from the Beeb; (1) *A Roller* was being read and considered, (2) it was on the shortlist, (3) it was one of five finalists. I hope I can share this experience without boring you. It was one of the great mornings of my life.

When I booked in at Wood Lane there were five names on a list. When you've been in dozens of print shops you learn to read upside down, right to left. Mine was the last name so was I fifth or the other finalists all had names starting with a letter before P? The plot thickens. I met the other finalists in a small room outside the presentation area, (1) a previous finalist, (2) a writer in residence at Wigan Pier Theatre Company, (3) a lady in black who seemed to be well known by the BBC people present, (4) a writer in residence at Liverpool University. I had to be fifth.

We were ushered into the presentation area, along with the radio short list. Princess Margaret was to present the cheques and there were strict instructions to call her Ma'am. Radio first then TV. I tried to rationalise my thoughts. The lady in black seemed to have a track record and I think she was a feature writer in the *London Evening News*. If I've got this wrong I apologise. The bloke who'd been a previous finalist, surely they wouldn't ask him twice and give him the wooden spoon a second time. The Wigan Pier man and the Liv Uni man nothing to choose between them.

> First up – the woman in black.
> Second up – the previous winner.
> Third up – Liv Uni so it's Wigan Pier and me.
> Fourth up – Wigan Pier.
> Excuse my excitement. I'd won! I'd Won! I'D WON! I went up for prize, a sealed envelope. The Princess gave me a funny look. There were tears in my eyes.

Pat was in Leicester with the family. I left the room to find a phone. I couldn't make it work. I hadn't dialled 0 for an outside line. A kindly commissionaire dialled the number. Now I have been known to over egg the pudding but all I could muster was "I've won." I calmed myself down by wandering through corridors full of pictures of celebs then went in for some grub. A middle aged lady said, "Well done. Can I touch you?" It was a dream. Most of the food had gone. I managed a sausage roll and some mushy trifle on the same plate. A tap on my shoulder. "The Princess is ready to meet you." Goodbye sausage roll and trifle mix.

The Princess started with the radio man and after a couple of minutes said to him, "Do you mind if I smoke?" Profuse "No Ma'am, not at all Ma'am etc."

"How about you?" I'd no intention of not toeing the line. These things just happen to me. "Will it make any difference?" Princess Mags threw her head back and said, "There speaks the Yorkshireman." The radio man was out of it. She was remarkably knowledgeable about Yorkshire and finally asked the BBC minder, "When's it going out?"

"About a year's time Ma'am."

"I shall hold you to that" was her final remark. I was flavour of the month. That's stretching it a bit, flavour of the week. Day is more like it.

I was asked to sign the visitor's book. HRH was in front of me. "You first" she said. "You're the star of the show."

"My Mother always taught me ladies first." As she put pen to paper I added, "That's so they get the bullet." Another big laugh from the Princess and a thank you for such a happy meeting.

Photographers, press men, Bill Cotton, Michael Grade, who I'd met when he worked for his Uncle Lew, were all full of "Well done, congrats" and so on. I was in a daze. What happens next? Calm down for a start.

Robert Young was to be director, Richard Broke the producer and Sarah Curtis script editor. That night I was on *Round midnight* which was recorded at 8:30pm. I got a big studio laugh by saying, "I thought I'd be lucky to get a BBC pen and pencil set." Why do I say these things? I asked for a tape of my bit to take home. I didn't expect to be staying the night. They put me up in a posh hotel. "You're on Breakfast TV at 8am." I went out and bought a fresh shirt. At dinner I ordered a bottle of wine. The waitress was full of it. She'd just won the waitress of the month award. I asked her to bring an extra glass and another bottle and each time she came to the table she had a secret slurp. It was just lovely. I drank most of the bottle and a half. I was definitely drunk. I decided to wash my underpants. I hadn't thought I would be staying the night. There were no radiators, the heating was from vents in the ceiling. I'm naked facing the window with wet underpants and a mouthful of pins from the shirt on a bouncy bed trying to fasten my underpants to the ceiling. I hadn't drawn the curtains. It's laff out loud time, you're allowed. I was still not sober at 4:30 am so got up and went for a walk. Oh, I dressed first.

Writer Germaine Greer actress Alexandra Pigg a chap my age very pleasant but I've forgotten why he was there were the others on the show, all very friendly. I was the last on, all very exciting.

I got back home from Leicester Friday afternoon. The phone was ringing. John asked where I'd been. He'd been trying to get me ever since Thursday. I explained. I began to see John's aggressive style. "Ron, I want this play of yours re-jigged. I don't want anything in it about double glazing. Turn it to DIY, solar panels, anything."

"John, I asked you if Margaret would type the play. I asked you to read it and said I wouldn't enter it if... You didn't read it. Andrew North read it and sent me a letter of appreciation, not a personal letter but one written on company notepaper. I asked Margaret if she'd ask Fred Hodges to read it. Entry date was approaching, I needed the script. Margaret handed it to me and said Fred had 'looked at it'. It took him almost two months to look at it. So John I've done everything possible to make key people in the agency to make comments. Zilch."

"Now I'm due at a script conference very soon where the director, the producer, the script editor and me will go through the script line by line. I'll let you know the outcome. If I try to swing the script to anything else but double glazing it will raise bigger problems and very good copy for journalists. If they want to make it more of a disaster movie I'll do my best to stand my corner." John was none too happy but saw the sense in this.

I opened the envelope with the cheque, it was for £4,500. I'd kept the write-up from Radio Times, first prize £6,000. I rang the radio winner. It was the same for him but he didn't want to cause any trouble. Obviously not a Yorkshireman.

I rang the BBC oik in charge of presentation. He said the standard was very low so there was no first prize. I was the winner. The oik also said if I didn't agree to £4,500 the production would be removed from the schedules. I've just remembered his name but I'll keep it to myself, his initials L.P. I was glad I had the tape where the oik said 'the standard was higher than ever and Ron's play absolutely superb'.

I rang my friend and solicitor Ian Whitson. He picked up the tape, wrote to the BBC. Final score I got the extra £1,500 and Ian put in a bill for his contribution.

Richard Broke rang and said, "Nobody likes the title." I came up with a dozen or so more including *Rainbow chasers*. All no good. I don't know how I got onto this, probably genius. I must have been looking at the cast list. Harry Jackson was the lead character, his secretary June King. You're ahead of me, aren't you? If not, you should be. Swap the surnames. He's now Harry King and she's June Jackson so *Harry's Kingdom* becomes the absolutely perfect title, job done.

The play opened doors just like our T.V campaign had done. Harry's Kingdom was repeated on BBC2 and U.K. Gold. Thirty years later I'm still getting cheques from far off places like Uzbekistan.

I got a rather harsh letter from the Sales Director, John Hart. The following week was an all-time record week for Anglian. Reps got a toe in the door by saying 'Did you see that thing about double glazing on T. V. last

Sunday? Our Advertising Agent wrote that'. Things calmed down. Money talks... particularly when you're on commission only.

It was a very different John Hart who bumped into me in Guernsey a year or two later, full of praise and offering to take Pat and I out to dinner. As with the German couple we had to refuse as he was tied up that night and tomorrow, we were on the plane home. He and his wife had gone to live there.

Switch now to shooting time. There was a strike on. Nothing was being made in England, Scotland or Wales. Michael Grade had read the script and found Northern Ireland was still working. Thanks Michael. I flew over for a few days. Timothy West, Peter Vaughan and Harry Fowler—remember him in the monkey suit?—couldn't have been pleasanter. So were the rest of the cast. We stayed up late and chatted into the early hours.

The shoot took 5 weeks. You're lucky to get 3 minutes a day in the can. I found it remarkable how the actors stayed in character. On stage you 'became' the character for two and a half hours. On T.V you 'become' the character for 3 minutes a day, providing you've got a fair sized part.

Read through of *Harry's Kingdom* and opening of the Charles Walls Advertising office in Jermyn Street, London. Richard Whiteley and Phil Carrick were the invited guests and I asked Phil if he was related to Arthur Carrick who was in my class at school and my batting partner at Moriah C.C.?

Phil: "I'm his son Ron and he was always known as 'Archie'."
Me: "That was his nickname at school. He must have been very proud when you first walked out of the Headingley Pavilion in your Yorkshire cap and sweater."
Phil: "Sadly Ron, he died just before that."

We chatted for a few minutes about Bramley. A thoroughly likeable man, who went on to captain the side and he too died at a youngish age.

Robert Young the Director, Richard Broke the Producer and Sarah Curtis the script Editor were present at the line by line reading. I got lucky. They knew little of the double glazing business and were intrigued by the set up. I was warned it could be a hatchet job. Only one line was queried. How much to pay the page 3 girl? It took 10 minutes. One or two lines were changed in production and a very short scene shot but then deleted.

All TV productions have a Director and a Producer and if, like me, you'd wondered who did what the simple answer is:

The Director is responsible for all you do see.

The Producer is responsible for all you don't see.

In other words, the Producer gets the cast together, arranged their fees, finds the locations and lots of minor but important jobs.

The Director takes the cast through the rehearsal and then directs the whole of the production and filming with the Producer on set to attend to any off-screen problems.

So now we both know.

One afternoon the page 3 girl sequence was shot. On screen there was shouting, clapping, lots of noise. In reality and there was director Robert Young, producer Richard Broke, script editor Sarah Curtis, the camera crew and me at this shoot. She was a very shy girl and asked for as few as possible to be present. Earlier she was panicking about her few lines and I went up to her room with Robert's permission, went through her lines and she was ok. When I left the filming stopped. Lots of kisses, from the ladies I hasten to add. Handshakes back slaps and I like to think they were not doing it out of politeness. A really memorable few days for me, business as usual for them.

I went to the rough cut preview at Pinewood and made a couple or three points which were accepted as long as there was footage to cover them. There was. The preview was in a proper cinema. Richard Broke made the opening remarks. The preview was unbelievable. The cuts Robert Young made as director worked. Lots of laughs and just wonderful. The screening was Sunday peak time, 9-10:30 BBC.

Let's get back to reality. I'd like to wallow a bit. If you don't like people who wallow turn the page until you get to the ordinary writing.

> Ron Pearson's excellent script – The Guardian.
> The plotting is Machiavellian and very funny – Independent.
> An hilarious and moving script – London Evening Standard.
> A terrific play. The end was quite chilling – Sunday People.
> An eye for detail and mastery of dialogue – Daily Mail.
> A splendidly observed black comedy – Time Out.
> Weekend viewing continued well with *Harry's Kingdom* – Daily Telegraph.
> It's a powerful play – The Stage.
> Ron Pearson's importance of dialogue in *Harry's Kingdom* – Plays and Players.
> What a series this would make – The Sun.
> So witty, well played was the fascinating *Harry's Kingdom – Sunday Express.*
> For sureness of touch, insight into character and narrative grip it ranks almost above every other TV play I've seen this year – personal note from Roger Waddis – Radio Times.
> We can't remember a play receiving so many good notices. *Harry's Kingdom* caused a sensation – BBC… so there.

So there.

"His clear darting eyes seem to take in everything, the kind of man you would describe as a character." I took some stick for that in the Radio

Times, particularly from my friend and solicitor, Ian Whitson. "Oh hello, is that the Mr Darting Eyes?" was his opening gambit in a number of phone calls.

The only downside to the play was from my Sister. She hated it and didn't go out for three days unless she met somebody who connected her name with that of the writer. At first I felt sad then unhappy that I had made her unhappy then I tried to analyse the situation. We'd always been different. I'd always had friends. She had none. She was uneasy with children or dogs. Scenery, countryside, made her ill. She admitted she was a loner preferring her own company to mixing with others. Put me down as the exact opposite of that and you get the picture but she is still my big Sister and there is a bond.

One day Richard Broke rang me up on a minor point – easily resolved. "What are you going to do with the money Ron?"

"I've just ordered some double glazing." He was still laughing when he put the phone down.

On the Monday after the showing I was invited down to discuss a series. I was both pleased and petrified.

I went down and was introduced to the lady producer on the series. Why not Richard Broke? I never found out. She seemed a very nice mid-twenties to mid-thirties something. I didn't think I was good enough to cope with six episodes to be shot on film – no expenses spared. I was introduced to a very likeable man in his late thirties with a faintly memorable face. He'd introduced himself at the original showing. How did he get on the invite list?

We decided on a 50/50 deal. I was to write the first episode and he would edit and together we would finalise then we would swop over but it didn't work out like that. "You've done so well Ron. Why don't you do episode two?" It's a long story but the most likeable of men was leaning on me. When he did work he was very good.

The scripts had to be in for the April Offers. They were. They missed the April Offers. Wait until October.

The producer, Katie, from now on, was always bright and cheerful but her only comment on the six hour long episodes was a line about Blue Stratos aftershave. Not much of a feedback on months of hard work. Whether the scripts were ever entered in the October offers I know not but they were now a dead duck.

I dialled the BBC and asked for the head lad Alan Yentob and amazingly got through to him. I told him how much money had been spent on a spin off series from *Harry's Kingdom*. He remembered HK said it was brilliant and "Leave it with me." Next day the series was re-instated but this time to be shot on video. Good news, bad news.

I worked my socks off on the first five episodes then I had a near breakdown. I rang Katie and said I couldn't go on. I was packing it in. The BBC found me a new partner, a Geordie living in Leeds.

I'd met him previously when I was writing for Emmerdale and that was another disaster. He was a likeable chap, Pat liked him, a big plus but there were problems. He was working on a series called Dangerfield shot in Bristol and was forever going back and forth. After 4 episodes the BBC pulled the plug on it, so that was that after a mere 10 years or so All that was left to be said was that the money was good. Katie said she was heading up a series of five minute no dialogue plays. I wrote one, "A man in a rain-coat and bowler hat plus violin case catches the tube gets off near the Albert Hall, poster of big orchestral concert, shot of stage door, man walks past it to front of Albert Hall, hat on ground, violin at neck, he's a busker'."

Katie thought it was brilliant and wanted more. What about some money for this one? Another blank. She was working on a full length single play shot mainly in a disused signal box near Ilkley. She invited Pat and me to lunch. The five minute thing never took off. I watched the signal box play. The disused signal box was immaculate. It went out Whit Monday, always a sign it was an also ran, not a winner.

My ex-writing partner, was such a genuinely nice bloke and at various times whilst we were working together he was writing a regular Saturday broadcast for the B.B.C. He was also working on a six parter for Griff Rhys Jones as a demobbed comedian on the variety circuit. I have a fair bit of knowledge on the subject and we had many long phone calls on this.

A series for Hale and Pace was another project which I think never happened as H and P split up, plus two things for Nigel Planer. The first was a half hour slot with Suzie Blake, a married couple who were lovey dovey on screen but rowed constantly off screen.

I pointed out that Alan Melville had written a play titled *Simon and Laura* on this subject. I'd appeared in it. His other work for Planer was a one man show at Hampstead Theatre. It started at 8 and finished about 9-ish. I enjoyed it but it was sly humour, not laugh out loud stuff. I don't laugh a lot neither did anybody else. Planer said 'and finally' the woman behind me said. "Thank gawd for that." the biggest laugh of the evening.

So what about Emmerdale? At this time the internal pub slots were filmed about two miles from where I lived and script meetings were held there. I don't know how it started but I was on the script writing team. We met every two or three weeks. A lot of my plot lines were taken on board but I didn't get any episodes to write. I became friends with a London writer Jimmy Chinn, a bit camp and he always got a laugh when the biscuit box was handed around, "Any chance of a gypsy cream?" was the line. He and a northern writer from Kirkbymoorside—James rings a bell—were my lunchtime companions when we went across the road to the pub for York-shire puddings in onion gravy. Jimmy said "You raise loads of plot lines but don't get any scripts." James said "I'm working on two of yours now."

Emmerdale was being updated. Originally Emmerdale Farm with lots of fairly ordinary everyday characters was changing. First to go was farm in the title, then the lady vet became a lesbian. A straightforward Yorkshire lass was to shorten her skirt, pick up a chap in the pub and go to bed with him. She walked out saying it would damage her image as principal boy in a forthcoming panto. A few of the old hands walked out or were pensioned off.

Jimmy raised the point of me contributing story lines but not getting any scripts. I got four, two back to back and another two the same. You got a brief story line for each episode.

I wrote the first two fairly quickly and a girl who had worked at Charlies lived in the village and did my typing. Whitsuntide was coming up and she very kindly agreed to stay at home if any corrections were needed. A new person greeted me. "Ron darling I'm in love" and a big hug. "Ello ello methinks." Thankfully it wasn't me and I'm not sure whether this middle aged romance was male or female.

If corrections were needed in the scripts they had coloured pages slipped in. Some scripts were known as "rainbows". Mine were almost clear, a couple of pink pages in each with minor corrections which Denise could do in 10 minutes that day. I came home, the corrections were done and scripts delivered.

Next day the man in charge rang me. "Ron there's quite a lot of corrections in your scripts. You've written a scene for the new parson in the pulpit. We can't have the church that day. You've also done a scene for the vet outed as a lesbian. She's on holiday for three weeks. There's a funeral scene for a young member of cast and his granddad had a few speeches. Unfortunately he's been ill for months and will wave from a car so we've a couple of minutes to fill there. There's a scene for a new member of cast (Chris Chittell) I think he's still there. His contract doesn't start…"

Me: "Hang on. None of these were in the brief and there were only a couple of minor corrections in each script corrected and delivered before the deadline." I offered to deliver the revised script two days after Denise returned. No go. It got nasty. I let go. "Listen it's a bank holiday weekend. I live in a bungalow I helped to design. No mortgage, I've a very good car in the driveway and a very healthy bank balance. It's your end that doesn't know what it's doing." So that's me over and out. The episodes went out 90% my work but credited to a fictional author. How cheap can you get? I got paid.

Back to the Beeb.

The Radio Times Drama Awards were held every two years. I missed on purpose 1988 but got a good idea for 1990. No problem about the title, it had to be *Errand boys*. The basic story line is that a Bradford businessman and a London gaming club are in conflict over a property owned by the Bradfordian in Morecombe. Remember the coal man with all sorts of irons in the fire including Morecambe? That's where the idea came from. He has a fish shop, a funeral directors, a tripe shop, a solicitors and a snooker hall. He also has a man called Little Billy who has a room at the snooker and runs errands. The London gaming club is owned by a Milan based baddie. The number 2 at the gaming club a smooth handsome dress suited young man is forever going up the M1 running errands for the syndicate. Good title, lots of plot lines, lots of humour and an original theme, I think.

No letters this time etc. A phone call from Debbie, "Ron you're a finalist in the Radio times etc". Flashback to November. Elizabeth who I'd run to school came to see me. She'd tried her hand at acting with a number of parts in Emmerdale, Tenko and the like but had now turned to writing. "You know that competition you won? A friend of mine won it this year She even mentioned a few of the cast."

So back to the call from Debbie. I said it's pointless coming down as a writer, called John Random is the winner. Silence. Quite a long silence. "How do you know that? It's not true. He is a finalist and you won't be wasting your time coming down." I went down. Debbie was heavily pregnant and wasn't there. I tracked down John Random and he made a poor attempt at not knowing. There were nine of us this time. I came third. Only the winner got any money. A likeable BBC man Tony Dinner came up to me and said, "Yours was far and away the best script but very expensive and needs to be shot on film. The winner is to be shot on video and of course you were a previous winner."

"Nothing in the rules about that Tony." Marmaduke Hussey a bigwig at the Beeb boomed, "You shouldn't be here. You won before." I gave the same reply. "Oh really." Was his comment as he walked towards another sausage roll.

A week later a chap from the BBC rang me. "Ron this *Errand Boys* of yours, we like it and want to get moving on it. Could you just bring the Southern characters a little more into focus?" I said I thought they were ok, could he give me an idea. Well he wasn't really in the ideas department but you know just bring them into sharper focus. He was a sort of errand boy. I did some work, sent it down. Errand Boy was delighted. Never heard another dicky bird. I've recently added a second episode—it keeps the old brainbox working—but nobody appears interested. Ring telephone ring.

According to my friend Elizabeth, now Lizzie Mickery, now a well-known writer in Los Angeles. John Random was so upset at the preview he walked out. It was another holiday showing. It was just about alright.

To finalise the RTDA I entered four years later with another unusual story line. A variety theatre with 9 acts and what happens when the Second World War broke out. I wrote a few minutes of each routine and researched the music and found a suitable theatre in Wakefield. One idea was the friendship between a German acrobat and a Jewish comedian. A young lady called Victoria Stewart came up from London to interview me and gave a very broad hint that I'd be the winner. I wasn't even invited down. I have a feeling the winning script was never produced and the drama awards is now the deadest of ducks.

So what's next? I got an idea to change a JB Priestley play into a musical. I told Ned Sherrin the presenter at the awards "Absolutely perfect subject" was his enthusiastic response.

The play was *When we are married* the hilarious story of 3 middle aged couples who are about to celebrate their silver weddings only to discover the curate who married them was apparently unqualified to do so. I had no difficulty of getting an option from Priestley's agent, his son Tom and Priestley's wife Jaquetta Hawkes who were interested. I met them at a Bradford Hotel and showed them the work I had done. They laughed a lot and wished me well.

There was a do at the Bradford Playhouse. I got chatting to Duncan Preston who said, "Peter Skellern is your man for the music." I met Peter in London; he lived in Devon and was very keen and suggested a 50/50 deal. I said he'd got the lion's share of the work in writing the music and songs whereas I was adapting an already written script and format. He was adamant. It was 50/50. What about your agent? "He'll do what I say" was Peter's comment. We decided on *La Di Dah* as a title and it was left for me to produce the general format of songs, chorus numbers, solos, script and a longish piece on how the musical would evolve. A friend of mine Bradford solicitor Roger Suddards a keen Priestley fan arranged a meeting at his London club. There was an investor and eight of us, a musical director, a theatre manager and a number of others involved in big time theatre. I couldn't believe it. I was out of my depth. I knew the play backwards. I'd appeared in it and also directed it at the Bradford Playhouse so that helped a bit.

Peter was touring with Richard Stilgoe and came to St George's Hall, Bradford for a one night stand. Early afternoon I picked him up and we had a very pleasant afternoon at my bungalow. He and Pat got on well and I'd got the studio to produce poster designs etc which he thought were terrific. Then it all went wrong.

Priestley's agents drew up a very complicated contract, everything from regional rights to world rights. It was beyond me completely however with my solicitor, Ian Whitson's, help we managed to get quite a few amendments in our favour. I was called down to see Peter's agent. I took my ex-writing partner's London agent with me. She smiled, but never spoke. He was a very unhelpful man and the meeting lasted less than half an hour and we were out on the pavement in pouring rain. Not even a cuppa and a gypsy cream.

This man wanted to see a script. I told him the script – or 90% of it, existed. It was in a play called 'When we are Married' and once Peter started writing the songs, the stage scripts would be adapted.

The project wasn't completely over. I met one of the theatrical people at the ill-fated Nigel Planer one man show. She said the Yvonne Arnaud theatre was interested. It all came down to money. It always does. Peter had a year out of touring to write an Indian based musical which never got very far. His hardnosed agent wanted him back on the road. I sent the 60 page outline, poster and programme designs to West Yorkshire Playhouse. No reply. That was the end of that. What a pity.

Oh, the national press got hold of the idea and I think it was the *Daily*

Telegraph interviewed Peter about the project. I believe Peter devoted the rest of his life to his local church in Devon and sadly died recently of a brain tumour. A lovely talented man, I'm sure we could have produced a winner, with his talent and my editing the script and overall planning of *La Di Dah*. You win some.

Chapter 34:
The Beginning of the
End at Charlie's

Watching the cricket one Saturday Don Alred said, "Is everything alright at your old place?"

I said, "Yes, as far as I know. What do you know?"

Don: I just heard it wasn't a very happy place to work.

Sometime later Pat and I were out to lunch when Liz Pratt and her husband were at a distant table. We waved and I sent the waiter over with wine. Afterwards they joined us.

Me: So how goes it at the old firm?

Liz: I'm not there anymore. It's so different, I just couldn't work there. She then listed quite a lot of names I knew, all gone.

I needed to do something about my pension or pensions, I had two. I also alerted Kenneth W and we had a foursome meeting. John, Kenneth, Me and Ian Whitson.

At first there was no deal. Ian handled the situation as only a quiet smooth thinking man can. John agreed both major pensions could be taken out. The smaller 'petrol money' pensions would stay in. Gradually we reached a sum agreeable to all. With my accountant's help I invested my take in a 5% annually rise on a more than substantial monthly sum.

Some years later I read in the paper that the business had gone into administration. Get this, I had to read it in the paper. I was astounded. The £1,500 pa petrol money went but thank goodness or rather thank Don Alred and Ian Whitson the major part of my pension was safe. How sad that the business was no more. That's life kiddo, just get on with it.

I was very annoyed with John. He always sent me a lavish Christmas card. I didn't send one. Bit little of me. Gradually the wound healed and he called to see me. He and his wife Sue another CWA employee now live in Australia as do their children and we are in regular communication.

Times were a'changing. And so was the advertising industry. Who's to say, I would have done any better? Agencies relied on 15% commission from media for their main source of income. Just before I retired, one of my clients was offered 33⅓% commission to place their business direct.

That's K.O before you get in the ring. Charlie died peacefully just before his 89th birthday. His wife took him up a cup of tea in the morning and he was gone. I've worked out he smoked over 10,000,000 cigarettes, at last knockings. How lucky can you get? A lovely man with a rather sad life.

Pat's Father also died about this time, in his case just before his 90th birthday. We'd moved him into fulltime care in Ilkley. He had £7,000 in the bank and we paid for his care when that ran out. Another lovely man everybody liked him but with absolutely no interest in the many businesses owned by the family. Happy to serve petrol and mend old cars as best he could. Always good company everybody liked Thomas Douglas Porter. You just couldn't help it.

I miss them both. Without that letter from Charlie in 1950, I've still got it, where would my career have gone? I wasn't the world's greatest advertising man. He gave me a chance. I took it. Again how lucky can you get?

So throughout the 1990s I was busy writing, gardening, acting, directing. Sheila Garnet, Pat's long time close friend became seriously ill. Her husband Ted who was President of the local Allotments Association asked me to take over for two years. Two years became four when the chap who took over from me died suddenly in his first weeks in the post. Sadly Sheila died, a great loss to Ted, the community and of course Pat and to a degree me. Nothing fazed Sheila and when Pat had the car accident she was truly brilliant.

Chapter 35:
The Incredible Limping Man

In 2000 something happened that was to change my life. We were on holiday in Guernsey when I developed a slight strain at the top of my right leg. The chemist's shop was opposite the hotel where we stayed and we were on good speaking terms. He recommended his version of E45 and then in a fairly busy shop said, "What kind of underpants do you wear?" I said, "Y fronts." He suggested a looser fit so off we went to Creaseys, the M&S branch in St Peter Port and bought half a dozen looser fit. They didn't help. On the Saturday before we flew back on Sunday I nearly passed out knocking the top off a boiled egg. It used to be said, "He couldn't knock the skin off a rice pudding." Trust me to go one better. Pat managed to find a doctor open on Saturday morning and off we went. Epididymitis was the verdict. Sounds like something Ken Dodd would have. Home on Sunday. Dr Keith Manchester on Monday. He agreed with the condition but changed the medication. It didn't help. I saw the vet. No this isn't a joke. We'd taken our dog Honey to the vet and he recommended a physio. Martyn Speight was wonderful. He kept me going for a couple of years.

One Sunday the dress rehearsal for a play I was in the leg became unbearable. I went to Yorkshire Clinic in Bingley hoping for a quick fix. I was kept in and missed the first week of *Stirrings in Sheffield on Saturday night*. I was playing a leading role but fortunately it was a male director who stood in reading from a clipboard. On Thursday I was allowed out and managed to hobble through the second week. I had to come down a few steps. I went dizzy for a few seconds but it wasn't noticeable. This told me I needed further help.

I think I saw four specialists. One diagnosed a hernia. I had the op no good. Eventually the problem was diagnosed as an ischium problem. That's part of the hamstring at the very top of the leg. The 'sitting down' bone. I had the op. It was a bit better but not right. I had treatment and MRI scans in Newcastle, West Hartlepool, Leeds, Bradford, Otley, Leicester and London.

I carried on acting for another five years, wrote a book about my early days in Bramley where I was born, drove until I was 93, gardened until 95 and as I'm writing this I'm fortunate to have full time care in my own home, the bungalow where Pat and I had almost 40 very happy years. As I look around me, the main room is full of things we bought together, pictures and Pat's wonderful tapestry items. So you get what life throws at you and get on with it.

I think we may have managed one more holiday in Guernsey, a few more theatre trips, some lunches out but then because of my inability to walk and sit down in comfort these became rare events. Martin Speight was wonderful and very practical. "It's doubtful this will ever get better but you never know." was a spot on diagnosis. Pat took it all in her stride and a very painful hip plus a new hip helped her somewhat.

I was two weeks in hospital with pseudo gout which it wasn't. Treatment, Voltoral, Diazepam, Paracetamol. I applied the Voltoral myself as they were too busy to do it. I couldn't reach my ankles so the solution was leave them.

Chapter 36:
Almost 66 Years

Pat was not well. She had lost her appetite. Our doctor visited and said it was unlikely to come back. He never gave an explanation for this but she couldn't taste the strongest of flavours.

A further problem is that one of her legs was painful and needed dressing by the district nurses. They were very helpful however the other leg started to weep and was painful. The district nurses said they were only here to do one leg and we'd need a recommendation from our doctor to treat the other one.

That night we watched TV, went to bed and at 2:30am I heard a cry, "Ron I've fallen out of bed." I tried for an hour or so to get her back in but it was not possible. The ambulance arrived and it was a hospital trip. I knew it was serious but like anybody in that situation hoped for the best. I rang my daughter and she and grandson Ben came up. Thursday Pat was sitting up and had eaten something. Friday she could hear me but couldn't talk. Saturday no difference. Sunday it was serious. Both Pat and myself had made Living Wills. If you don't know about these, they are drawn up by solicitors. The crucial part is, in laymen's terms "That if in the opinion of two doctors there is no chance of recovery the patient should be allowed to sleep and drift off." The last words Pat spoke to me were "Let me go." I'd no option. We'd each promised each other we would not let each other suffer longer than possible. It was the worst moment of my life. "Let me go" comes back to me even now on a regular basis. I found a couple of nurses. They told me two doctors were on their way so it was really a done deal. I didn't have to produce the Living Will and Pat died peacefully early Monday morning.

We'd been married a month short of 66 years, mostly very happy years. Ask anybody who has been married that long if there was never any problems and they say no it means three things. They'd led a very tedious 66 years, or they are lying or, they are choosing not to remember.

What a wonderful happy person Pat was. She knew her father was letting the businesses drift away but he had been a wonderful Dad when she was little. Pat's mother developed Agoraphobia when she was 50 and only went out in the car, never getting out.

Pat's funeral was a private one with family and close friends. I managed better than I expected. The one thing I couldn't do was to see the coffin. Women are much braver than men in their personal sorrows.

I think my daughter made a speech. I know all my grandchildren did and was told they spoke well. I can't remember a word of any of them. I do remember I found the old 78 recording of Fats Waller singing '*My very good friend the milkman*' which we both bought on the same day unknown to each other. It contains a line about having a cottage with country views. We helped to design and had Cliff Cottage built in our garden and it had country views. I got through that but only just.

After the funeral I wrote to my doctor criticising the system rather than The District Nurses. I was still in shock. I think he agreed with me.

Chapter 37:
I'd Never Fried an Egg

Being unable to stand without a Zimmer frame learning to cook on an Aga was never a possibility. There is also the fact that I didn't want to.

Since Pat died, I've been in hospital 3 times for 1 night, the diagnosis being irregular heartbeat. By the time the ambulance took me down the heartbeat had eased off and no further treatment necessary.

The first two visits were to LGI and just about acceptable. The third visit to St James was unacceptable. I was on a trolley from 6:30pm to 3:30am. I gave the nurses my essential tablets. I wasn't given any during my stay nor to take home. I was on a gluten free diet. They tried to 'source' some. I suggested supermarkets, not on their schedules. At 3:30am I conned a nurse to bring me a glass of water and two digestive biscuits. Breakfast, a fruit jelly. Lunch a badly baked potato. On arrival a male doctor told me I had to stay in overnight because the x-ray department was closed until the morning. In the morning a lady doctor said there was no need for an x-ray. The first toilet was filthy and unusable, the second toilet slightly better but no toilet paper or paper towels. A visiting nurse wasn't surprised by this. Throughout my stay I stayed in my own clothes. Was I glad to get home, have a shower and something to eat after more than 24 hours.

> A few days later, "Good morning, Mr Pearson I'd like to discuss your visit to St James." Me: "Yes I've a few complaints." They hung up.

Life has to be lived. I got out the *Errand Boys* TV script and made a few revisions. I then wrote an extra episode and got myself a new agent in Leeds. The London agent talked a lot but did absolutely nothing to earn her commission on the fourteen *Harry's Kingdom* scripts. Basically TV companies are looking for six episodes as a starter. I don't think I have another four *Errand Boys* episodes in me. In my mind a script is never actually finished. I thought advertising was a pressure business but writing good material is even more so. Will *Errand Boys* ever reach the screens? Doubtful, everything is haywire due to Covid, but I know in my own mind I have written two better than average scripts.

So what else? Well, I'm writing this aren't I and you're reading it? If you've got so far you must be getting some pleasure from it. So what about life in care? Nobody wants it.

If like me you've walked the dog, gardened most days, done loads of household bits and pieces plus a time consuming hobby of directing acting, and trying not to bump into the scenery it comes hard to be stuck in a chair all day but there are only two alternatives. You go on about it and make other people miserable or you get on with it. That's the way the biscuit breaks. OK, so it's cookie crumbles, but I like to be just a midge different, that's the way the doughnut dunks, your turn.

I've had some ups and downs with some of these carers. One girl tried her hand at baked Alaska in the Aga. It didn't work. One girl tried to boil a kettle on the polished lid of the Aga etc., etc., etc. I've changed carers a time or three. There is the occasional slip, the blame is equally shared between them and me. It's a good relationship.

There are bound to be minor problems but these are in the main easily resolved. You may find it hard to believe I've made mistakes. I've made them by the sackful. I've a good memory and often an unrelated moment will trigger off an error I'd sooner forget. I'd like to think I've done more good than bad but of course, I'm not the only judge. Let's leave it at that.

I have never cooked so it was obvious something had to be done to stop me living on tea and ginger biscuits. I decided I could manage a simple cold breakfast and at first the care company to provide lunch, tea and supper. After a few weeks I cut out supper but after a year or so it became obvious as my lack of balance and pain level got worse, I needed full time care.

My first full-time carer was a very pleasant Rumanian who had two disadvantages, she couldn't cook and she was a cleaner who never stopped cleaning. One day I was having my usual after lunch rest when I felt grit on my face. The ceiling was being swept with an outside brush. I could go on. Please don't. I won't.

The company said they would send somebody in to provide lunch and tea but would have to charge me. I disagreed. I also pointed out Laura didn't drive and supplies were running out. Sainsbury's was only half a mile away but she was frightened to walk down the main road. It wasn't working out. The company never charged me for the extra lunch and tea carers for meals and I got them to agree to a 50 per cent discount on the general care.

I changed carers. The first girl was very good and stayed nine weeks then a personal problem then she decided to leave, stay, left, stayed six time in one morning and I had to ask my good friend and neighbour Monica down to try and calm her down. Monica came down from the bedroom, she's staying. Wonderful. She went. I know she was a secret smoker. She swore on God's name she wasn't. I've never smoked. I found an unsmoked cigarette on my bedroom floor. It wasn't hers. After she'd gone I found a half full bottle of wine on a ledge in the garage. Ah well, you lose some then you lose some more.

The next lad who came was a Buddhist from Poland. He said the bush by the front window didn't exist nor did the Victorian lamppost in the garden though it lit up every night. He doubted if we existed. I said, "Let me stab you with these scissors and see if you bleed." He said that needed some thought. After a couple of weeks he left for Nottingham or was it Derby or Luton or Norwich? On the Tuesday he rang to see if he could come back.

The next carer was a very pleasant man. I ordered steak pie and vegetables. I got vegetables and two jam tarts on the same plate. You'd better believe this. I stumbled out to the freezer in the garage, found the frozen steak pie. Would I like it warming through? And so it went on.

Chapter 38:
On a Lighter Note

Here's a couple of rhymes that may raise a smile. All the kids at school were singing bits of songs and silly rhymes. They all had radios. We didn't. Dad saw no point. He was hardly ever in but Mum finally got him to agree to Radio Relay. You got a loudspeaker plus a switch that gave you BBC London and North National. It cost 1/6 per week. On Saturday teatime one channel went over to Radio Luxembourg and I remember this.

> Sung: Take Carter's little liver pills.
> Just the thing to cure your ills.
> Get out of bed a rarin' to go.
> Make yourself a nice person to know.
> Healthy folk are happy folk.
> They sing, they dance, they play.
> So if you don't feel good.
> Well then I bet you would.
> If you took Carter's little liver pills.

Spoken in a strong American voice:

> And he did and lived happily ever after.
> So if you don't feel good.

> Sung: Take Carter's liver pills.

This jingle was a memory from Radio Luxembourg in 1937. Carter's Little Liver Pills were first marketed in the U.K. by American, John Morgan Richards in the 1880's. In 1951 the brand name was amended to Carter's Little Pills, so this jingle was no longer viable.

Here's another from a play on black and white TV that had a lad singing.

> Hark the herald angels sing.
> Beecham's pills are just the thing.
> They are gentle, meek and mild.
> Two for adults one for a child.

If you want to go to heaven.
You should take about seven.
If you want to go to hell.
Take the b... y box as well.
Hark the herald angels sing.
Beecham's pills are just the thing.

Many years later I was in London, auditioning for a TV commercial and this lad, now a man, turned up. I would have used him the director thought differently. He won. I don't recall ever seeing this chap on TV. Mind you I don't watch TV until 7pm. I once saw someone smile in 'Hollyoaks'.

Another one up for audition was a tall, handsome actor in black and white films in the late 1930s. Still tall and handsome he made an entrance in a white roll neck sweater and navy blazer, plus of course trousers. His opening words were "I've spent Summer crewing for a chum on the Med". So he wasn't working then? Once again, the director wasn't impressed.

Chapter 39:
Family Update

After her education at Bradford Grammar School Louise went to Art College at elegant Harrogate, then gritty Bradford (David Hockney's Alma Mata), then finally to study Fine Arts at Leicester Polytechnic.

After graduation she taught in state and private schools, loving her work and getting a lot of reward from helping her students to attain their potential. Lo has lived in both town and country houses and the interior design of all the houses has been a lifelong interest.

Art has continued to be her passion, being involved in various art organisations and enjoying visiting exhibitions and galleries and pursuing many creative projects. Her personal life has involved two marriages and the product of these were three amazing children. My daughter is now very happy with her partner plus 2 dogs, Bella a wire haired terrier and Basil, a whippet who go everywhere with them.

I love my Daughter and my Grandchildren and Great-grandchildren and I accept them all for what they are as they accept me. The grandchildren's careers are:

Grandson number 1 is in the Metropolitan Police... He will be promoted to Inspector later this year. I think this was inspired by "adventure" walks in the woods behind my bungalow. It was usually 'cops and robbers', but if I tried to change into 'pirates' and 'Superman' after a few minutes it always ended up with 'C and R's'. Number 2 grandson is now an entrepreneur in Australia in the drinks trade. (Inspired by me – the entrepreneur – not the booze).

Finally, my granddaughter got a degree and works as a social worker (inspired by her Father). I am immensely proud of them professionally and their different but lovely personalities.

I've always been lucky and can add three great grandchildren to my brood, two in UK and one in Oz.

After Dad died in 1972 Eileen struggled along on her own in the dreary, below street level oblong Council house with unkempt garden. I think she mowed the front lawn and that was it. In 1973 she asked me to get some details of a flat development almost in the town centre and in walking distance from her work, theatres and cinemas. She was in Brighton on holiday, on Wednesday evening I got a rather garbled phone call. "Ron, I hope you don't think I'm awful but I want to live down here. You see I'm Pisces and want to be near the sea." So Brighton it was. She soon got a job at a solicitors then moved again to another solicitors until her retirement. As in Leeds it seemed a rather lonely life but then it always was. She became secretary of the Military Bands Association and became a fan of the Blues and Royals going to their Sunday morning religious services in London for a while.

On one occasion the band played in Brighton on a Monday and Bradford on the Friday. Despite gale warnings and not to travel by train she attended both venues to hear, I suppose the same concert. She also became a fan of electric organs and went all over to organ festivals, Squires Gate, North Blackpool being one of the venues. She would come to us for a night then I would take her to the local station for a through train.

She thought she would try a direct route by bus. I got the following card, "You know what I'm like with scenery. I read most of the way and then looked inwards and got through it that way." That was her preferred route from then on. It was just about acceptable that she didn't want marriage or children but for the countryside to make her ill I found very difficult to accept. I love the countryside. That was the last time we met, about 17 years ago.

However coming up to her 99th birthday she lives alone in an upstairs flat with one caller a week and manages a short walk. Margaret a distant relative is the visitor and also rings every day. This is a great help to me. I've spoken many times to Margaret and she is a very kind and considerate companion. So where are we now?

In January 2022 Eileen had a fall and was taken to Hospital and then moved to a Care Home. She was seriously ill and lost her power of speech. However, on the week I write this she managed to say a few words on the phone. The Care Home looks very nice and I have had several conversations with a very considerate carer.

Sadly in April 2022, my Sister Eileen Margaret Pearson died peacefully in the Care Home. Just over one month after her 99th birthday. She had a long, active life until the end of 2021. In our younger years she was always my 'big Sister'. In later years after Dad died she seemed to live a somewhat strange and lonely life. But who am I to judge, it was her choice and we were 'best friends' and had many happy times together in our younger days.

Chapter 40:
All Done and Dusted

What will I do when I've finished this? Believe me I won't sit in a chair feeling sorry for myself. At least I hope I won't. It doesn't pay any dividends and although there are low moments, more of frustration than anything else, life has to be lived. If the next 98 years are as good as the last 98 there'll be no complaints from me.

"That's all folks." As Mel Blanc said at the end of countless film artoons. If you don't believe me take a trip to the US of A where you'll find "That's all folks" on his gravestone.

If dear reader you are known to me and your name doesn't appear in this tome please forgive me. At the very beginning I stated I did not do research so some of these rambles go back over ninety years. Who did I sit next to at school? All I can recall is Douglas Ward in Standards 7 and 8. So there you are Douglas, you've got a mention. Douglas was right handed, I was left and my left arm was continually in battle with his right. I suggested we change places. No dice. He had the number one spot, I was number two. When I started work in Bradford we often travelled on the same bus. He was an engineer working for a big weighing scales company. How about that for memory Douglas? Or son of Douglas or daughter or grandson or... *Oh shut up Ron and say Cheerio to the readers.*

Chapter 41:
A Few Big Thank Yous

First and foremost, my wife. Pat put up with me for almost 66 years. What a marathon. What a constitution.

What a wonderful calming influence she was.

Next my family. I'm both lucky and proud to have them as very good friends.

Thanks also to the Doctors, Nurses and staff at Calverley Medical Centre for their kindness over a twenty year period. Special thanks to Dr John Keene, Dr Martyn Speight at Wharfedale Clinic and Mr. Tom Taggart at Yorkshire Clinic.

I've been to Newcastle, Hartlepool, Leicester, Barnsley, London and all the Leeds and Bradford Hospitals but to no avail.

In the village both Pat and I had lots of good friends. Sadly most of them are no longer with us. Here I must mention Peter Clayton. Nothing beats Peter, he's that sort of chap. Anything from a dodgy pond pump to a wonky drawer that refuses to close. Peter invariably has 'something at home' that might, and always does do the trick. In his spare time Peter makes the long trip to 'Radio Caroline' where he is Chief Engineer, it says so on his overalls.

Friends like Peter are hard to come by and it's easy to take them for granted. To Peter a very big thank you for being my friend and making my life more enjoyable.

Monica our near neighbour who lives in our old house, is a wonderful neighbour. Her husband John died two or three years ago. For over 40 years not a bad word has been spoken between us. Always ready to help particularly in between carers when she came down to provide breakfast, lunch and tea for several days always with a smile. I cannot thank Monica enough for what she has done and continues to do for me.

In my long career as an Actor, Director and General Muggins cum set builder, I made many friends and hopefully no enemies. If I list some names I am bound to leave some out so all I can say is thank you for your friendship and many, many Happy Memories.

I did get very low, particularly when Pat died, but eventually you just have to get on with it. I'm lucky to be writing this, watching evening TV, never during the day. I could be much worse off so in an odd way, I'm lucky.

A big thank you to my carers – in particular Ann King who has been a tower of strength for the last couple of years. She's a very good Rummy player and our contests are always happy, but fiercely fought.

Ann is now with me 39 weeks with the ever-reliable Ande helping me for the remaining 13.

Thank you to my typist, Kathryn Brooke who, after some wobbly starts at my end, with a variety of typists made what you are reading, readable.

If you find a few bijou mistakettes or something out of context, please forgive me. It's been a helluva task remembering this lot and with Kathryn's help getting it down in some sort of order.

Here are couple a of northern 'poems':

Red Rose:

Lancashire born, Lancashire bred,
Strong in thi arm, weak in thi 'ead.

White Rose:

Hear all, see all, say nowt,
Eat all, sup all, pay nowt.
And if ever tha does owt fer nowt,
Always do it fer thi'sen.

They can, of course, and often are, transposed.

I'd like to end with a couple of quotes.

…First

From veteran American comedian, George Burns on reaching 90.
"If I'd known I was going to live this long, I'd
have taken better care of myself."

…Then

"You can always tell a Yorkshireman… but you can't tell him much."

And finally:

Thanks for being a devil and giving it a go… No Returns.

Ron.

Obituary and Disclaimer

The first draft of this book was completed on 12 February 2022, with amendment during the next few months. On hearing the sad news of the death of Queen Elizabeth II on 9 September 2022, certain amendments have been made but the titles of Queen Elizabeth and Prince Charles remain as they were at the time of writing.

In accordance with current practice real names have been omitted in many cases.

Stop Press....Stop Press...Stop Press...Stop Press...Stop Press...Stop Press...Stop Press...Stop Press...Stop Press....Stop Press....Stop Press.... Stop Press....Stop Press....Stop Press....Stop Press

Tuesday 5th July 2022

Several big wows. I have been offered a contract by an international publisher – Austin Macauley. They absolutely loved it. *Calm down Ron, stop wowing, it happens every day to other people.*

So great moments in my life:

Meeting my wife
Marrying her
Birth of my daughter
The "Harry's Kingdom" saga

Then:

Holding the book in my hand.
Counting the money.